THE AVAILABLE MEANS OF PERSUASION

NEW MEDIA THEORY
Series Editor, Byron Hawk

The New Media Theory series investigates both media and new media as a complex ecological and rhetorical context. The merger of media and new media creates a global social sphere that is changing the ways we work, play, write, teach, think, and connect. Because this new context operates through evolving arrangements, theories of new media have yet to establish a rhetorical and theoretical paradigm that fully articulates this emerging digital life.

The series includes books that combine social, cultural, political, textual, rhetorical, aesthetic, and material theories in order to understand moments in the lives that operate in these emerging contexts. Such works typically bring rhetorical and critical theories to bear on media and new media in a way that elaborates a burgeoning post-disciplinary "medial turn" as one further development of the rhetorical and visual turns that have already influenced scholarly work.

OTHER BOOKS IN THE SERIES

Mics, Cameras, Symbolic Action: Audio-Visual Rhetoric for Writing Teachers, by Bump Halbritter (2012)
Avatar Emergency by Gregory L. Ulmer (2012)
New Media/New Methods: The Academic Turn from Literacy to Electracy, edited by Jeff Rice and Marcel O'Gorman (2008)
The Two Virtuals: New Media and Composition, by Alexander Reid (2007). Honorable Mention, W. Ross Winterowd/*JAC* Award for Best Book in Composition Theory, 2007.

THE AVAILABLE MEANS OF PERSUASION

Mapping a Theory and Pedagogy of Multimodal Public Rhetoric

David M. Sheridan, Jim Ridolfo, and Anthony J. Michel

Parlor Press
Anderson, South Carolina
www.parlorpress.com

Parlor Press LLC, Anderson, South Carolina, USA

© 2012 by Parlor Press
All rights reserved.
Printed in the United States of America

SAN: 254-8879

Library of Congress Cataloging-in-Publication Data

Sheridan, David M. (David Michael)
 The available means of persuasion : mapping a theory and pedagogy of multimodal public rhetoric / David M. Sheridan, Jim Ridolfo, and Anthony J. Michel.
    p. cm. -- (New media theory)
 Includes bibliographical references and index.
 ISBN 978-1-60235-308-4 (pbk. : alk. paper) -- ISBN 978-1-60235-309-1 (alk. paper) -- ISBN 978-1-60235-310-7 (adobe ebook) -- ISBN 978-1-60235-311-4 (epub)
 1. Persuasion (Rhetoric) 2. Persuasion (Rhetoric)--Study and teaching. 3. Communication--Study and teaching. 4. Communication--Technological innovations. I. Ridolfo, Jim, 1979- II. Michel, Anthony J. III. Title.
 P301.5.P47S54 2012
 808--dc23
                                    2012005615

                       1 2 3 4 5

Cover design by Jim Ridolfo and David Blakesley.
Cover image: Photograph by Jim Ridolfo. Used by permission.
Printed on acid-free paper.

Parlor Press, LLC is an independent publisher of scholarly and trade titles in print and multimedia formats. This book is available in paper, cloth and eBook formats from Parlor Press on the World Wide Web at http://www.parlorpress.com or through online and brick-and-mortar bookstores. For submission information or to find out about Parlor Press publications, write to Parlor Press, 3015 Brackenberry Drive, Anderson, South Carolina, 29621, or email editor@parlorpress.com.

Contents

Acknowledgments   *vii*
Introduction   *xi*

Part I: Foundational Terms   *3*

1 Kairos and the Public Sphere   *5*

Part II: Kairotic Inventiveness and Rhetorical Ecologies   *23*

2 Multimodal Public Rhetoric and the Problem of Access   *25*

3 Kairos and Multimodal Public Rhetoric   *50*

4 Composing with Rhetorical Velocity: Looking
  Beyond the Moment of Delivery   *75*

5 Challenges for an Ecological Pedagogy of Public Rhetoric:
  Rhetorical Agency and the Writing Classroom   *99*

**Part III: The Challenges and Possibilities
  of Multimodal Semiosis**   *121*

6 A Fabricated Confession: Multimodality,
  Ethics, and Pedagogy   *123*

7 Public Rhetoric as the Production of Culture   *144*

Part IV: Practice and Pedagogy: A Synthesis   *159*

8 Case Study: The D Brand   *161*

9 Multimodal Public Rhetoric in the
  Composition Classroom   *170*

Notes   *189*
Works Cited   *193*
Appendix   *211*
Index   *215*
About the Authors   *225*

Acknowledgments

In this book we join with a growing number in our field who argue that writing is not the result of a single individual working in isolation, but necessarily involves multiple collaborators, technologies, texts, and discourses. It is particularly fitting, then, that we take a moment to name some of the more salient ways that others supported this book. First, we are grateful for the support of David Blakesley, founder and publisher of Parlor Press, and Byron Hawk, the editor of Parlor's New Media series. The guidance David and Byron provided, from their review of our proposal to the finished product contained here, was invaluable. Similarly, we are grateful to the two reviewers who read an early draft of this manuscript and made many useful suggestions for revision, and to Terra Williams, who meticulously copyedited the final manuscript. This book is stronger because of their input.—D.M.S., J.R., A.J.M.

I have been very lucky over the past nine years to have worked in an intellectually rich culture created by colleagues (undergraduates, graduate students, staff, faculty, and community partners) in the Michigan State University Writing Center, the Rhetoric and Writing program, and the Residential College in the Arts and Humanities. I am grateful to all of the many people who, over the past several years, have been willing to engage with me in conversation about the issues we take up in this book. I'm reluctant to name names, for fear of leaving someone out. I do, however, want to say a special word of thanks to Bump Halbritter, Bill Hart-Davidson, John Monberg, and Terese Monberg, who read early drafts of various portions of this book and provided useful feedback. Additionally, I would like to thank Ann Folino White for graciously sharing her research on "Cotton Patch," an example of multimodal public rhetoric that we discuss in the introduction. I am indebted to Adam Sheridan for drawing my attention to Bruno Latour's "Where Are the Missing Masses? The Sociology of a Few Mundane Artifacts." I would like to thank Mark Sleeman for agreeing to share the SearchMTR materials we discuss in chapter 9.

Finally, thanks to my coauthors and to my family for putting up with me throughout the process of writing this book. I know I wasn't always easy to deal with. —D.M.S.

When I was a MA student at Michigan State University, I started to argue and pick fights with Dave Sheridan. These arguments were some of the most productive and enjoyable moments of my graduate experience and this book is a record of some of them. I'm thankful to Dave for taking the time to argue with the younger version of myself and guiding the transformation of those discussions into this book. I'm also indebted to my graduate faculty at Michigan State, specifically Julie Lindquist, Malea Powell, Jeff Grabill, Dean Rehberger, Dànielle DeVoss, Bill Hart-Davidson, and Ellen Cushman, as well as my undergraduate mentors Libby Miles and Bob Schwegler. Their mentorship and support has been a constant source of strength for me. I would also like to acknowledge my life partner Janice Fernheimer for her love, encouragement, and sense of humor during the duration of this project. Janice, thank you. —J.R.

It would be impossible to locate the moment when our collective work on this book began, let alone the many people who have supported me in the process. I am particularly grateful to David Sheridan, the architect of this project, and Jim Ridolfo, who, as both rhetorician and activist, inspired it. In addition, I owe a debt of gratitude to the many faculty, students, and staff at the institutions where I have been fortunate enough to work over the past ten years, including Michigan State University, California State University, Fresno, and Avila University. I am particularly grateful to the faculty and students with whom I worked for four amazing years at Fresno and over the past five years at Avila. While there is not adequate space to name all of the people who deserve my gratitude, I would be remiss if I did not make mention of a few people without whose extraordinary generosity I would never have had the opportunity to do the kind of work I love so much. I am particularly indebted to Daniel Mahala who introduced me to the field of composition and rhetoric almost two decades ago and who has had no small impact on the work in this book. I am also grateful Dean Rehberger, Diane Bruner, Rick Hansen, Jody Swilky, Jeff Myers, and the members of the "Rhetoric Society" at California State University for their enduring support and intellectual generosity. Finally, this work would not have been possible except for the love, encouragement and support of my parents, Anthony N. and Leone L. Michel, and my two beautiful children, Leo and Kate. —A.J.M.

We are grateful for permission to reprint portions of this book that were previously published in "Kairos and New Media: Toward a Theory and Practice of Visual Activism." *Enculturation* 6.2 (2009): n. pag. and "'The Available Means of Persuasion': Mapping a Theory and Pedagogy of Multimodal Public Rhetoric." *JAC* 25.4 (2005): 803–844 (Reprinted in *Plugged In: Technology, Rhetoric, and Culture in a Posthuman Age*. Ed. Lynn Worsham and Gary Olson. Cresskill, NJ: Hampton Press, 2008. 61–94).

Introduction

The 'magic' of the Internet is that it is a technology that puts cultural acts, symbolizations in all forms, in the hands of all participants; it radically decentralizes the positions of speech, publishing, film making, radio and television broadcasting, in short the apparatuses of cultural production.

—Mark Poster

FIRST THINGS FIRST

In 1964, something remarkable happened: a small segment of the culture industry decided to revolt. This group of "graphic designers, photographers and students" signed a "manifesto" calling for a "reversal of priorities" (Garland 154, 155). Entitled "First Things First," this manifesto notes that the "skill and imagination" of creative professionals is typically harnessed for ridiculously trivial matters, "to sell such things as: cat food, stomach powders, detergent, hair restorer, striped toothpaste" and other frivolous products (154). Thirty-six years later, a revised version of "First Things First" was published in various professional venues, such as *AIGA*, *Émigré*, and *Adbusters*. The revised text is more philosophical, proclaiming that

> Designers who devote their efforts primarily to advertising, marketing and brand development are supporting, and implicitly endorsing, a mental environment so saturated with commercial messages that it is changing the very way citizen-consumers speak, think, feel, respond and interact. To some extent we are all helping draft a reductive and immeasurably harmful code of public discourse. (*Adbusters*)

The authors of the manifesto propose "a reversal of priorities," in which designers and other cultural workers eschew commercial discourses "in favor of more useful, lasting and democratic forms of communication" (*Adbusters*).

The FTF statement draws attention to a key problem: that we are immersed in discourses produced by technically proficient and highly creative culture workers whose talents serve media institutions that are ultimately interested in profit. To address this problem, the FTF authors recommend revolt. Graphic designers, illustrators, videographers, scriptwriters—all of the specialists responsible for producing commercialized discourse should simply opt out, should refuse to place their talents in service of capital. This is an admirable response as far as it goes. The problem is that it assigns responsibility to a small group of highly trained specialists (cultural workers) and fails to address the larger structures of power in which those specialists are embedded.

This book is about a different solution. We propose that instead of leaving the work of cultural production to graphic designers, illustrators, photographers, videographers, and other creative specialists, this work should be considered the proper domain of ordinary people. In making this proposal, we attempt to connect the possibilities associated with multimodality to traditions in composition that emphasize, in Rosa A. Eberly's words, the "praxis of rhetoric as a productive and practical art" ("Rhetoric" 290). Eberly argues that deploying a pedagogy founded on such an approach "can be a radically democratic act" and "can form collective habits" which in turn "can be experienced as pleasurable" and "can sustain publics and counterpublics—on campus and beyond campus" (290, 294). In this book, we argue for a more substantial integration of multimodal rhetoric into our collective public-rhetorical habits. As multiply-situated subjects positioned within various and overlapping publics and counterpublics, we contend that ordinary rhetors should appropriate the rhetorical tools of graphic designers, illustrators, photographers, and videographers in order to assume responsibility for the production of culture.

As Nancy Fraser observes, historically disenfranchised groups have the most at stake in addressing the problem of commercialized media. "In stratified societies," Fraser observes, "unequally empowered social groups tend to develop unequally valued cultural styles" (64). These inequalities are compounded by the fact that for-profit media control the conversation:

> the media that constitute the material support for the circulation of views are privately owned and operated for profit. Consequently, subordinated social groups usually lack equal access to the material means of equal participation. Thus,

political economy enforces structurally what culture accomplishes informally. (64–65)

Fraser introduces the idea of multiple "subaltern counterpublics" as an alternative to the singular and exclusive liberal bourgeois public sphere outlined by Jürgen Habermas in *The Structural Transformation of the Public Sphere: An Inquiry into a Category of Bourgeois Society* (67, 79).[1] Subaltern counterpublics are "parallel discursive arenas where members of subordinated social groups invent and circulate counterdiscourses, which in turn permit them to formulate oppositional interpretations of their identities, interests, and needs" (67). As many scholars have observed, subaltern counterpublics seek out a wide range of rhetorical practices as they oppose dominant discourses. For instance, in his contribution to *The Black Public Sphere: A Public Culture Book*, Houston A. Baker, Jr., explores the role of "music," "spectacle," and "performance" as tools for establishing publics and achieving the goals of the civil rights movement (19–22). Focusing "attention on issues of equality and justice," according to Baker, requires "[r]adically new forms of visibility" (33–34).

The rhetorical practices Baker describes are not limited to the words-on-paper rhetoric that has historically characterized the writing classroom and the field of composition studies. Baker outlines an intensely multimodal, multimedial, multigeneric set of practices that exploit the full range of rhetorical potential available at any given moment. The question we want to ask is this: *Is there a way for rhetorical education, as practiced in contemporary academic settings, to make itself relevant to the needs of rhetors who might want to use multimodal rhetoric in the various and overlapping publics and counterpublics within which they are situated?* However, this question implies a prior question, one of rhetorical theory. An effective pedagogy will be one grounded in an effective model of how rhetoric happens. Therefore, the second question that occasions this book is, *What, if any, revisions must be made to traditional models of public-rhetorical practice in light of multimodality?*

MULTIMODAL RHETORIC AND THE PUBLIC TURN IN COMPOSITION

As we use the term, *multimodal rhetoric* refers to communicative practices that integrate multiple semiotic resources. Films, for instance, routinely integrate music, moving images, still images, spoken words, written words, gestures, facial expressions, and more. A multimodal composition does not achieve its rhetorical effects through simple addition (text + image + sound = message). The holistic effect of a multimodal text is achieved through, to borrow David Blakesley's word, the "interanimation" of semiotic components, resulting in a whole that is decidedly greater than the sum of its parts (112). Focusing on multimodality, as Rick Iedema observes, "is about recognizing that language is not . . . at the centre of all communication" (39). Multimodality "provides the means to describe a practice or representation in all its semiotic complexity and richness" (39).

Multimodality is not new. Humans experience the world through multiple senses simultaneously, and practices of sociality (including rhetoric) have always reflected this. A speech delivered in a public forum is a complex performance that involves not just words, but gestures, facial expressions, intonation, and more; young Cicero was trained by a theatrical performer (Hughes 129).[2] Nor is public oratory, which figures so prominently in stories that emphasize the Western evolution of rhetoric, the only ancient category of rhetorical production. Angela Haas, for instance, explores the American Indian tradition of wampum as a rhetorical form that prefigures what we now call "hypertext." Haas writes, "[A] wampum hypertext constructs an architectural mnemonic system of knowledge making and memory recollection through bead placement, proximity, balance, and color" (86). Haas sees wampum as a "digital" rhetoric in the sense that it pertains to the fingers (or digits); thus, wampum is both visual and tactile (84).

Part of Haas's purpose is to critique narratives that depict hypertext as a Western "discovery" (83). Mindful of Haas's critique, we want to be careful in making any claims about the newness of the communicative practices facilitated by the networked personal computer and other digital technologies. New technologies build on earlier traditions even as they broaden rhetorical options. Consider the way the tradition of storytelling has evolved in recent years. In *The Moth* performance series, individuals tell stories in front of live audiences, as humans have always done. These stories are recorded, broadcast on public radio, and podcast on the Internet. Listeners access these stories on personal computers, car radios, smart phones, iPods, and more. *The Moth*, then, blends ancient (live performance), "old" (radio), and "new" (Internet podcast) media. Similarly, the artist David Hockney "paints" landscapes with his iPhone and iPad. These paintings have been widely distributed via email and the Web; they are also enlarged (using special software that prevents pixelation) and then printed in sizes suitable for traditional gallery shows (Gayford). Bathsheba Grossman uses computer-aided design (CAD) software to design sculptures, then "prints" hard copies of her designs. Grossman uses a direct-metal printing process that converts the digital designs to fully-formed, three-dimensional sculptures made of a steel-bronze alloy (see Grossman). In all of these cases, traditional forms of multimodal human expression (storytelling, painting, and sculpture) are produced, reproduced, and distributed via processes that fluidly incorporate ancient and contemporary practices, older and newer media.

A rich body of scholarship in composition and rhetoric explores the potentials of visual, aural, and multimodal rhetoric.[3] Not too long ago, Cynthia Selfe warned that "[t]o make it possible for students to practice, value, and understand a full range of literacies . . . English composition teachers have got to be willing to expand their own understanding of composing beyond conventional bounds of the alphabetic. And we have to do so quickly or risk having composition studies become increasingly irrelevant" ("Students" 54). Emerging alongside this interest in multimodality is a renewed interest in public rhetoric. Some have even referred to a "public turn" (Weisser) or better yet, in honor of rhetoric's roots in communal life, a "public *return*" (qtd. in Mathieu).[4]

These two major trajectories of conversation within composition-rhetoric and adjacent fields, however, do not often intersect. Many scholars explore the relationship between digital technologies and the public sphere, but these discussions tend to ignore the implications of multimodality. Discussions of "e-democracy" and "digital democracy" tend to focus on undifferentiated conceptualizations of "information," "communication," and "knowledge" without attending to the specific forms (aural, visual, alphabetic, etc.) this material takes. Katrin Voltmer, for instance, observes that "[w]ithout reliable information, it would be impossible for citizens to use their power effectively at election time, nor would they be aware of the problems and issues that need active consideration beyond voting" (140). Similarly, in their introduction to *Digital Democracy*, Barry N. Hague and Brian Loader provide a list "of the key features of interactive media that are claimed to offer the potential for the development of a new variety of democracy" (6). The list includes "Interactivity," "Global network," "Free speech,"

"Free association," "Construction and dissemination of information," "Challenge to professional and official perspectives," and "Breakdown of nation-state identity" (6). But there is no reference to multimodality (or associated concepts of visuality, aurality, multimediality, etc.) as one of the assets afforded by new media (for a similar list, see Hacker and van Dijk 4). In her recent study, *Rhetoric Online: Persuasion and Politics on the World Wide Web*, Barbara Warnick provides a useful overview of how public rhetoric changes in light of the Internet. While Warnick alludes to the use of multimedia on the Internet, she does not explore the implications of this in any detail. Instead, she focuses on the categories of credibility, interactivity, and intertextuality. Even the New London Group, so instrumental in drawing attention to visual, aural, and multimodal literacies, is strangely silent on multimodality in its discussion of "changing public lives" (13–15).

On the other hand, discussions of multimodal (or, more typically, visual) rhetoric occasionally invoke the idea of a "public." For instance, W. J. T. Mitchell devotes a chapter of *Picture Theory: Essays on Verbal and Visual Representation* to "Pictures in the Public Sphere," and Robert Hariman and John Louis Lucaites explore visual rhetoric and "public culture" in *No Caption Needed: Iconic Photographs, Public Culture, and Liberal Democracy*. These works, however, focus primarily on visual rhetoric that emerges from commercialized, professionalized, and centralized media channels. One example that Hariman and Lucaites examine, for instance, is the famous *Raising the Flag on Iwo Jima* photograph, but this photograph was taken by a professional photographer (Joe Rosenthal) employed by an official institution of the commercial media (Associated Press) and was distributed to the public through technologies of distribution owned by the commercial press (the AP wire service, newspapers, and other media). In this vision, public conversation is driven by centralized, for-profit media institutions rather than by the participation of lay actors.[5]

Our book, then, is positioned at the intersection of the field's interests in multimodal rhetoric, on the one hand, and in public rhetoric, on the other. We contend that these two strands of the conversation need to be read in relation to each other. Multimodality raises distinctive complexities and challenges for the theory and practice of public rhetoric; and the *public* nature of public rhetoric raises distinctive concerns for multimodality. As our exploration of the FTF manifesto indicates, at stake here is nothing less than *who owns culture*. We can continue to conceive of public rhetoric as a largely word-based affair, but to do so would cede large portions of the culture to commercialized media. What we explore here is a model in which public rhetoric is conceived of as "the making of culture" (Spellmeyer 7) or "poetic world making" (Warner 114), a model in which all public rhetors, not just well-capitalized corporations, play a role in the production of culture through imaginative and ethical use of words, images, and sounds.

Problems Introduced by Multimodality

We argue that to realize the full potential of multimodal public rhetoric, the field of composition and rhetoric needs a wide range of solutions to a number of intellectual and practical problems. One set of problems pertains to our ability as a field and as a culture to confront the wide range of options available to us. Once we look beyond writing, we find a dizzying array of choices. Teachers need to decide what to teach. Rhetors need to decide what to use in any given situation. These decisions are made more complex and more urgent by the reality that options continually change in response to new cultural practices and new technologies. What is off limits one day is routine the next.

Additionally, multimodality gives new urgency to considerations of what happens when the composition is done. Deciding whether or not to use a given mode or medium requires going beyond the question, *Can I make it?* We must also ask, *Once I make it, how will it get where it needs to go in order to do the work it is meant to do?* Questions about the circulation of rhetorical compositions quickly foreground material considerations that have typically been elided in discussions of rhetorical theory and pedagogy. As rhetors struggle to choreograph a wide variety of resources that include money, space, time, technologies, and collaborators, rhetorical practice begins to feel less like a cognitive-symbolic activity (Would an argument from ethos work here? An enthymeme?) and more like a set of arcane project-management skills. Rhetorical agency, in turn, needs to be reconfigured, understood in relation to a web of contingencies that are largely beyond the control of the rhetor.

A different set of problems pertains to the distinctive way semiosis happens when words, images, and sounds interact. In multimodal compositions, the whole exceeds the sum of the parts, resulting in both challenges and new possibilities. Some of these challenges con-

cern a set of ethical considerations that emerge from multimodal semiosis. Some of the potentials concern the reality that culture itself is
multimodal, as are the cultural products of identity and consciousness.

In the remainder of this chapter, we briefly illustrate each of these
problems by examining three examples or cases. Indeed, this book relies heavily on our interpretation of case examples as a means to convey
ideas about rhetoric, pedagogy, publics, and new media. This kind of
evidence has its own limitations and affordances, as James E. Porter
has noted. Drawing on Albert R. Jonsen and Stephen Toulmin, Porter
observes that any "principles derived in such a way [i.e., through case
analysis] do not hold 'universal or invariable' status, but they do have
heuristic power" (*Rhetorical* 20). This book aims to develop heuristic
strategies for teachers, scholars, and practitioners by examining multiple cases of multimodal public rhetoric.

Case #1: 3D Printers (Or, What Forms of Composing Are NOT Relevant to Writing Courses?)

There's a new kind of printer on the market, a rapid-prototyping technology that prints fully-formed three-dimensional objects. Inkjet and
laser printers, like typewriters before them, place a layer of ink on the
surface of paper. 3D printers spray a very thin layer of plastic and then
continue to add layer upon layer until the composition is rendered
complete with height, width, and depth. Some commentators have
claimed that this turn to desktop *manufacturing* will be just as "revolutionary" as desktop *publishing* has been (see Gershenfeld 42; Morris).[6]

Should composition and rhetoric participate in this revolution? We
routinely ask students to print papers. Should we ask them to print 3D
compositions as well? We suspect that many readers will be skeptical
about the relevance of 3D printers for the composition classroom or the
field of composition studies. Indeed, skepticism toward new rhetorical
forms is historically typical. Plato was skeptical about writing. More
recently, those who have explored the importance of visual, aural, and
multimodal rhetorics have found it necessary to address various forms
of skepticism. Writing eight years after the New London Group drew
attention to the importance of visual, aural, and multimodal literacies,
Bruce McComiskey begins a discussion of visual rhetoric by recounting conversations with colleagues who claim that visuality is irrelevant
to writing ("Visual" 188).

Intellectual skepticism is healthy when it engenders critical reflection. It is counterproductive, however, when it forecloses emergent rhetorical forms that students might usefully deploy in the publics and counterpublics with which they identify. So how do we, as a field, tell the difference between new rhetorical forms that we can safely ignore and forms that force us to reconfigure our pedagogies? The question is an important one. Those of us who help facilitate rhetorical education are assigned the sobering task of deciding which rhetorical practices, forms, and tools are valued in the classroom and which ones are not. The set of values we install in classroom contexts, to some degree, shapes the broader culture outside the classroom. So how do we decide what to value? Maybe it's okay for rhetorical education to ignore 3D printers. How would we know?

While we find 3D printers interesting, our goal here is not to advocate their use in the writing classroom, but instead to raise an important intellectual problem that rhetors, rhetorical theorists, and rhetorical educators need to face. *Given that we are continually confronted with new rhetorical modes, practices, and technologies, how do we decide what to teach and use?* As we map a theory and pedagogy of multimodal public rhetoric, we find it essential to address this question.

Case #2: Not a Box (Or, The Distribution of the Message Is the Message)

Dutch designer David Graas is known for innovative designs that exemplify sustainable practices. One of his designs is the *Not a Box*—a lamp made from a cardboard box (figure 1). In a gesture of postmodern humor, the sides of the box contain cutouts in the shape of a traditional lamp. When the bulb inside the *Not a Box* is turned on, the cutouts light up. To understand the rhetoricity of the *Not a Box*, we need to see that the package for the product (the cardboard box) *is* the product. The *Not a Box* is an example of no-waste packaging; as such, it functions to raise awareness of sustainable practices. The rhetorical message embodied and performed by the *Not a Box* might be paraphrased as *we need to (and can!) find creative ways to avoid waste.*

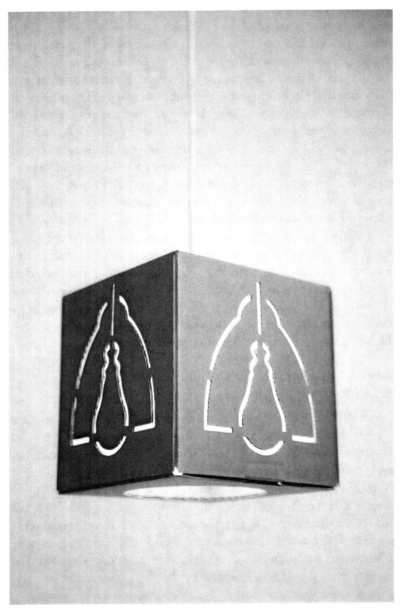

Figure 1. David Graas's *Not a Box*. Photograph by Tim Stet. © 2010 David Graas. Used by permission.

Traditional models of rhetorical theory and pedagogy are of limited use in helping to facilitate a critical reading of the *Not a Box*. The rhetorical success of the *Not a Box* cannot be accounted for based on compositional considerations alone. It's a simple cardboard lamp, a novelty item. Imagine that the *Not a Box* was submitted by a student in response to the assignment, *Produce a composition that helps raise awareness about sustainable practices*. Teachers who sought out the message of the *Not a Box* through the usual methods—by examining the composition—would be forced to conclude that there was no message. The *Not a Box* would certainly receive a failing grade.

It is only when one takes into account how the lamp was distributed—that the lamp was its own package, and therefore generated zero waste—that the *Not a Box* communicates a socially relevant message. This case points to the relationship between composition and distribution—between the message and how that message travels through material-cultural contexts. In this case, composition *anticipates* circulation. Graas didn't design a lamp and then inquire into how it could be shipped. He first inquired how it could be shipped and then created a design that exploited that process. Considerations of composition follow considerations of distribution.

As we map a theory and pedagogy of multimodal public rhetoric, we find that it is essential to revise models of rhetorical invention so that they adequately account for the relationship between composing and the processes of reproduction and distribution that happen when the composition is done. While the relationship between composition and distribution is particularly pronounced in the case of Graas's *Not a Box*, we contend that this relationship is always an essential one. Based on cases we explore below, we go one step further, claiming that the *composing process* is exceeded by the *rhetorical process*. The work of rhetors is not done when the composition is done, but continues in the labor rhetors invest in processes of circulation.

Case #3: "Cotton Patch" (Or, The Latourian Mystery of Page 48)

Our third case is a bit more involved. It concerns a New Deal-era theatrical vignette called "Cotton Patch," as explored by theater historian Ann Folino White. Belonging to the "living newspaper" genre, "Cotton Patch" offers a theatrical rendering of current issues of the day. Specifically, it focuses on the irony that results when government programs undermine each other. An African-American farmer named

Sam has received a mule through a government loan program, but because Sam owes taxes, a sheriff is sent to repossess the mule. As the sheriff leads the mule away, he asks Sam what the animal's name is. "Guv'ment," Sam replies—a gesture that, according to White, "characterizes the Roosevelt Administration a jackass" (246). "Cotton Patch," White concludes, "represents the national situation as inane" (247). In many ways, then, "Cotton Patch" conforms to a standard model of public rhetoric; it is a vehicle used by citizens to critique social issues of common concern.

"Cotton Patch" appeared as part of *Triple-A Plowed Under,* a production of the Federal Theatre Project, one of the arts programs sponsored by Roosevelt's Works Progress Administration. It premiered on March 14, 1936 at New York City's Biltmore Theatre, but was cut from *Triple-A* after opening night and was not included in subsequent Biltmore performances. According to White, the only direct explanation for the cut can be found on Page 48 of an archived copy of the script, which contains a typed note from Director Joseph Losey:

> We are not using this scene as it was impossible to get actors to play it with the necessary simplicity. The scene is conceived to be played entirely without props, with vaudeville technique, but not to be played up or plugged. If this scene is to be used, it should be played in front of a cyclorama [i.e., a neutral screen often used as a backdrop] framed with blacks [i.e., black curtains], and the subsequent Sharecropper Scene, should be played in front of Blacks. (qtd. in White 244)

White's account takes the form of a detective story. The mystery concerns why "Cotton Patch" was cut from *Triple-A,* and the note from Joseph Losey is the principal clue. White examines this clue from a variety of angles, offering various possible interpretations, but none of these interpretations is altogether satisfying; the mystery is ultimately unsolvable. We could, for instance, take Losey at his word and assign blame to the actors. This becomes problematic, however, when one considers that the script itself seems to demand a comedic style derived from conventions of "light minstrel comedy" (246). Sam's character is established through song, pantomime, and "stereotypic dialect that abounds in 'sho'nuffs' and syntactical disorder," making it difficult to reconcile with Losey's direction that the scene is "not to be played up or plugged" (246). The script, actors, and director seem to be at odds with each other.

While the case of "Cotton Patch" uses the traditional tools of theater rather than the digital tools of new media, it illustrates the important reality that multimodal public rhetoric often emerges from a complex network: multiple actors, multiple technologies, multiple discourses, and multiple semiotic resources. Traditional models of rhetorical production tend to emphasize stable relations between rhetor (usually a single, rational, autonomous subject), message, and audience, but the mystery of Page 48 points to the limitations of this model. Page 48 is mysterious, as White cleverly shows, because it lies at the intersection of a hundred threads in a material-cultural-performative-semiotic web that includes various collaborators (director, writers, actors, stage designers, and audience members), theatrical genres (vaudeville, minstrelsy, political satire, and other dramatic forms), and staging technologies (cyclorama, black curtains, and no props). "Cotton Patch" cannot be theorized in terms of a single rhetor's purposeful actions. Instead, "Cotton Patch" emerges from a complex network of human and nonhuman agents. In chapter 5 we draw on actor-network theorists like Bruno Latour, John Law, and others to explore the distributed nature of rhetorical agency.

The case of "Cotton Patch" also reveals that ethical issues are often at stake in rhetors' struggles to confront multiple contingencies. In this case, a failure to effectively choreograph a constellation of human and nonhuman actors could result in the promotion of racist perceptions. If the actors, with guidance from the director, do not effectively transmediate the script provided by the writers, the portrayal of rural African-Americans will slip from productive social commentary to the pernicious representational practices of minstrelsy. While representational ethics are implicated in all rhetorical actions, many of the challenges here derive precisely from the multimodal and distributed nature of the performance: the particular configuration of disparate elements of theatrical production (song, dance, props, make-up, costumes, and performed script). As we map a theory and pedagogy of multimodal public rhetoric, then, we find it crucial to confront a set of peculiar ethical considerations raised by multimodality.

Mapping a Theory and Pedagogy of Multimodal Public Rhetoric

We begin, in chapter 1, with a discussion of *kairos* and *public sphere*, two keywords that will inform our exploration of multimodal public rhetoric throughout this book. *Kairos* is often defined as "the opportune moment," but this is shorthand for a complex and generative concept that helps us accomplish three major objectives: (1) to explore certain aspects of the rhetorical context that have often been overlooked; (2) to adopt a critically reflective disposition toward new possibilities in a given situation that may not conform to received wisdom; and (3) to examine not just the efficaciousness of various rhetorical responses, but ethical dimensions as well.

Equally generative, the *public sphere* has come to signify a social space for addressing "issues of common concern." *Public sphere*, however, is a highly contested term that warrants careful consideration. In response to the liberal bourgeois public sphere introduced by Habermas—in which public opinion is formed through rational-critical debate—we draw on Michael Warner, Nancy Fraser, and others to paint a picture of multiple publics and counterpublics characterized by what Warner calls "poetic world making" (114).

In chapter 2, we use the case of 3D printers as a starting point for examining what we might call, the *problem of newness*. In a time of rapid technological change, we as a field and as a culture are continually confronted with new modes, media, and technologies. Faced with this newness, it is not always easy to discern the kairotic opportunities that confront us. *Are 3D printers revolutionary or irrelevant? Should we redesign our curricula to account for them or should we simply ignore them?* These questions are important, in part, because they speak to the issue of access: will 3D printing remain the purview of a small group of specialists (industrial designers and engineers) or will it be appropriated by the students who fill our composition classrooms? We turn to the case of two "old media" technologies—the still camera and the movie camera—in order to demonstrate the way multiple material and cultural pressures open up certain opportunities and foreclose others. Scholars who have examined the case of still and movie cameras have demonstrated that the potential of those technologies to function as tools of multimodal public rhetoric was severely limited by a variety of cultural forces.

As Eric Charles White says, "*kairos* regards the present as unprecedented, as a moment of decision, a moment of crisis, and considers it impossible, therefore, to intervene successfully in the course of events merely on the basis of past experience" (14). If past experience is our only guide, 3D printers are a non-starter. In the past, composition has been about the spoken and written word, not about the production of fabricated plastic prototypes. But kairos forces us to suspend the habits, routines, and attitudes that characterize our thinking and ask, *How is this moment different? What new possibilities present themselves?*

To help facilitate the kinds of inquiry that lead to locally situated and provisional answers to such questions, we offer a four-part heuristic aimed at helping stakeholders (rhetors, students, teachers, administrators) confront the *problem of newness*. Faced with new rhetorical technologies like 3D printers, we might ask whether they are available, affordable, and easy-to-use. These are questions that pertain to the *infrastructural accessibility* of a given rhetorical form. Alternatively, we might ask whether or not 3D rhetoric can accommodate the kind of persuasive strategies (e.g., arguments from pathos, ethos, and logos) that we desire. These questions pertain to the *semiotic potentials* of the rhetorical form. We might also ask whether or not 3D rhetoric is valued in the personal, academic, professional, and public contexts within which we hope to succeed. These questions pertain to the *cultural position* of the rhetorical form. Finally, we might ask whether or not teachers trained in the field of writing properly have any business teaching 3D rhetoric. If 3D rhetoric is to be taught at all, shouldn't it be taught by engineers and industrial designers? These questions pertain to the practices of *specialization* associated with a given rhetorical form. We argue that these topoi or commonplaces can help open up kairotic opportunities for stakeholders.

While the heuristic we offer can be used in specific rhetorical contexts, we see it as most useful in generating broader inquiries and dispositions pertaining to the design of curricular structures (e.g., syllabi, courses, programs) and co-curricular structures (e.g., multiliteracy centers, humanities computing labs, living-learning communities) that might facilitate a robust praxis of multimodal public rhetoric. But rhetors working in specific situations will require more concrete strategies to facilitate what Jeffrey Walker calls "kairotic inventiveness"—strategies that form the focus of chapter 3 (49). Based on our reading of several cases of rhetorical intervention, we argue that kairotic considerations need to include questions that emerge *before* the rhetor commits to words on paper as well as questions that pertain to what happens *after* the composition is complete. Before they commit to words on paper, rhetors need to consider a wide range of options, including written and spoken words, moving and still images, music, ambient noises, color, typography, layout, diagrams, charts, graphs, and more. Rhetors also need to anticipate and plan for the way their compositions can be reproduced and distributed *after* those compositions are complete. A color photograph might work well on a webpage, but might be totally ineffective as part of a brochure that is destined to be reproduced using a cheap black-and-white photocopier. These considerations of reproduction and distribution force us to reconfigure existing models of rhetorical invention. We go one step further, arguing that rhetors not only need to *anticipate* reproduction and distribution, but to *involve themselves in* processes of reproduction and distribution.

The multiple and related shifts we explore in this chapter—from alphabetic rhetoric to multimodal rhetoric, from composition to circulation, from the discursive to the material—ultimately lead us to conclude that rhetors need to see themselves as part of a larger web of considerations that include audience, exigency, modes, media of production, media of reproduction and distribution, infrastructural resources, other collaborators, and other compositions. Rhetors participate in complex networks of human and nonhuman actors. We draw on and reconfigure Dilip Parameshwar Gaonkar's understanding of the rhetor as "point of articulation" to capture the rhetor's participation in this complex network (263).

In chapter 4 we continue our exploration of how rhetorical compositions circulate. We introduce the term *rhetorical velocity* to account for the speed and direction of compositions as they travel through material-cultural spaces. Related to rhetorical velocity is the concept of *rhetorical recomposition*, which refers to the way compositions are reused by subsequent rhetors. Our reading of three rhetorical interventions suggests that considerations of rhetorical velocity and recomposition inform the composing processes of successful rhetors. At the same time, rhetors never have full control over what happens to their texts once they enter into circulation.

Chapters 2–4, then, explore a number of complexities that are arguably overlooked by traditional rhetorical theory. In this reconfiguration, rhetoric is not a function of a single rhetor designing texts in response to exigencies and audiences. Instead, it emerges from a larger *ecology*: linguistic, aural, and visual semiotic resources; multiple technologies; multiple humans; multiple compositions and recompositions; multiple channels of reproduction and distribution. One risk of this ecological understanding of rhetoric is that rhetorical agency seems to evaporate. Rhetorical action is no longer the result of a rational autonomous subject who achieves a desired result by strategically adopting the right rhetorical techniques. Instead, it's the uncertain outcome of a web of contingencies, many of which are beyond the control of a single rhetor. Indeed, at times rhetoric fails to happen, as the case of "Cotton Patch" suggests.

In chapter 5, therefore, we turn to the problem of rhetorical agency. We draw on discussions of agency that are informed by postmodern conceptions of subjectivity, ideology, and discourse to theorize the way agency "exceeds the subject" (Herndl and Licona 142). We then draw on actor-network theory to more deeply understand the way agency is distributed across networks of human and nonhuman actants. This reconfiguration of agency, however, has important implications for pedagogy. In the second half of this chapter, then, we explore ways rhetorical education might productively be transformed to address the challenges faced by rhetors as points of articulation, the challenges that result from orchestrating or "choreographing" (Cussins) multiple actors, multiple compositions, multiple modalities, and multiple infrastructural resources. How can we help students confront the challenges associated with rhetoric's radically distributed nature?

Having explored the complex web of contingencies that surround processes of rhetorical invention, production, reproduction, and distribution, we focus our attention, in chapters 6 and 7, on the composition itself, seeking to understand the way the peculiar dynamics of multimodal rhetoric articulate with previous models of public rhetoric. We start by invoking traditions of rhetorical ethics. Kairos, after all, dictates that a rhetorical response be not just effective, but also fitting. In chapter 6 we explore distinctive ethical considerations that emerge in the context of multimodality, focusing on a particular multimodal composition used by the prosecution in the trial of Michael Skakel. We demonstrate the ways the particular dynamics of multimodality were exploited by the prosecution to create a "fabricated confession" (Santos, et al. 67). Based on cases like "Cotton Patch" and the Skakel case, we conclude that existing models of rhetorical ethics need to be reconfigured to account for multimodality. Moreover, if teachers want to encourage ethical practices in students, they will need to find ways for students to explore the ethical challenges distinct to multimodality.

As we explore rhetorical ethics, however, we want to avoid the narrow and limiting construction of public rhetoric that sometimes results from the "goal of reaching a rationally motivated agreement" (Habermas, *Moral* 88). Too often, public-sphere theorists sacrifice important communicative practices in the name of the "rational." Pathos, visuality, and even rhetoric itself are often excluded in rigid and impoverished understandings of public discourse as rational-critical argument. In this narrow model, there is little room for multimodality to flourish.

In chapter 7, therefore, we explore an alternative model in which public rhetoric is conceived broadly as "the making of culture" (Spellmeyer 7) or "poetic world making" (Warner 114). In this model, rhetoric becomes "the mobilization of signs for the articulation of identities, ideologies, consciousnesses, communities, publics, and cultures" (De-Luca 17). As such, rhetoric is more than a rational-critical means of shaping public opinion. It fundamentally shapes our identities and the way we experience the world. We see this alternate model as a useful foundation for establishing a richer tradition of multimodal public rhetoric.

Finally, in chapters 8 and 9, we attempt to bring all of these strands together, to synthesize the various facets of our argument about the practice and teaching of multimodal public rhetoric. We offer a close reading of one large-scale rhetorical intervention—the D Brand (an attempt by a non-profit organization to rebrand Detroit)—that attends to all of the considerations we have been exploring. The D Brand, we suggest, takes seriously the task of poetic world making and offers compelling strategies for confronting rhetoric as complex ecology.

In chapter 9 we describe a particular approach to teaching multimodal public rhetoric that attempts to address the various concerns raised throughout the book. This approach attempts to provide students with an expanded understanding of kairos, with opportunities to make kairotic assessments of modes, media, and technologies of production, reproduction, and distribution. It asks them to think beyond single modes and single compositions—indeed, to think beyond the moment of composition to the ways their work might circulate through channels that are simultaneously material (in their reliance on the body, on geography, and on technologies) and cultural (in their reliance on structures of sociality, ideology, and legitimation). We situate this approach in a tradition of teaching what Eberly calls the "praxis of rhetoric as a productive and practical art" ("Rhetoric" 290). Along with Rosa A. Eberly, James A. Berlin, Bruce McComiskey, and others, we hope that teaching rhetoric as productive art "can be a radically democratic act" that "can sustain publics and counterpublics—on campus and beyond campus" (Eberly, "Rhetoric" 290, 294).

THE AVAILABLE MEANS OF PERSUASION

PART I

Foundational Terms

1 Kairos and the Public Sphere

In this preliminary chapter, we explore *kairos* and the *public sphere*—two theoretical concepts that will inform discussion throughout the book. Tracing the ways these terms have been discussed in both historical and contemporary contexts helps demonstrate their usefulness for a theory of multimodal public rhetoric. Ultimately, we argue that both *kairos* and *public sphere* need to be reconfigured if they are to serve multimodal public rhetors effectively.

DEFINITIONS OF KAIROS

Virtually all sustained discussions of kairos begin by observing, as James L. Kinneavy does, that "*kairos* is a complex concept, not easily reduced to a simple formula" ("A Neglected" 85). In his introduction to *Rhetoric and Kairos: Essays in History, Theory, and Praxis*, Phillip Sipiora observes that

> *kairos* is typically thought of as "timing" or "the right time," although its use went far beyond temporal reference. . . . A fundamental notion in ancient Greece, *kairos* carried a number of meanings in classical rhetorical theory and history, including "symmetry," "propriety," "occasion," "due measure," "fitness," "tact," "decorum," "convenience," "proportion," "fruit," "profit," and "wise moderation." (1)

Cynthia Miecznikowski Sheard (292) and Jane Sutton (413) each provide lists that are similarly various and copious. Kinneavy notes that to appreciate the full relevance of kairos for rhetoric, we need to take into account the "ethical, educational, epistemological, and aesthetic levels [of kairos], all of which are linked to each other" ("A Neglected" 87). In their explorations of kairos, rhetorical scholars have linked the concept to Sophistic, Platonic, Aristotelian, and Ciceronian traditions

(Hughes; Kinneavy, "A Neglected"; McComiskey, "Dissassembling"; Sipiora and Baumlin; Sutton). Kairos is a complex and richly generative concept that stubbornly resists simple definitions.

Many theorists emphasize that kairos includes both temporal and spatial dimensions, beginning with the original metaphors that inform the concept. Kinneavy asserts, "a second meaning of *kairos* was 'the right place' in addition to the right time" ("Revisited" 83; see also, Miller, "Kairos"; Sheard). Eric Charles White usefully addresses the various temporal and spatial metaphors that merge in the concept:

> *Kairos* is an ancient Greek word that means "the right moment" or "the opportune." The two meanings of the word apparently come from two different sources. In archery, it refers to an opening, or "opportunity" or, more precisely, a long tunnel-like aperture through which the archer's arrow has to pass. Successful passage of a *kairos* requires, therefore, that the archer's arrow be fired not only accurately but with enough power for it to penetrate. The second meaning of *kairos* traces to the art of weaving. There it is "the critical time" when the weaver must draw the yarn through a gap that momentarily opens in the warp of the cloth being woven. (13)

Richard Broxton Onians similarly explores the roots of kairos in weaving and in archery, noting that "Euripides refers to a part of the body where a weapon can penetrate to the life within" (343). White, Onians, and others establish that in addition to "the opportune moment," kairos is the opening or gap that allows passage to a goal or desired destination.

Most contemporary accounts of kairos are explicitly informed by ongoing discussions of the rhetorical situation (see Bazerman; Miller, "Kairos"; Sutton). Kinneavy flatly asserts that "the concept of situational context" is "a modern term for *kairos*" ("A Neglected" 83). Many of these accounts draw specifically on the conversation about the rhetorical situation begun by Lloyd Bitzer in the inaugural issue of *Philosophy and Rhetoric*. Indeed, this debate has become so codified that Charles Bazerman refers to it as the "Bitzer-Vatz-Consigny debate" (174). Other theorists link kairos to rhetorical context via Kenneth Burke's concept of scene and the pentad (e.g., Sheard; Herndl and Licona). After citing the work of Bitzer, Burke, and others, Kinneavy concludes: "All of these voices saying ultimately the same thing ought to convince us that some consideration in any rhetorical theory must be given to the issue raised by the concept of *kairos*—the appropriateness of the discourse to the particular circumstances of the time, place, speaker, and audience involved" ("A Neglected" 85). Sheard offers a concise encapsulation of many of these concerns in her summary of the concept:

> *Kairos* is the ancient term for the sum total of "contexts," both spatial (e.g., formal) and temporal (e.g., epistemic), that influence the translation of thought into language and meaning in any rhetorical situation. *Kairos* encompasses the occasion itself, the historical circumstances that brought it about, the generic conventions of the form (oral or written) required by that occasion, the manner of delivery the audience expects at that time and place, their attitudes toward the speaker (or writer) and the occasion, even their assumptions about the world around them, and so on. (291–92)

Kairos, then, provides a way of exploring how rhetors shape their actions in response to a number of factors. As we expand the scope of kairos to account for multimodality, new factors come into play, introducing new layers of complexity. Many kairotic determinants are beyond the rhetor's control, a reality that complicates models of rhetorical agency. Indeed, the delicate nature of rhetorical agency is one of the abiding preoccupations of this book. Accordingly, we offer a preliminary look at agency here.

KAIROS AND RHETORICAL AGENCY

We sometimes talk about writing and rhetoric as if everything depends on rhetors and their compositions. Rhetors are constructed as rational autonomous subjects who craft efficacious compositions based on their mastery of the art of rhetoric. Kairos, however, reminds us of the numerous factors that rhetors do not control but that nevertheless determine what is rhetorically possible at a given moment. Kairos draws attention to rhetoric's "bondage to the occasion and the audience" (qtd. in Sutton 415). Kinneavy explores this issue in an interview focused on kairos. Asked if kairos is "beyond the rhetor's control" or if it can be "manufactured" by the rhetor, Kinneavy replies,

> Well, I can see that a rhetor can choose the right time, and in
> that sense he can create it. He may realize *this* is not the right
> time to bring *this* up yet, but if he waits too long it's going to
> be too late. So timing, or the right time, is sometimes in the
> hands of the rhetorician, but not always. Sometimes a situa-
> tion just arises, and if a rhetorician wants to persuade, he has
> to use the time, and so in that case what he can do is simply to
> adapt himself to that time. Or, sometimes, say these times are
> not very good or not very favorable to *this* idea, then he may
> show you back historically how this has been a very important
> idea, and we should not forget that. So, there are different
> things a rhetorician can do with regard to time. It is not *totally*
> in his control. ("Revisited" 77–78)

Kinneavy goes on to explain that if the time is not right, the rhetor
can "tell people, 'you people nowadays don't think very much of the
importance of this particular concept, but it is important'—you can
create that kind of a timing" (78). Kinneavy acknowledges that attention to kairos means candidly confronting the constraints within
which the rhetor operates. But he ekes out a space, however uncertain
and contingent, for rhetorical agency. The rhetor "reads" the situation
to determine what opportunities are and are not available.

Moreover, in Kinneavy's view, kairos doesn't fully precede rhetoric. Instead, rhetoric plays a role in helping to *construct* the moment of
kairos. In Kinneavy's example, referring to the lack of kairos becomes
a way to create kairos. An audience might be resistant; a skilled rhetor
might artfully address that resistance. Some audiences, however, might
be so resistant that no amount of rhetorical skill will be sufficient.

JoAnne Yates and Wanda Orlikowski are among the most opti-
mistic about rhetoric's ability to create its own kairos. Yates and Orlikowski, citing Carolyn R. Miller, emphasize a "constructivist" view
in which "situations are created by rhetors; thus, by implication, any
moment in time has a *kairos*, a unique potential that a rhetor can grasp
and make something of" (Miller, "Kairos" 312). Yates and Orlikowski
give the following example to illustrate the role of rhetoric in fashion-
ing kairos:

> An especially eloquent statement of this action-centered no-
> tion of time comes from a keynote speech made by Dr. Ben-
> jamin Mays, the president of Morehouse College, to a 1946

convention of the Young Women's Christian Association (YWCA) at which delegates were debating a proposed (and, at the time, very progressive) interracial charter. In this speech, he successfully overcame inertia and motivated action, in part through his characterization of time as something to be manipulated: "I hear you say that the time is not ripe . . . but if the time is not ripe, then it should be your purpose to ripen the time." (109)[7]

Yates and Orlikowski can be seen as testing the limits of rhetoric's ability to, as Kinneavy says, "create that kind of timing." Moreover, their example reveals the danger of citing situational constraints as an excuse for inaction.

Thus, there is a negotiation—or, as Carolyn R. Miller, drawing on Eric Charles White and Scott Consigny, calls it, a "struggle"—between the rhetor and the situation. "As an art," Miller concludes, "rhetoric engages the phenomena of concrete experience and itself is engaged by the force of human motivation; it is thus the site of interaction between situation and rhetor" ("Kairos" 313). Reviewing Gorgias's understanding of kairos, White echoes this more dynamic notion of the rhetor-situation relationship, stating that "[f]or Gorgias, *kairos* stands for a radical occasionality which implies a conception of the production of meaning in language as a process of continuous adjustment to and *creation of* the present occasion . . ." (15, emphasis added).

The crucial idea that rhetors might "ripen the time" is usefully illustrated in Miller's discussion of the rhetoric of science. Miller draws on the work of John Swales, whose research focuses on how scientific articles are framed. Swales finds that one of the primary "rhetorical moves" scientists make in their introductions is to "indicate a gap in the previous work" that "is turned into the research space for the present article" (qtd. in Miller, "Kairos" 313). For Miller, Swales's gap corresponds to the kairotic gap: the opening through which the arrow passes. "Kairos as opening," therefore, "is actively constructed by writers and readers" ("Kairos" 313).

The kairos or opening might present itself to the archer at a particular moment in time, but exploiting it depends on all of the training and preparation the archer has received prior to that moment. Similarly, the ability of rhetors to exploit kairotic moments depends, in part, on their past experiences and training. Sharon Crowley invokes the notion of the "prepared rhetor," a phrase we find particularly apt (84). Preparation is required to read the situation effectively, to discern what opportunities are available, and to know how to frame a rhetorical response that is appropriate. As McComiskey demonstrates in his discussion of Gorgias's use of kairos, an approach that works in one situation may not work in another, therefore "it is necessary for the Gorgianic orator to know and be able to apply all of the different literary devices (*metra*) to any *logos* in any kairotic situation" ("Disassembling" 213). Walker alludes to the issue of preparedness in his discussion of the enthymeme. He notes that the verb form of enthymeme (*enthymeomai*) includes the concept of "forming plans," hinting at rhetoric's "strategic intentionality." Crucial to this "strategic intentionality" is "kairotic inventiveness": "an inventiveness responsive to . . . the 'opportune' at any given moment in a particular rhetorical situation" ("The Body" 49). In many ways, this is a book about how "kairotic inventiveness" changes in the context of multimodality.

Kairos, finally, refers precisely to the moment when theory becomes practice, the moment when all of the rhetor's preparation, knowledge, and training is applied within a particular situation. This is hinted at in a passage from the *Phaedrus* cited by Kinneavy:

> But it is only when he has the capacity to declare himself with complete perception, in the presence of another, that here is the man and here the nature that was discussed theoretically at school—here, now present to him in actuality—to which he must apply *this* kind of speech in *this* sort of manner in order to obtain persuasion for *this* kind of activity—it is when he can do all this and when he has, in addition, grasped the concept of propriety of time . . . —when to speak and when to hold his tongue . . ., when to use brachylogy, piteous language, hyperbole for horrific effect, and, in a word, each of the specific devices of discourse he may have studied—it is only then, and not until then, that the finishing and perfecting touches have been given to his science. (qtd. in "A Neglected" 86)

Given the role of preparedness, rhetorical education can be seen as fundamentally consistent with a kairotic approach. By rhetorical education, we mean the totality of experiences that prepare a rhetor to act effectively within any given situation. In this broad sense, rhetorical education begins early. Infants enter into social environments in which a variety of rhetorical practices and tools are modeled. As they grow older, they continue to be immersed in rhetorically rich settings in which they experience and practice a wide range of rhetorical activities. School settings encourage various kinds of rhetorical practices, from drawing pictures to writing essays to giving oral presentations. At the college level, rhetorical education is potentially distributed across the entire curriculum. We can, of course, point to certain locations that function as key sites, including first-year composition, upper-level writing, and other writing-intensive courses. In many ways, the idea of the "prepared rhetor" is the motivation for our book. This book is primarily addressed to those who play a role in rhetorical education: writing teachers, writing program administrators, writing center consultants and administrators, WAC coordinators—those who are charged with fostering in rhetors the subjectivities and practices necessary for "kairotic inventiveness" (Walker, "The Body" 49) and "improvisational readiness" (E. C. White 14).

Our understanding of kairos and agency, then, references the "struggle" of the prepared rhetor within complex and multifaceted contexts that are simultaneously material, discursive, social, cultural, and historical. This struggle calls for the prepared rhetor to be kairotically inventive. We ourselves are somewhat skeptical about rhetoric's ability to "ripen the time," particularly in light of a number of complexities that are elided in most accounts of kairos. In the three chapters that immediately follow this one, we attempt to demonstrate that rhetorical success is contingent upon networks of human and nonhuman actors, including multiple semiotic modes and multiple media of production, reproduction, and distribution. These networks can be complex, unpredictable, and chaotic. After exploring this networked understanding of rhetorical practice through a close reading of a number of specific cases, we revisit the concept of agency in chapter 5. We begin with the way agency, as Carl G. Herndl and Adela C. Licona (following Paul Smith) put it, "exceeds the subject" (142). Drawing on Herndl and Licona, we explore the ways postmodern understandings of ideology, subjectivity, and discourse force us to posit "constrained agency" (134). We then turn to actor-network theorists like Latour and Law, who help us understand the way agency is distributed across human and nonhuman actors. We find this understanding particularly useful in our discussion the way of multimodal public rhetoric is linked to the material concerns of technology and space.

Finally, we should note that if kairos refers to the opportune moment, it is not about simple opportunism. As already hinted at in the definitions provided above, kairos is inextricably linked to ethics. Kairos is not just about what is effective, but what is fitting. Kinneavy, for instance, traces the relationship between kairos and justice from sophistic through Ciceronian rhetorics. He claims that for the sophists, justice was situational, coming close at times to "complete relativism" ("A Neglected" 87). While Plato worried about this relativism, his own system of ethics was grounded in "proper measure and right time— the two fundamental components of the concept of *kairos*" (88). This "aspect" of kairos "continued in the Latin concept of propriety, especially in Cicero" (88). A kairotic understanding of ethics is consistent with postmodern models that emphasize the situational nature of ethics. As Porter puts it in *Rhetorical Ethics and Internetworked Writing*

> By ethics I do not mean a particular moral core (as in the articulation "Christian ethics"). I am referring, rather, to rhetorical ethics—a set of implicit understandings between writer and audience about their relationship. Ethics in this sense is not an answer but is more a critical inquiry into how the writer determines what is good and desirable. Such inquiry necessarily leads toward a standpoint about what is good or desirable for a given situation. (68)

An understanding of ethics as situated becomes important to us in chapters 6 and 7, when we connect multimodal public rhetoric with models of the public sphere. We examine a multimodal composition used by the prosecution in the Michael Skakel trial to explore the ways multimodality potentially undermines the ethical goals of making reasoning transparent to an audience. We do not offer these goals as universal and transcendent, but rather as particular goals rhetors might want to embrace in certain situations. In chapter 7, we examine a different tradition of the public sphere that is not based on rational deliberation and that privileges goals aside from transparency of reasoning.

Publics, Publicity, and Public Spheres

If *kairos* allows us to characterize the inventiveness of the prepared rhetor, *public sphere* allows us to frame the broader social contexts within which rhetors operate. A highly contested and thoroughly vexed term, the public sphere is commonly defined as the space in which "the citizens of a pluralistic polity speak from and across their differences productively" (Ivie, "Rhetorical" 278). The term owes its popularity, in no small degree, to the work of Habermas, especially *The Structural Transformation of the Public Sphere*, published in English in 1989. We agree with Kevin Michael DeLuca that something akin to the "concept of the public sphere is indispensible for theoretical and practical reasons" (21; see also Fraser 57). In the remainder of this chapter, we review contemporary conversations about the nature of publics and publicity in order to establish what we have in mind when we use the concept of the *public sphere*. We begin with a brief outline of the defining features of Habermas's original model and then trace five broad areas of critique that public-sphere scholars have offered in response.

Habermas and the Liberal Bourgeois Public Sphere

In Habermas's original model, the liberal bourgeois public sphere is a social space in which private citizens (as distinct from state actors) come together to address issues of "common concern." Public-sphere activity could be witnessed in the salons of France, the coffee houses of Great Britain, and the "table societies" and "literary societies" of Germany (31–34). These institutions "organized discussion among private people" in such a way that social status was "disregarded altogether" (36). Not social status, but "the authority of the better argument" ruled the day (36). The "rational-critical debate" (160) that took place in coffeehouses and salons resulted in "public opinion" which in turn exerted political force on the state (52–55). The public sphere, in this conception, mediates between the private lives of ordinary citizens and the state.

Critical Responses to the Liberal Bourgeois Public Sphere

The model of the public sphere offered by Habermas in *Structural Transformation* has been critiqued along many lines. For the purposes of our exploration of multimodal public rhetoric, five broad areas of critique are particularly relevant.

Critique #1: The ontology of publics. The first set of critiques concerns the fundamental nature of the public sphere: What is the manner of its existence? Is it a sphere? Network? Rhizome? (Brouwer and Asen 1–23). The question is so vexing that some theorists recommend giv-

ing up the search for a definitive answer. Borrowing a term from Slavoj
Žižek, Jodi Dean recommends treating the public sphere as a "zero
institution": "an empty signifier that itself has no determinate meaning but that signifies the presence of meaning" (105). We find the
approach of Daniel C. Brouwer and Robert Asen more productive.
Brouwer and Asen begin the introduction to their recent collection,
Public Modalities: Rhetoric, Culture, Media, and the Shape of Public Life
by observing that

> The public organizes through metaphor. Both its practitio-
> ners and theorists employ a rich range of metaphors when en-
> acting and analyzing public activity. *Spheres, lines, networks,*
> *screens*—these terms render distinctly intelligible the quali-
> ties, realms, collectivities, or processes signified by multiple
> meanings of public. (1)

Brouwer and Asen resist the temptation to assert a single metaphor
as superior. Instead, they consider multiple metaphors, reviewing the
possibilities that each one opens up and forecloses.

As Brouwer and Asen note, the metaphor of the "sphere" has been
criticized by a number of scholars. Hariman and Lucaites complain
that spheres are "abstract, formally elegant, inherently rational, self-
completing and self-regulating entities imagined to be freestanding
in abstract space and seen from a macroscopic perspective" (qtd. in
Brouwer and Asen 4). Moreover, the insistence on spatiality that is
implied by a sphere (as a geometrical shape) can be both productive
and counterproductive (Brouwer and Asen 3–5). If we're not careful, we begin to speak of "entering" the public sphere, as if one could
physically move in and out of it in the same way one enters and leaves
a coffeehouse (for critiques of space- and place-based metaphors, see
Calhoun, "Rethinking" 4; Edbauer Rice, "Unframing" 9–12; Mah).
It will become clear in subsequent chapters that the metaphor of the
network or *web* has a special resonance for us. As Brouwer and Asen
observe, "Network and web metaphors invite greater consideration of
relationality and temporality" (7). *Network* is consonant with our understanding of kairos as involving a complex configuration of relationships between rhetors, audiences, places, and contextual resources and
constraints at a particular moment in time. We are also attracted to
Brouwer and Asen's use of modality, which "foregrounds productive

arts of crafting publicity," though we avoid this term because of possible confusion with "multimodality" as it is used in this book (17).

A danger of metaphors like "sphere" and "network" call to mind entities that exist (like a geophysical places) independently of the performances that occur "in" them, in the same way a theater exists even when there is no performance occurring there. But several theorists take issue with the implication that the public sphere exists independently of rhetorical performances. Warner, for instance, emphasizes the way a public is coaxed into existence via the operation of multiple texts circulating in relationship with each other over time:

> It's the way texts circulate, and become the basis for further representations, that convinces us that publics have activity and duration. A text, to have a public, must continue to circulate through time, and because this can only be confirmed through an intertextual environment of citation and implication, all publics are intertextual, even intergeneric. (97)

Audience and attention, in this model, become crucial: "Because a public exists only by virtue of address, it must predicate some degree of attention, however notional, from its members" (87). In Warner's conception, the public sphere has a fragile quality. It is always in danger of evaporating. Should channels of textual circulation become blocked or attention be diverted, the public will fade away. In this sense, a public is different from other forms of sociality, such as a "nation," which "includes its members whether they are awake or asleep, sober or drunk, sane or deranged, alert or comatose" (87). This emphasis on circulation and attention drives much of the subsequent discussion in our book. In chapters 3–5, we offer a revised model of rhetorical invention based on links between the composing process and considerations of circulation, of what happens when the composition is done.

Critique #2: The nature of access to the public sphere. The second critique concerns how publics are accessed. The liberal bourgeois public sphere is founded on the idea that participation is not reliant on social status. One did not need to be a duke to enter the coffeehouse and introduce arguments. But as many have pointed out, and as Habermas himself concedes, the allegedly egalitarian nature of this public had severe limitations: It only applied to white male property owners. The ideal model of the public sphere described by Habermas insists on what Seyla Benhabib calls a "symmetry condition," which includes the related tenets that "each participant must have an equal chance to initiate and to continue communication" and "each must have an equal chance to make assertions, recommendations, explanations, and to challenge justifications" (87). Likewise, Craig J. Calhoun writes that "[i]n a nutshell, a public sphere adequate to a democratic polity depends upon both quality of discourse and quantity of participation" ("Introduction" 2). Access is partly a function of material resources. As Nicholas Garnham observes, contemporary models of the public sphere must include provisions for "the problem raised by all forms of mediated communication, namely, how are the material resources necessary for that communication made available and to whom?" (361).

Habermas's "symmetry condition" is premised on the idea that social status and cultural difference can be bracketed or ignored and that participants can enter into rational-critical exchanges as equals. Fraser famously argues that it is impossible to achieve this form of equal access because "even after everyone is formally and legally licensed to participate," there will continue to be "informal impediments to participatory parity" (63). As an example of these impediments, Fraser cites Jane Mansbridge's finding that "[s]ubordinate groups sometimes cannot find the right voice or words to express their thoughts, and when they do, they discover they are not heard. [They] are silenced, encouraged to keep their wants inchoate, and heard to say 'yes' when what they have said is 'no'" (qtd. in Fraser 64). Fraser concludes that "[w]e should question whether it is possible even in principle for interlocutors to deliberate as if they were social peers in specially designated discursive arenas, when these discursive arenas are situated in a larger societal context that is pervaded by structural relations of dominance and subordination" (65). Rather than ignoring differences, it would be better to "explicitly thematiz[e]" them (64; see also, Sanders 360-2; Young, "Activist"; Young, "Communication" 122–3).

Combining Gayatri Spivak's "subaltern" with Rita Felski's "counterpublic," Fraser proposes the term "subaltern counterpublics" to denote the "parallel discursive arenas where members of subordinated social groups invent and circulate counterdiscourses, which in turn permit them to formulate oppositional interpretations of their identities, interests, and needs" (67, 79). Rather than a model that emphasizes a single, all-inclusive public, Fraser proposes a model comprised of multiple, oppositional publics. This proposal is not intended to signify the desirability of a hopelessly fractured society in which groups only talk amongst themselves; instead, "the concept of a counterpublic militates in the long run against separatism because it assumes an orientation that is *publicist*. Insofar as these arenas are *publics* they are by definition not enclaves" (67). Therefore, "subaltern counterpublics have a dual character. On the one hand, they function as spaces of withdrawal and regroupment; on the other hand, they also function as bases and training grounds for agitational activities directed toward wider publics" (68; see also, Felski 167; Asen and Brouwer 7).

In this book, we have no interest in reinscribing a naïve liberal ideal of equal access for all participants. Our pedagogy is kairotic, aimed at creating the conditions within which students—as members of various and overlapping publics and counterpublics—can theorize their own situated decisions about public participation. In the approach we propose, students read public contexts and make decisions about if, when, and how to participate. These forms of participation will be various and, to a certain extent, unpredictable. At times participation might take the form of tactical planning and value formation within small, highly focused groups, while other moments might be opportune for addressing wider publics.

Critique #3: The product of public-sphere participation. Habermas suggests that rational-critical debate leads to the formation of public opinion (54). Fraser, however, broadens this goal, emphasizing that public-sphere activity leads to "decision-making" on the one hand and "identity formation" on the other (75, 68). For Fraser, productive entrance into the public sphere "means being able to speak 'in one's own voice,' thereby simultaneously constructing and expressing one's cultural identity through idiom and style" (69). This function of the public sphere is not merely incidental, but an important political opportunity. "It seems to me," Fraser writes, "that public discursive arenas are among the most important and under-recognized sites in which social identities are constructed, deconstructed, and reconstructed" (79).

For Warner, identity is both the occasion for the public sphere and a product of it. Warner writes that "conditions of gender and sexuality can be treated not simply as the given necessities of the laboring body but as the occasion for forming publics, elaborating common worlds, making the transposition from shame to honor, from hiddenness to the exchange of viewpoints with generalized others, in such a way that the disclosure of self partakes of freedom" (61). Furthermore, a

> public, or counterpublic, can do more than represent the interests of gendered or sexualized persons in a public sphere. It can mediate the most private and intimate worlds of gender and sexuality. It can work to elaborate new worlds of culture and social relations in which gender and sexuality can be lived, including forms of intimate association, vocabularies of affect, styles of embodiment, erotic practices, and relations of care and pedagogy. It can therefore make new forms of gendered or sexual citizenship—meaning active participation in collective world making through publics of sex and gender. (57)

Indeed, for Warner, the proper business of the public sphere is "poetic world making" (114). Warner contrasts his model of the public sphere with Habermas and those who view public-sphere practice as limited to "conversation." In the liberal bourgeois model, publics "exist to deliberate and then to decide" and "require persuasion rather than poesis" (115). For Warner, however, "the perception of public discourse as conversation obscures the importance of the poetic functions of both language and corporeal expressivity in giving a particular shape to publics" (115).

Critique #4: The nature of public-sphere discourse. If diversity and difference demand that we speak of multiple publics and if these publics engender not just public opinion, but identity, consciousness, and culture, then the kind of discursive practices we should expect to find in the public sphere are themselves diverse, extending well beyond rational-critical deliberation. For Fraser, it is crucial that subordinated groups participate on their own terms, using their own "idiom and style" (69). To insist that groups adopt a single set of norms dictated by the dominant culture would amount to "discursive assimilation," which would lead to "the demise of multi-culturalism" (69). Late twentieth-century feminism, for instance, was not limited to a narrow understanding of rational-critical deliberation, but included such things as "festivals" and "film and video distribution networks" (67). Fraser's insistence on valuing participants native "idiom and style" is reminiscent of conversations in composition and rhetoric that led to and were fueled by CCCC's "Students' Rights to Their Own Language."

In "Reason and Passion in the Public Sphere: Habermas and the Cultural Historians," John L. Brooke usefully reviews a range of historical research that explores the role of expressive practices that go far beyond the coffeehouse conversations Habermas examines. As summarized by Brooke, David Waldstreicher locates public-sphere practices of post-Revolution U.S. in such things as "celebrations, parades, toasts, songs" (50). Similarly, David Shields "finds the sociability of the eighteenth-century [colonial American] public sphere defined by wit, humor, theatricality, and satire" (53). Shields reveals a sociality formed out of "the pursuit of pleasure" that includes social, affective, and aesthetic dimensions (qtd. in Brooke 53).

For Warner, the radical potential of publics is linked precisely to the ability of groups to introduce their own forms of expressivity: their own styles, forms, and practices of semiotic exchange. Warner writes that counterpublics "might not be organized by the hierarchy of faculties that elevates rational-critical reflection as the self-image of humanity; they might depend more heavily on performance spaces than on print" (123). "A queer public," writes Warner, "might be one that throws shade, prances, disses, acts up, carries on, longs, fantasizes, throws fits, mourns, 'reads'" (124). One of the most striking examples Warner explores is a performance of "erotic vomiting" at a leather bar (206–08).

For Warner, identity is maintained through particular forms and styles of discourse. Therefore, embracing the terms of rational-critical discourse required by a mainstream public sphere amounts to sacrificing identity; as counterpublics seek political agency, they "adapt themselves to the performatives of rational-critical discourse. For many counterpublics, to do so is to cede the original hope of transforming not just policy but the space of public life itself" (124). In contrast to "deliberation" or "conversation" Warner uses "poesis" to encapsulate all of the various forms of expression available to would-be participants in various and overlapping publics (115).

As we demonstrate in chapter 7, critiques #3 and #4 are crucial to our own argument about multimodal public rhetoric. If we limit the definition of the public sphere to the social space where rational-critical debate leads to public opinion, we are likely to dismiss multimodal public rhetoric as of very limited value indeed. In such a case, multimodality would be relegated to a supportive role: charts, graphs, diagrams, and figures meant to lend clarity to word-based arguments. But if the proper function of public-sphere practice is poetic world making that shapes consciousness and identity through the captivation of attention, multimodality becomes quite relevant indeed. Films, animations, fabricated objects, games, virtual reality compositions, and mixed media performances—these multimodal forms might play central role in public-sphere practices. Byron Hawk, for instance, explores the ways a punk rock album (Refused's *The Shape of Punk to Come*) functions as "both an example of and a call to create a public rhetoric through poetic world making . . ." (11).

Critique #5: The nature of agency. Habermas has been widely criticized for embracing a "modernist" understanding of the subject as an autonomous, rational agent. The philosopher Noëlle McAfee, for instance, draws on Julia Kristeva's notion of "subject-in-process" to develop an alternative model of agency as relational (153–54; see also MacAvoy's review). For Warner, agency is vexed, fragile, and problematic on several levels. Warner rejects the Habermasian model in which publics appear to derive agency through rational deliberation. Moreover, Warner is insistent that no single rhetorical act can bring a public into being. Texts never exist in a vacuum, but are read in relation to other texts, forming an intertextual network, much of which is beyond the control of single individuals or groups. "Every sentence," Warner writes, "is populated with the voices of others, living and dead, and is carried to whatever destination it has not by the force of intention or address but by the channels laid down in discourse. These requirements often have a politics of their own, and it may well be that their limitations are not to be easily overcome by strong will, broad mind, earnest heart, or ironic reflection" (128).

In our discussion of kairos above, we began to explore the notion of agency as struggle within various local and global contexts. In chapter 5, we revisit the concept of agency in the context of ideology and technology. We synthesize conceptions of agency offered by Warner with models offered by postmodern conceptions of the subject and with actor-network theory.

CONCLUSION

In this book we describe a kairotic approach to public rhetoric, by which we mean an approach that seeks to discover in each situation what kind of rhetorical action is appropriate. In our deployment, kairos refers to a struggle between rhetors and their contexts. Many of the factors in this struggle are beyond the control of any one individual or group; all situations demand kairotic inventiveness from prepared rhetors.

Public-sphere theorists have outlined a wide range of practices that are available to rhetors. A kairotic approach to public rhetoric means being aware of available options, aware of possibilities and constraints that operate at any given moment of action. The work of Habermas, Warner, Fraser, and others helps increase awareness of some of those possibilities and constraints. In this book, we continue to use the term "public sphere" despite the problems that inhere in that term. We certainly do not mean to emphasize "formally elegant, inherently rational, self-completing and self-regulating entities" (qtd. in Brouwer and Asen 4). Indeed, in many ways even *network* or *web* are too neat, calling to mind the elegant symmetry of a spider web or the efficiency of information traveling through the Internet at the speed of light (Latour, "On Recalling" 15–16). We continue to use the term *public sphere*, as many scholars do, not as a zero institution, but self-consciously as a shorthand expression for a set of social practices that are complex, multifaceted, and dynamic—often chaotic and inelegant.

To exploit the potentials of multimodal public rhetoric, we need to move past a narrow model of the single, universal public sphere constituted by physically co-present interlocutors who engage each other in rational-critical debate for the purpose of forming public opinion. Synthesizing the post-Habermasian models described by Fraser, Warner, and others, we have sketched a version of the public sphere that accommodates multiple publics whose identities and desires lead them to exploit a wide range of expressive forms: erotic, corporeal, extravagant, performative. This notion of a public is consonant with DeLuca's definition of rhetoric as "the mobilization of signs for the articulation of identities, ideologies, consciousnesses, communities, publics, and cultures" (17). Thus, we see the public sphere as inherently rhetorical. For us, referencing the *public sphere* is a way to avoid the repeated awkwardness of saying something like, *a set of contested and complementary, affective and desire-laden imaginary social phenomena brought into being through multiple acts of rhetorical poesis, addressed to strangers and occurring over time and in spaces that are simultaneously discursive, cultural, and material.*

PART II

Kairotic Inventiveness and
Rhetorical Ecologies

2 Multimodal Public Rhetoric and the Problem of Access

Public rhetoric is increasingly dominated by centralized commercial media. Many important channels of communication—spanning across film, TV, radio, and print media—are owned and operated by a small number for-profit firms. This reality severely limits who can enter into public conversations and on what terms. Conditions dictating access, however, are not fixed, but are always shifting, always in a state of flux. Changes in cultural practices and in communication technologies open new opportunities even as they foreclose others. The nineteenth century saw the invention of the camera, for instance, potentially opening up new forms of visual expression for public rhetors. A kairotic approach demands that we see each moment as, to some degree, new—characterized by new opportunities as well as new constraints. But this is much easier to say than to do. In this chapter, we attempt to confront the complex and shifting nature of access as it relates to material, cultural, and pedagogical conditions.

THE WONDER OF IT ALL: CONFRONTING RHETORICAL OPTIONS IN A MOMENT OF CRISIS

In our introduction, we called attention to a new kind of printer that outputs fully-formed, three-dimensional plastic prototypes. We posed a few questions for rhetorical practitioners, theorists, and educators: *Do you plan to integrate 3D printing into your rhetorical practices, models, and classrooms? Why or why not? How would you make such a decision? Why should printers that output ink on paper be privileged over printers that output 3D plastic prototypes?*

We use the 3D printer as an example precisely because it combines the familiar with the strange. Printers have become a normalized technology in writing instruction, evolving seamlessly (or so it might appear) from earlier technologies like the typewriter. Yet we expect that many readers will laugh at the proposition that this new kind of printer—which produces not words on a page, but 3D plastic proto-types—is relevant to composition students, teachers, or theorists.

We are not interested, here, in advocating for the adoption of 3D printers. Rather, we aim to focus on the broader intellectual problem that scholars and practitioners face when confronted with new rhetorical options in an era of rapid cultural and technological change. Technologies (like 3D printers) that appear marginal, esoteric, and laughable one day appear mainstream, common, and important the next. Given that, how do we decide what to emphasize in our rhetorical theories, pedagogies, and actions?

This is a sobering question to us—partly because it speaks to the question of access. We can't teach everything, especially in an era when new technologies continually make available new options. But the decision to teach certain genres, modes, media, and technologies instead of other available options constitutes an important cultural intervention. Every time we select a particular rhetorical option to teach, we intervene in two ways: we give students opportunities to practice that option and we normalize it. Conversely, when we decide not to teach an option, we withhold from students the opportunity to practice that option and we marginalize it. Whether or not rhetors see 3D rhetoric as a productive rhetorical option depends in part on whether the sum total of their educational experiences has provided them with the necessary knowledge and competencies to use 3D rhetoric effectively. But it also depends on whether rhetors view 3D rhetoric as a legitimate option to begin with, and this legitimacy derives, in part, from the way 3D rhetoric is (or is not) treated in institutionally sanctioned spaces of education (e.g., first-year writing).

In an age of rapid technological change, new rhetorical options become available daily. We can chose to ignore them, to rely on established traditions and practices that have become comfortable to us, but this runs counter to a kairotic approach. According to Eric Charles White, a commitment to kairos demands that we be willing to suspend accustomed habits of thinking and interrogate the moment to see what new possibilities it contains:

> [K]airos regards the present as unprecedented, as a moment of decision, a moment of crisis, and considers it impossible, therefore, to intervene successfully in the course of events merely

on the basis of past experience. How can one make sense of a world that is eternally new simply by repeating the readymade categories of tradition? Tradition must answer to the present, must be adapted to new circumstances that may modify or even disrupt received knowledge. Rather than understand the present solely in terms of the past, one should seek to remain open to an encounter with the unforeseen spontaneity we commonly describe as the "mother of invention." (14)

Honoring kairos, then, has a destabilizing effect, forcing us to question past practices in light of new possibilities. In an age of rapid techno-logical change, these new possibilities include things like 3D printers, wrap-around virtual worlds, multiplayer online games, and other op-tions that at first seem strange, newfangled, irrelevant.

Diana George, in "Wonder of It All: Computers, Writing Cen-ters, and the New World," eloquently captures the stunning effect of rapid technological change. George observes that "[c]hange is difficult, mostly because we just don't know how to change" (331). Drawing on the work of Stephen Greenblatt, George suggests that our encounter with new technologies is analogous to Europeans' encounter with the so-called "new world" (332). The "wonder and amazement" that ac-companied this encounter induced a kind of cultural and intellectual paralysis, akin, as Greenblatt puts it, to "the 'startle reflex' one can observe in infants: eyes widened, arms outstretched, breathing stilled, the whole momentarily convulsed" (qtd. in George 332). Likewise as we encounter the new world of emergent technologies "we are in dan-ger of either recreating the old or staring at the new in wonder" (333). The only cure for this paralysis the hard intellectual work that enables us to make sense of this "new world." We need "theory building" for without it, "we have no way of understanding the New World—the world of marvels, of wonder" (334).

This chapter heeds George's call for theory building. We offer a four-part heuristic aimed at supporting a kairotic approach—an ap-proach, that is, in which we experience each moment as a moment of crisis, full of possibilities that might not be self-evident. Our heu-ristic derives from analysis of earlier moments in history when new rhetorical technologies, namely the still camera and the movie camera, emerged as tools potentially available to public rhetors. Before we turn to these old new technologies, however, we want to establish a more general understanding of the dynamics of access and the way recent developments in media technologies are shifting those dynamics.

Two Technological Divides

In recent years, it has become common to refer to the "digital divide"—the gap between the technological "haves" and "have nots." Discussions of this divide often suffer from simplistic, acultural understandings of technology and from an uncritical reliance on problematic constructions of race and class. As Barbara Monroe and others demonstrate, much "digital divide" discourse relies on "bootstraps" narratives in which success is the simple result of an individual's hard work. In this formulation, once the "have nots" are given computers they will automatically secure lucrative jobs and a high quality of life. And if they don't, it's their own fault (Monroe 5–30).

The issue of access is further complicated by another kind of "divide." The rise of technologically-intensive mass media (e.g., TV, film, print media, and the Web) has meant that culturally important channels of communication have increasingly been owned by large, centralized, for-profit media firms. These firms command resources of capital, technology, and talent that far exceed what ordinary people possess. We now take it for granted that media conglomerates (e.g., Time Warner, Disney, and News Corp.) have access to vastly more resources than ordinary people, but this system is not inevitable, nor is it universal throughout human history (see, for instance, Hauser, *Vernacular* 14–24).

Many media scholars have explored the problems of a system that relies on centralized, conglomerated, and commercialized media institutions (see Bagdikian; Eberly, "Rhetoric"; Habermas, *Structural*; Hauser, *Vernacular*; Herman and Chomsky; Howley; Keane; Louw; McChesney; Norris). Edward S. Herman and Noam Chomsky, for instance, argue that the post 1980 period, marked by neoliberal politics of deregulation and globalization, has resulted in a significant erosion if not wholesale annihilation of the public sphere. The centralization of the media industry from fifty companies in the early 1980s to eight transnational conglomerates in 2002 has allowed what Kevin Robins and Frank Webster refer to as "the displacement of a political public sphere by a depoliticized consumer culture" (qtd. in Herman and Chomsky xviii). Robert W. McChesney draws similar conclusions in *The Problem of the Media: U.S. Communication Politics in the Twen-*

ty-First Century, arguing that neoliberal policies of deregulation and globalization have strengthened the cultural power of advertising and marketing, thereby allowing consumerism to overtake public interest.

As Fraser observes, the cultural marginalization of some groups is "amplified" by the reality that "the media that constitute the material support for the circulation of views are privately owned and operated for profit" (64–65). Similarly, Eberly alludes to this problem when she quotes a lengthy passage from McChesney that is worth repeating here:

> The market is in fact a highly flawed regulatory mechanism for a democracy. In markets, one's income and wealth determine one's power. It is a system of "one dollar, one vote" rather than "one person, one vote." Viewed in this manner, the market is more a plutocratic mechanism than a democratic one. In communication this means that the emerging system is tailored to the needs of business and the affluent. . . . The market is assumed to be a neutral and value-free regulatory mechanism. In fact . . . a commercial "marketplace" of ideas has a strong bias toward rewarding ideas supportive of the status quo and marginalizing socially dissident views. Markets tend to reproduce social inequality economically, politically, and ideologically. (qtd. in "Rhetoric" 297)

As solutions to the problems of corporatized and centralized mass media, a number of theorists have proposed more effective governmental regulation and the importance of publicly owned media (see, for instance, Keane; McChesney). These are important components of a solution, but there are other possibilities to consider as well. Without buying into the myth that "[t]he Internet . . . will set us free," we would like to summarize the ways new technologies potentially open up new forms of access to various and overlapping publics and counterpublics (McChesney 10).

SHIFTING DYNAMICS OF ACCESS: CAN YOU REMEMBER THE TWENTIETH CENTURY?

At heart, industrializing communicative processes (beginning with newspapers, but reaching its zenith with television) led to mass communication, which is inherently top-down and manipulative. Industrialization reduced

> *the spaces for 'ordinary' people (non-professional commu-*
> *nicators) to engage in meaning-making as anything other*
> *than audience.*
>
> —Eric Louw

Many new developments in rhetorical practices that have been enabled by emergent technologies—despite their newness—have already become so naturalized that it's easy to overlook their significance. Think, for instance, of how routine the posting and sharing of videos has become in the era of YouTube. It requires serious effort to recall the pre-Web, pre-home computer era. In this context, it is interesting to revisit works like Richard A. Lanham's *The Electronic Word: Democracy, Technology, and the Arts*, which attempt to record important shifts in access brought about by digital technologies. Lanham's work is suffused with a kind of wonder that emerges from the way new digital technologies make available forms of visual, musical, and multimodal expression that had previously been reserved for highly trained specialists. "Digitization," Lanham writes, "has rendered the world of music-making infinitely more accessible to people who before had not the talent or the resources to make music and hear how it sounds" (107). More generally, the personal computer can be seen as a "way to open levels of symbolic transformation . . . to people hitherto shut out from this world" (108).

A full understanding of access needs to include attention to the full cycle of rhetorical circulation, including production, reproduction, and distribution. In the case of mass media, each stage of the process is associated with a unique set of barriers. Successful TV and film *production*, for instance, has historically required expensive cameras, lights, microphones, editing equipment and so on; these technologies, in turn, required sound technicians, lighting technicians, camera operators, editors, and other specialists. Likewise, producing sophisticated print artifacts (e.g., magazines, brochures, books) required access to cameras, printing presses, inks, papers, die cutters, and more; a sophisticated print artifact might require the contributions of copywriters, graphic designers, photographers, illustrators, typesetters, and press operators.

Shifting attention to the way mass media compositions were *reproduced* and *distributed* reveals yet another set of variables that limit access. Once a film (for instance) was created, it was expensive and difficult to get it to audiences. Professional production companies had elaborate, resource-intensive systems for copying reels of film and distributing them to theaters, which themselves were increasingly owned by regional and national chains, and which contained expensive, highly specialized equipment (e.g., projectors, screens, sound systems).

The question of access is further complicated by problems related to the specific nature of certain media technologies themselves. Many mass media platforms were designed to facilitate few-to-many rather than many-to-many communication. As Bertolt Brecht observed eighty years ago:

> The radio would be the finest possible communication apparatus in public life, a vast network of pipes. That is to say, it would be if it knew how to receive as well as to transmit, how to let the listener speak as well as hear, how to bring him into a relationship instead of isolating him. On this principle the radio should step out of the supply business and organize its listeners as suppliers. (2)

Echoing Brecht, Hans Magnus Enzensberger contends that "[i]n its present form, equipment like television or film does not serve communication but prevents it. It allows no reciprocal action between transmitter and receiver" (97).

As many have noted, however, emergent technologies are fundamentally altering the dynamics of access by providing nonspecialists the resources necessary to produce, reproduce, and distribute rhetorically effective multimodal compositions (see, for instance, Anderson; Gershenfeld; Lanham, *Electronic*; Poster; Shirky). The personal computer allows lay actors to manipulate visual and aural semiotic elements in ways historically reserved for highly-trained specialists. Communicators who hope to make use of photographs, for instance, can turn to a host of free or inexpensive applications that provide access to a palette of options previously reserved for darkroom specialists: enlarging, cropping, adjusting color and contrast, and more. Likewise, many of the editing operations crucial to rhetorically effective uses of film—the ability to sequence footage, to cut between shots, to add music and voiceovers—are now easy to perform using a standard computer and free or inexpensive software. In unprecedented numbers, nonspecialists have access to applications that allow us to draw, paint, compose music, create animations, and even design and manufacture three-dimensional objects.

Problems related to reproduction and distribution are also increasingly addressed by the Internet and other digital technologies. Communicators can distribute a wide range of multimodal content via the Internet for a tiny fraction of what it would have cost in the past. Colors, images, and other semiotic elements do not add to the cost of reproducing digital compositions. A standard personal computer, configured as a Web server, can distribute millions of copies of a webpage without incurring additional cost. In contrast to TV, film, or radio, content on the Internet can be made available twenty-four hours a day without adding significant costs and without displacing other content. Even print documents are cheaper to produce, reproduce, and distribute than they were only a few years ago. A full-color brochure can be distributed to a wide audience as a PDF document. End users can output the composition on their own inkjet printers, which are now capable of producing sophisticated documents that include color, font, layout, photographs, charts, and more. Moreover, the concerns articulated by Brecht and Enzensberger are partially addressed by the Internet, which, in contrast to traditional radio and television, is a many-to-many, rather than a one-to-many technology. The predominant metaphor for new media is not a pipeline distributing content from a central location, but a web or network that connects multiple users to each other.

To sum up, recent technological changes mean that across a wide range of media, from videos to posters, production is cheaper and easier, reproduction is cheaper and easier, and distribution is cheaper and easier. Public rhetors potentially(!) have access to powers of production, reproduction, and distribution that only a few years ago were not readily available outside of commercial media. As Mark Poster writes, the Internet "radically decentralizes the positions of speech, publishing, film-making, radio and television broadcasting" (211). It is now possible to talk about the "demassification" and "mass amateurization" of media—to borrow terms from Bruce McComiskey ("Visual" 199) and Clay Shirky respectively.

As the preceding discussion should make clear, we are very interested in new media and the way new technologies open up new possibilities for rhetorical action, but we use the lens of *new media* generatively (to make visible more options) rather than as a filter (to reduce options). While new media may have distinct affordances, we are not suggesting that any category of media is preferable for all rhetorical situations. The term *new media* is typically reserved for practices that are "purely" digital, such as digital video, digital animation, webpages, virtual reality, etc.; however, focusing too narrowly on digitality is problematic. Sometimes "old media" options are better, and many compelling options are hybrid forms. Desktop publishing, for instance, ultimately leads to hardcopy ink-on-paper compositions, but the production of hardcopies is made much easier by the fact that the design process takes place within the digital environments provided by graphic design software. In chapter 4, we examine a case in which a message is communicated through a complex rhetorical chain that includes electronic and faxed (i.e., hard copy-to-digital-to-hard copy) press advisories, live performances, and alphabetic-photographic accounts published in both print and online newspapers. The approach we advocate is not characterized by a single-minded allegiance to new media, but by a commitment to a deep process of rhetorical invention that takes into account all available options.

INVISIBLE TOOLS: A SHORT HISTORY OF CAMERAS

In the previous section, we focused narrowly on technologies themselves. Our goal was to review the way recent technological shifts alter the dynamics of access, partially upsetting asymmetries between the power of large, conglomerated, for-profit media firms and ordinary people. As Barbara Jean Monroe observes, however, technologies do not exist in a vacuum. Reminding us that class inequality "is at once economic, racial, discursive, and epistemological in character," Monroe suggests that "[r]esituating the [digital] divide within the landscape of larger social and political formations should allow for a richer, more complicated discussion of a host of issues that attach themselves to Internet access per se but are actually constituted by these larger formations" (5). To better understand the way technologies are inextricably linked to the cultural, the social, and the discursive, it is useful to examine the adoption of earlier media tools: the analog still camera and the motion picture camera. An examination of how these older tools were and were not assimilated reveals important insights into how both cultural and material logics circumscribe the adoption of emergent technologies and rhetorics.

In his 1909 talk "Social Photography, How the Camera May Help in the Social Uplift," reform photographer Lewis Hine implores his audience to use photography as a political tool. Visual rhetoric, Hine claims, "brings one immediately into close touch with reality" and the photograph in particular "has an added realism of its own," an "inherent attraction not found in other forms of illustration" (111). Hine remarks that although his own era belongs to the "specialist," there is much to be gained "by the popularizing of camera work" (112).

Contemporary theorists like John Tagg and Don Slater agree with Hine's earlier assessment that the camera, in the hands of ordinary citizens, can be a powerful political tool. In Slater's words,

> the camera as an *active* mass tool of representation is a vehicle for documenting one's conditions (of living, working and sociality); for creating alternative representations of oneself and one's sex, class, age-group, race, etc.; of gaining power . . . over one's image; of presenting arguments and demands; of stimulating action. (290)

Slater and Tagg, however, both argue that the political potential of the camera has not been fully realized. To be clear, Slater and Tagg are not arguing that ordinary citizens have never used cameras for political or activist purposes. Instead, they are making a more general claim about the way a number of material and cultural pressures circumscribe political uses of the camera.

Tagg explains that technologies relevant to the photographic process "only passed into popular hands in the crudest sense of the term" and important "technical and cultural knowledge" remained unavailable to ordinary camera-users (17, 18). Anyone could snap a photograph, but in the age of film-based photography, most camera-users did not (for instance) own a darkroom equipped with the chemicals, enlargers, papers, and filters necessary to take advantage of the full range of photographic expression. Instead, most amateur photographers had their prints developed at local photomarts, thereby relinquishing the ability to make the rhetorical decisions that professional photographers routinely made in the darkroom: the ability to adjust contrast and tonality, to make precise determinations about how an image is cropped, to select an appropriate size and shape for the print, and more. Moreover, photography has been situated within a cultural hierarchy that privileged professionals and artists while it relegated amateurs to the domain of "kitsch" (19).

Slater examines other forces that have limited the ability of non-specialists to deploy in photographic rhetoric, pointing to the effects of "high pressure mass marketing of photographic equipment" that relegates the use of cameras to nonpolitical purposes (290). Slater concludes that the "enormous productive power" of the camera "is effectively contained as a conventionalized, passive, privatized and harmless leisure activity. The mass of photography—snapshooting—is hardly a conscious activity at all: it is an undeliberated moment spliced into the flow of certain ritual events: watching the baby, being at a tourist site, spending Sunday with the grandparents" (289; see also, Tagg 18).

The case of the motion picture camera is strikingly parallel to the case of the still camera. Early on, observers were aware that the movie camera could potentially be appropriated by ordinary citizens to effect social change (Winston 67). As Brian Winston and others have demonstrated, however, a complex set of cultural and material pressures severely curtailed radical use of the movie camera and related technologies. Winston argues against the "technological determinist view" that sees technologies as having self-evident and self-realizing potentials. In this view, "[w]hat the technology *can* deliver is what the technology *will* deliver" (86). "On the contrary," Winston argues, "technology is always responsive to forces outside itself" (86). The practice of using 35mm film is a case in point. Winston shows that the 35mm standard was perpetuated not because of "utility" but because of "unexamined cultural prejudice" including technology developers' tendency "to work with film strips in culturally familiar widths" (59). Initially the result of a one-inch wide image plus sprocket holes, the 35mm standard was "naturalized" and continued to be enforced throughout subsequent decades. Amateurs paid the price for this naturalization. Using 35mm film, "required cameras (and, of course, projectors) somewhat too large to be sold to the public, inhibiting the growth of amateur cinematography" (60).

Eventually alternate standards more conducive to amateur cinematography were developed—16mm and 8mm films that were less expensive and more portable—but these formats were seen as substandard and nonserious. Echoing Slater's analysis of the still camera, Patricia Rodden Zimmermann shows that the "definition" of nonprofessional use of film "narrowed . . . to a nonserious, leisure-time activity bolstering family solidarity and consumption" (145). Amateur film was "marginalized . . . as a hobby to fill up leisure time and as a retreat from social and political participation" (145–46). This marginalization was not inevitable, but was accomplished through the complex set of cultural and material forces, including "[t]echnical standards, aesthetic norms, socialization pressures, and political goals derailed its cultural construction into a privatized, almost silly, hobby" (157). Despite these pressures, Zimmermann ends with the hope that future constructions of amateur film "may liberate it as a more accessible and meaningful form of personal expression and social and political intervention" (157).

The same cultural pressures that limited the political use of cameras remain operational in the digital age. Apple, for instance, has developed a remarkable suite of applications packaged as iLife. These applications include tools for archiving and manipulating still images, making videos, composing music, and burning DVDs, but they are marketed via images of leisure-time consumption that recall the Kodak marketing Slater discusses. A recent advertisement asks, for instance, "What if you could command an entire world of music, photos, movies and DVDs—all from your sofa? Now you can share the good life with friends and family on a . . . new iMac G5" ("Mac Expo"). Like the camera, iLife is positioned within a discourse that tends to render it politically innocuous rather than one that underscores its radical possibilities. GarageBand, an iLife application for composing music, seems to locate itself, by its very name, in the domain of trivial recreation rather than serious social action.

The evolution of digital technologies themselves also strikingly echoes the evolution of the camera. Slater notes that in its pursuit of the widest possible market share, Kodak's goal was to make the camera as easy to use as possible. This imperative simultaneously resulted in cameras that were more restrictive (lacking features and settings available to professionals) and in consumption practices characterized by unthinking, unreflective use. "Point-and-shoot" became both a technical achievement and a (passive, depoliticized) mode of use. Likewise, newer versions of iMovie lack useful features available in older versions, rendering it easier to use, but more restrictive. That is, certain rhetorical options that were available in earlier versions were lacking or more difficult to access in later versions.

To sum up: the cases of the still and movie cameras reveal that a complex web of forces interact to shape the way a technology is developed and adopted. Technologies never have a completely independent "life of their own"; they do not inevitably yield their full potential to society (Winston 86). Instead, a constellation of cultural and material factors influence how they are used and by whom. To operationalize the full potential of technologies on behalf of social justice, we need to better understand the material-cultural dynamics that govern the development and uses of technologies. Slater, following Raymond Williams, observes, "any medium must be analysed not only in terms of its present use (a restriction which encourages technologism) but also in terms of its *potential* forms" (289-90, emphasis added).

Education, broadly conceived, plays a key role in shaping our conception and use of technologies, both at the systemic/macroscopic level (e.g., citizens voting on policies that dictate access to the Internet) and at the microscopic level of the individual and small group (e.g., an individual activist deciding to use or not use a particular rhetorical form). Every time a teacher asks a student to use a technology in the classroom, that technology is to some degree legitimated and alternate possibilities are, to some degree, marginalized. The practice of requiring first-year writing courses and of defining rhetorical practices in those courses narrowly (as words on paper) normalizes writing and marginalizes other rhetorical forms that are potentially valuable.

A HEURISTIC FOR CONFRONTING THE MOMENT OF CRISIS

Eric Charles White tells us that "kairos regards the present as unprecedented . . . a moment of crisis, and considers it impossible, therefore, to intervene successfully in the course of events merely on the basis of past experience. How can one make sense of a world that is eternally new simply by repeating the readymade categories of tradition? Tradition must answer to the present . . ." (14). As the cases of the still and motion picture cameras illustrate, however, it is not always easy to determine the new possibilities opened up by new rhetorical technologies. Numerous cultural and material pressures conspire to ensure that some uses will be apparent while other uses will not. The still and motion picture cameras were quickly naturalized as innocuous, depoliticized tools for nonserious leisure-time pursuits. If we abstract from this brief history of cameras, we can derive at least four fundamental lines of critical inquiry that need to be opened up in order to achieve a fully realized multimodal public sphere.[8]

1. *Semiotic potentials:* The particular processes of semiosis that a given rhetorical option (mode, medium, genre, or technology) makes available.

    Example: Hine claims that the photograph "has an added realism of its own," an "inherent attraction not found in other forms of illustration" (111).

2. *Cultural position:* The value assigned to a particular rhetorical option by various and overlapping cultural logics.

    Examples: Slater and Zimmermann show that the dominant culture treats photographic and filmic rhetoric (respectively) as appropriate for the domain of personal leisure, not political engagement.

3. *Infrastructural accessibility:* The material and intellectual resources necessary for a given rhetorical option to be deployed by a rhetor.

    Examples: Tagg demonstrates that technologies associated with the photograph are withheld from rhetors. Winston and Zimmermann both demonstrate that filmic technologies were withheld from rhetors.

4. *De/specialization:* The range of perceptions concerning the use of a given rhetorical form by nonspecialists.

    Example: Zimmermann demonstrates that even when access to filmic technologies was theoretically possible, "[t]he construction of media expertise limits and intimidates" production by nonspecialists (148).

In our discussion below, we offer a meta-discursive analysis of how we (as a field and as a society) respond to shifts in rhetorical technologies and practices. We examine key moments of change, including Plato's response to writing and more contemporary responses to visual and multimodal rhetoric. The point here is to demonstrate that the four heuristic categories we name are operational in our field, in related fields, and in the broader culture. They are rhetorical commonplaces, but they typically operate *unsystematically* and *tacitly*. By making them systematic and explicit, we hope to provide teachers, scholars, rhetors, and other stakeholders (parents, students, school board members, principals, deans, department chairs, etc.) with a heuristic tool for increasing critical reflectiveness, for opening up the kairotic possibilities in perpetual moments of crises. We do not conceive of these lines of inquiry as rigid and radically distinct, but as heuristic categories that fluidly overlap.

(1) Semiotic Potentials: *The particular processes of semiosis that a given rhetorical option makes available.*

Lewis Hine is often quoted as saying "If I could tell the story in words, I wouldn't need to lug a camera" (qtd. in Stott 30), which seems to imply that there is something special about the nature of photographs that make them better, for Hine's purposes, than language. Our culture is replete with similar expressions: "A picture is worth a thousand words." "If I could say it in words there would be no reason to paint" (commonly attributed to Edward Hopper). "Music is the universal language of mankind" (qtd. in N. Shapiro 17).

Common sense suggests that modes, media, and technologies have different affordances and constraints; in the words of Gunther Kress, they "bestow different powers on the makers and remakers of representations" ("Gains" 16). Arguments for or against a given rhetorical option frequently invoke these different powers. In "From Analysis to Design: Visual Communication in the Teaching of Writing," for instance, George raises the issue of affordances right from the start, in the epigraph that opens her piece: "In some respects . . . words cannot compare in effectiveness with pictures. The mere outlines in a Greek vase painting will give you a more immediate appreciation of the grace and beauty of the human form than pages of descriptive writing" (11).

Arguments from affordance are not, of course, limited to the contemporary moment. Plato argues that writing lacks the affordances of oral dialectic. "I cannot help feeling," Socrates tells Phaedrus, "that writing is unfortunately like painting; for the creations of the painter have the attitude of life, and yet if you ask them a question they preserve a solemn silence" (278). Nor are such arguments limited to our field. Legal scholars Neal Feigenson and Richard K. Sherwin, for instance, examine the affordances associated with visual rhetoric in the courtroom. Noting that "[l]awyers want to (and do) communicate implicitly for all sorts of reasons," they assert that "visual representations can create . . . implicit meanings very differently, *and in some ways better*, than (spoken) words alone can" (295–96, emphasis added).

Determining the affordances of a given mode, medium, or technology, however, is difficult. This "slipperiness" (Wysocki "Awaywithwords" 60) of affordances is raised in a special issue of *Computers and Composition* devoted to exploring the work of Gunther Kress. In the article that opens the issue, Kress examines the relative affordances and constraints of new and traditional media. He notes that print forms, like the book, tend to be sequentially and linearly ordered with a single point of entry, while more visual forms associated with newer communicative practices (like the Web) tend to be spatially constructed with multiple entry points ("Gains"). Paul Prior usefully complicates Kress's argument, providing examples of print-based rhetoric that seem to possess the very affordances Kress assigns to digital, imagistic rhetoric. Similarly, Anne Frances Wysocki demonstrates that Kress's analysis suffers from the use of rigid binaries.

Prior and Wysocki trace the introduction of *affordance* to James Gibson who "stressed that affordances are relational, ecological, and tendential (not determinative)" (Prior 26). Wysocki observes that designer Donald Norman distinguishes between "real and perceived affordances as well as among physical, logical, and cultural constraints" (60). Norman candidly concedes that "none of us know all the affordances of even everyday objects" (qtd. in Wysocki 60). As Kress himself warns, things that seem so similar (like speech and writing) might actually be substantially different. Indeed writing itself might contain so wide a variety of phenomena as to make impossible any generalizations about the affordances associated with it as a means of representation ("Gains" 12).

The types of heuristic questions we find useful for exploring the semiotic potentials of modes, media, and technologies include the following: *What semiotic work can this mode, medium, or technology perform? What communicative or persuasive power does it possess compared to other modes, media, and technologies? What are its limitations? How are the potentials of this new option revealed or masked by cultural practices? What cultural practices endow this mode, medium, or technology with potentials or impose on it limitations? Who has a stake in using this rhetorical form? Who benefits and who loses when affordances and constraints are assessed?*

(2) Cultural position: *The value assigned to a particular rhetorical option by various and overlapping cultural logics.*

Our discussion of affordances moved from the material qualities of rhetorical forms to the cultural values and practices associated with those forms. Without denying that affordances are inextricably bound up with culture, we would nevertheless like to suggest that there is heuristic value in designating a separate category for what we will call *cultural position.* There are at least four axes along which to measure the cultural position of a given mode, medium, or technology: prevalence (how common is it?), status (what value is accorded to it?), role (in what cultural spheres—personal, academic, professional, public—is it used?), and practice (what behaviors are associated with it?).

The rhetorical commonplace of *cultural position* occurs frequently in arguments for paying greater attention to visuality or multimodality, including arguments in both academic and nonacademic contexts. Kress, for instance, contends that "[i]f English is to remain relevant as the subject which provides access to participation in public forms of communication, as well as remaining capable of providing understandings of and the abilities to produce *culturally valued texts*, then an emphasis on language alone simply will no longer do" ("English" 67, emphasis added). In support of this claim, Kress attempts to demonstrate "that written language is being displaced from its hitherto unchallenged central position in the semiotic landscape, and that the visual is taking over many of the functions of written language" ("English" 68). Kress's argument, then, rests on the premises that (1) visual modes are gaining *status* (are increasingly "culturally valued") and (2) are becoming more *prevalent* (they are "taking over"). Similarly, prosecutor Christopher Morano, defending his use of multimodal rhetoric in the high-profile murder trial of Michael Skakel (which we discuss in chapter 6), observes that such rhetoric is the norm within "real life" contexts such as the "evening news." "This is what people are comfortable with now," Morano explains, "And that is why this is what has to be brought into the courtroom" (qtd. in Orson, "Multimedia in the Courtroom").

Arguments in favor of paying greater attention to visuality often involve a critique of a hierarchy that assigns visual rhetoric a lower cultural status than alphabetic rhetoric (see, for instance, George, "From Analysis to Design"; McComiskey, "Visual"; Stroupe; Trimbur. "Delivering"; Welch; Westbrook; S. Williams). In this hierarchy, all of the privileged connotations belong to alphabetic rhetoric:

Table 1. The relative cultural positioning of alphabetic and visual rhetoric.

Alphabetic Rhetoric	Visual Rhetoric
high culture	low culture
academic	popular
serious	recreational
sophisticated	simplistic
intellectual	emotional
logical	expressive
clear	ambiguous

Diana George, for instance, exposes the exclusionary nature of academic culture by citing the example of a composition instructor who asks his students to analyze comic books. The instructor reports that "[o]nce the students realized how influential comic books were, some of them began to inquire why they couldn't write their own comics." The instructor replies that "the reason they [students] were in college was not to learn comic book writing, but to counter the comic book mentality of our age with a more educated vision. The classics provide that vision. The classics are classics because they represent the finest and most humane statement on the universal human condition . . ." (qtd. in "From Analysis to Design" 27)

Immersed, as he is, in the Arnoldian values of the academy, this instructor is able to attribute only limited worth to comic books, despite his recognition of their rhetorical power. To adequately assess the prospect integrating comic books into sites of rhetorical education, we would need to interrogate the system of value that deprivileges comic books, to ask where it comes from and whether it should be embraced or resisted.

In Plato's *Phaedrus*, a similar set of oppositions operates, except that oral dialectic enjoys the location of privilege instead of writing. Socrates says that one "who knows the just and the good" will write "only for the sake of *recreation* and *amusement*" (279, emphasis added).

Socrates aligns himself with the one "who thinks that . . . only in principles of justice and goodness and nobility taught and communicated
orally for the sake of instruction and graven in the soul . . . is there
clearness and perfection and *seriousness* . . ." (281, emphasis added).

To invent and assess arguments for or against particular modes,
media, and technologies, then, we need to interrogate the cultural logics that inscribe them. We need to ask heuristic questions like, *What
images and metaphors do we associate with this mode, medium, or technology? What is our initial response to it? Where does this response come
from? How is this mode, medium, or technology depicted within the myriad representational practices of the culture? What roles and status has it
been assigned? Why? How prevalent is it? What practices are associated
with it? How have these come to be? What systems of cultural values privilege or deprivilege this particular mode, medium, or technology? Why and
how did this valuing come about? To what extent should this valuing be
embraced? Critiqued? Reconfigured? How could things be otherwise? Are
there potentials for this rhetorical form that are invisible to us, that are
untapped? At our most imaginative, what uses can we envision for this
rhetorical option?*

(3) Infrastructural accessibility: *The material and intellectual resources
necessary for a given rhetorical option to be deployed by a rhetor.*

We borrow "infrastructure" from Dànielle Nicole DeVoss, Ellen
Cushman, and Jeffrey T. Grabill, who use the term to cover a cluster of
material, cultural, and intellectual resources, including but not limited
to "computer networks," "operating systems," "computer programs,"
"the design and arrangement of computer classrooms," and "time pe-
riods of classes" (21). As we use the term, infrastructure refers to time,
space, technologies, money, and raw materials, as well as the cultural
and intellectual capital necessary to take advantage of these resources.

Appeals to what we are calling "infrastructural accessibility" are
common in discussions of modes, media, and technologies. For instance, George observes that "more recent access to the Internet and
to desktop publishing has given teachers ways of incorporating visual
thinking into the writing class, but even that will take time and money
and equipment and training" ("From Analysis to Design" 32). Likewise, Daniel Anderson, in exploring the rhetorical potential of digital video, contends that, "the emergence of consumer-friendly digital

video editing applications and low-cost digital video cameras changed the dynamics of who was able to produce video materials." George and Anderson both point to the fact that infrastructural investment is shifting in ways that allow rhetors greater semiotic freedom (see also Kress and Van Leeuwen 2; Lanham, *Electronic* 107).

Infrastructural concerns are perhaps more obvious in technology-intensive composing practices, but all types of rhetorical instruction and practices make assumptions about infrastructure—even writing with paper and pencil. At first glance, paper and pencil may seem like simple technologies, cheap and easy to operate, but in fact a substantial infrastructural investment is required to use them effectively. David, for instance, apparently learned to use paper and pencil through many years of guided practice. He remembers a stretch of years where he was met every morning, in his public school classrooms, with a paragraph written on the board by the teacher. His task was to copy the passage and submit it to the teacher, who would evaluate it and correct it. Over the years, the state of Michigan invested many thousands of dollars to ensure that David could use a pencil effectively. If a low threshold of infrastructural investment is a criterion for selecting which modes, media, and technologies we should pay attention to, perhaps writing itself should be reexamined.

We need to be mindful, then, that dynamics of infrastructural accessibility are continually shifting. Moreover, infrastructural accessibility is never merely a question of ease. The case of paper and pencil reveals that ease is a relative term; degree of difficulty needs to be weighed against other matters, such as semiotic potentials and cultural position. Heuristic questions that open these issues up for critical reflection include, *What technologies are—and are becoming—available? How much of an investment would need to be made in order to use these technologies effectively? How much time, money, space, effort would this rhetorical option involve? What raw materials (paper, ink, envelopes, etc.) are necessary? What people (e.g., IT support staff) and spaces (e.g., computer labs) would need to be accessed to accomplish rhetorical goals?*

(4) De/specialization: *The range of perceptions concerning the use of a given rhetorical form by nonspecialists.*

Arguments for or against the integration of new modes, media, and technologies frequently evoke particular models of specialization: the way human intellectual and physical labor is organized at the level of individuals and of institutions. W. J. T. Mitchell alludes to the need to rethink traditional models of specialization in light of changing representational practices:

> Recent developments in art history, film theory, and what is loosely called "cultural studies" make the notion of a purely verbal literacy increasingly problematic. A bureaucratic answer to this problem would insist that students take a "double major" in the textual and visual disciplines. The clear separation of "faculties" (corporeal and collegial) on the basis of sensory and semiotic divisions is becoming obsolete and is now being replaced by a notion of humanistic or liberal education as centrally concerned with the whole field of representations and representational activity. (*Picture* 6)

Similarly, in his discussion of typography, John Trimbur examines shifts in the way rhetorical labor has been divided in the professional world: "Typography was traditionally a craft, an artisan's labor that belong[ed] to the print shop" ("Delivering" 268), but "in the twentieth century, typography settled into the division of labor under corporate capital, becoming a career path for graphic artists in design studios . . ." (269). "With the rise of desktop publishing," however, "the division of labor is beginning to flatten and distinctions between author, designer, and printer are starting to collapse" (269; see also, Kress and Van Leeuwen 2).

As Trimbur implies, changes in understandings of specialization are often related to changes in technology. Anderson observes that "prosumer" technologies allow "those who have less to do things that professionals might have in the past only been able to do." He notes that "[t]he emergence of consumer-friendly digital video editing applications and low-cost digital video cameras changed the dynamics of who was able to produce video materials." This link between specialization and technology is important; there is, however, heuristic value in treating them as separate categories, partly because our systems of specialization often lag behind changes in infrastructural accessibility. Video production, for instance, might be kept separate from writing long after technological barriers have dissolved.

Arguments from de/specialization often focus on the changing nature of the identity of "ordinary" people. This is evidenced in the increasingly common refrain: "Anyone can be an X," where X is a form of rhetorical production that has historically been the domain of specialists. So we have such assertions as:

> Everyone can be a video game developer. (National Institute on Media and the Family 6)
>
> They say anyone can be a filmmaker these days, all you need is a camera and a computer. ("Making Movies")
>
> Anyone can be a graphic designer, all you need is a computer (or so they would have you believe). (Swistock)
>
> This is a world where everyone can be a designer, a manufacturer and a consumer all at once. (Davey 16)

In each of these cases, the writer is making the claim that emergent technologies are democratizing a particular set of practices—or are perceived to be doing so. Importantly, while three of these writers are endorsing and celebrating this democratization, Janet Swistock, as her parenthetical implies, is writing to challenge it. Indeed, it is easy to find examples of professionals challenging (often vehemently) claims that nonspecialists can appropriate a given rhetorical option. Shifts in professional identity are often accompanied by struggle, resistance, and defensiveness.

A heuristic inquiry into practices of specialization questions the fixity of notions of the expert, the professional, the credentialed, the licensed, the authorized, and the legitimate. These discussions are fruitfully connected with more general critiques of specialization itself. In his proposal for "reinventing the humanities," for instance, Kurt Spellmeyer critiques the "culture of specialization" that characterizes the academy and champions the notion of the amateur or "ordinary citizen" who is charged with the task of "making culture" (7, 222).

The struggle between specialists and "anyone," then, gives rise to the question, *Who is able/allowed/encouraged to be a producer of any given rhetorical form?* A separate but related question is, *Who is responsible for* preparing *'anyone' to be a producer of X?* This raises issues of the way institutional space is ordered and the way human knowledge is organized.

McComiskey addresses this second question as it relates to visuality:

> In many conversations, I have heard colleagues and friends admit that visual communication is ubiquitous in public,

> private, and even academic discourse, but (they always say),
> "What can I do? I teach *writing*. What role could images pos-
> sibly play in the *writing* class?" My reply is often unsettling at
> first, partly because I say it in a tone of feigned indignation:
> "Writing? I don't teach *writing*. I teach *rhetoric*." ("Visual" 188)

McComiskey's strategy for resolving the contradiction perceived
by his colleagues mobilizes the capaciousness of the term *rhetoric*.
Rhetoric, McComiskey observes, "is not bound to a particular mode
of representation; . . . it may be practiced in any medium, including writing" (188). In an interesting appropriation of institutional
turf, McComiskey seems to be saying that, as a teacher and scholar
of rhetoric, his expertise, his academic credentials, and his role within
the academy authorize him to teach non-alphabetic modes. Robert E.
Scholes (16) and Richard A. Lanham (*Electronic* 8, 25) make similar
moves on behalf of English studies.

   A full exploration of expertise and institutional space is beyond the
scope of this discussion; the essential point we wish to make is that
the realities of de/specialization are not inevitable, natural, or fixed.
Indeed, both the intensity and the system of specialization that characterizes the contemporary academy are relatively new (Klein 20–22;
Spellmeyer 222). Arguments for or against new modes, media, and
technologies, then, need to balance an appreciation of the dynamics of
specialization with an appreciation for the fact that structures of specialization can be reformed and transformed. To invent and assess arguments from specialization, we need to ask questions like, *What forms
of specialized knowledge and skills are associated with the effective use of
this mode, medium, or technology? What institutional and professional
structures govern access to this specialized knowledge and these skills? On
what is this system based? What material and cultural realities does it reflect and reproduce? Who stands to gain from it? Is this system desirable?
Should it be embraced or resisted?*

CONCLUSION (OR SHOULD WE TEACH 3D PRINTING IN THE WRITING CLASSROOM?)

Rhetorical options are never merely present, but are made visible or
invisible by a complex array of material and cultural forces that are
themselves situated within larger discourses and ideologies. Assessing
options is difficult intellectual work, but is precisely the work that

kairos demands. Sites of rhetorical education have a role to play in facilitating the critical assessment of rhetorical options. Teachers and administrators continually make decisions about what to teach and what to leave out. These decisions can support or question the status quo, opening or foreclosing new opportunities. At stake in these decisions is the issue of access. When a teacher leaves out a mode, medium, or technology, s/he is foreclosing an opportunity for students. Choosing, however, is inevitable: we can't teach everything. The choices we make have serious cultural consequences.

We hope that the heuristic we offer in this chapter will help stakeholders make reflective choices about what rhetorical options to theorize, teach, and practice. We see this heuristic as a tool for facilitating kairotic inventiveness and a response to George's call for the kind of "theory building" that helps us change productively. Heuristic approaches are typically contrasted with algorithmic ones. The later are formulaic, precise, rigid, authoritative, and limiting, whereas the former are flexible, open-ended, and generative. Algorithmic approaches tend to be well-suited to situations that are relatively simple, stable, and known, whereas heuristic approaches are needed for situations that are uncertain, contingent, and not fully understood (Rose 391–92; Selber, "Technological" 172). In Mike Rose's words, "[a]lgorithms are precise rules that will always result in a specific answer if applied to an appropriate problem" (391). Heuristics, on the other hand, "offer solutions that are good enough most of the time" (qtd. in Rose 392).

The Greek *heuresis*, of course, closely corresponds to *invention* (Lanham, *Handlist* 91), and our aim in offering this heuristic, with its four topoi, is to help stakeholders invent arguments for and against the use of available rhetorical modes, media, and technologies. Should we teach 3D fabricated rhetoric in the writing classroom? Those who say no might argue that 3D objects (including clothes, shoes, jewelry, toys, figurines, gadgets, decoratives, furniture, cars, and more) do not facilitate communication as effectively or powerfully as writing. Those who say yes might cite the work of anthropologists like Grant David McCracken, who claims that "material culture as a means of communication works in more understated, inapparent ways than language" and therefore "allows culture to insinuate its beliefs and assumptions into the very fabric of daily life" (68–69). These are arguments from *semiotic potential*. Additional arguments might focus on the *infrastructural accessibility* of 3D rhetoric. Some might argue that the tools of 3D design and production are too difficult or too expensive. Others might note that 3D printers have fallen below the $1,000 price point and CAD software, like Google's SketchUp, is free and easy to use. Inquiring into the *cultural position* of 3D rhetoric opens up yet another line of argument. Echoing critiques of visual rhetoric, some might dismiss the three-dimensional objects that fill our lives as mostly commercial, nonintellectual, and even destructive. Responding to such claims, Mc-Cracken contends that "[i]t is time to take a more intelligent view and to see that consumer goods capture us because they capture meanings with which we construct our lives" (4). Finally, we might turn to arguments from *de/specialization.* Some writing teachers might argue that their background does not prepare them to teach 3D rhetoric. Others might claim that their background in rhetoric provides an excellent framework for understanding the persuasive power of 3D fabricated objects (see Blair; Buchanan; González, "Rhetoric"; Grier). The larger point is that a heuristic helps us be systematic and explicit about decisions that are otherwise frequently made without fully reflecting on the underlying logics that inform them.

3 Kairos and Multimodal Public Rhetoric

Making copies changes everything.

—Bump Halbritter and Todd Taylor

In the previous chapter, we offered a heuristic designed to open up possibilities for public rhetoric. Our basic argument was that possibilities don't simply present themselves. Instead, a wide range of material-cultural pressures reveals certain options and masks others. Critical reflection is required to open up kairotic opportunities that may at first seem foreclosed. Are cameras relevant to rhetorical education? Are 3D printers? The heuristic we offer is intended to be used as a tool to help stakeholders systematically consider options that might otherwise remain hidden. We see it as most useful in designing curricula, pedagogies, and policies.

In this chapter, we turn our attention from this more abstract inquiry to the more specific forms of invention practiced by rhetors as they work individually or in concert with others to address public exigencies. As we discussed in chapter 1, we use the term kairos to refer to the way rhetors negotiate or "struggle" with and against their contexts as they seek a particular outcome (Miller, "Kairos"). This struggle calls for the prepared rhetor to exercise "kairotic inventiveness" (Walker, "The Body" 49) and "improvisational readiness" (E. C. White 14) within contexts that are comprised of many elements beyond the rhetor's control. We find in kairos a rich and generative heuristic tool. At the same time, we contend that the concept of kairos needs to be expanded if it is to serve as an appropriate tool for thinking about multimodal public rhetoric.

Typical applications of kairos in rhetorical analysis locate the kairotic struggle in the rhetor's deployment of "specific devices of discourse" (Plato) or "linguistic techniques" (McComiskey, "Disassembling" 213) that are tailored to a particular situation at a particular moment in time. Joseph J. Hughes, for instance, explores the way "considerations of *kairos* might, on occasion, override the necessity of

maintaining *decorum*" (136). Hughes examines "The Eating of Lar-
gus's Limb," a humorous anecdote embedded in a speech given by
Crassus (130). The anecdote uses "comedic characterization, language,
and plot structure" and reflects the comedic devices, such as the "love
triangle" of Roman New Comedy (133). This use of humor is praised
by Cicero, despite the fact the it seems to violate Cicero's own valoriza-
tion of *decorum* and *dignitas*, and despite the fact that it runs counter
to a more general Roman tendency to distinguish between the theater
and rhetoric (129, 136).

Similarly, Julie Nelson Christoph applies the concept of kairos in
her exploration of how autobiographical writings by pioneer women
function as public arguments. Christoph nicely illustrates the kairotic
struggle between rhetors and the contexts within which they operate.
Her analysis begins with an acknowledgement of various constraints
imposed on pioneer women, noting that "[a]s disenfranchised women,
these writers did not have the educational background or access to
information necessary to participate in public debates about westward
expansion on an equal basis with men" (668–69), but they overcome
these constraints, to some degree, by adopting a particular set of rhetorical strategies that establish their ethos. Pioneer women's "personal
experiences on the frontier gave them a measure of authority, which
they were able to use effectively to convey their views on westward
expansion to a general audience . . ." (669). Pioneer writer Annie Pike
Greenwood, for instance, "is aware . . . of *kairos* and the need to present herself as a person whom her audience might view as trustwor-
thy" (675). To establish her ethos, Greenwood uses what Christoph
calls "identity statements" such as "the antiputrefactive woman" and
"a sagebrush woman" (675).

We find this understanding of kairos useful. Indeed, we turn to
close readings of multimodal compositions in future chapters as a
means to better understand ways rhetorical choices reflect and help
constitute kairotic opportunity. At the same time, we argue that our
understanding of kairos needs to be expanded along several lines if it
is to fully support the use of multimodal public rhetoric. Specifically,
we argue that a full assessment of kairos in a given context needs to
include questions that arise *before* the rhetor commits to writing as a
mode, as well as questions that arise *after* a rhetor is finished with the
composition. To illustrate this expansion of kairos, we examine several
cases of kairotic struggle.

Before we proceed, we should clarify that when we invoke a *be-
fore-after* framework, we do not intend to impose a rigid, linear struc-

ture on the composing process. Indeed, in our view, the composing process, especially in the context of technology-intensive multimodal rhetoric, is actually even messier and more iterative than the way it is represented in traditional models (e.g., a rhetor might invest hundreds of hours in creating an elaborate website, only to discover that a simple flyer is a better rhetorical approach). Our reference to a temporal sequence is a simplification that we employ for explanatory convenience and is not meant to be taken as a rigid formula.

Case #1 Jim Ridolfo's Free Trade of the Americas Documentary. As a political activist, Jim Ridolfo noticed that mainstream media representations of protests are often characterized by a pattern of distortion resulting in part from the distanced perspective of the camera. Aerial shots from helicopters do not adequately capture the experience of facing police in riot gear. To counter these representations, Jim decided to create a documentary film based on his participation in the 2003 Free Trade Area of the Americas (FTAA) protests in Miami. Using video footage that he shot and digitized himself, Jim produced a short film and distributed it via the Internet using the file-sharing application LimeWire (figure 2).

Figure 2. Still frame from Jim Ridolfo's documentary of the 2003 FTAA Protest in Miami.

Within months, over 3,000 people had downloaded the film, and at least one independent bookstore began distributing it on CD, alongside more traditional leaflets and tracts. This simple case of multimodal public rhetoric suggests that kairos might be productively expanded in several ways.[9]

Kairotic Expansion #1: The Moment before Composition

At first, cases like Jim's FTAA documentary might seem to call for relatively minor shifts to rhetorical theory and pedagogy. We might envision updating Lanham's *Handlist of Rhetorical Terms* to include, alongside *chiasmus* and *zeugma*, devices of filmic rhetoric, such as *extreme close-up* and *dolly shot*. We contend, however, that cases like this one suggest a process of rhetorical invention that is fundamentally different from traditional models. Jim's kairotic struggle did not begin as an attempt to discern what linguistic strategies would be effective within a particular context. *It began even before he committed himself to the use of a particular mode and medium.* Jim's kairotic inventiveness began with explorations of multiple possibilities, including options that had little to do with words on paper.

The selection of documentary video as the best form of rhetorical intervention was not a single decision, but encompassed a set of related decisions, including decisions about modes, media, and genres:

- **Modes**: Jim selected the multimodal rhetoric of video rather than committing himself to a single mode (such as an aural recording or a written essay).
- **Media of production and delivery**: Jim opted to use a camcorder, microphone, and nonlinear video-editing application to produce a digital video intended to be viewed on a computer screen, as opposed to (for instance) ink on paper.
- **Genre**: Jim opted to produce a serious documentary rather than other filmic genres (such as a mocumentary or fictional narrative) or other non-filmic genres (such as a white paper, leaflet, or poster).

These new concerns were read in relation to more traditional kairotic concerns like *audience* and *exigency*. Jim felt that his target audience of young people would be more likely to value a multimodal documentary than, for instance, a written essay. The rhetorical ex-

igency that occasioned the documentary had to do with the representational practices of network television. Jim could have critiqued
those practices in a written essay, but, as Raymond Williams insists,
"[c]ritical demystification can take us only part of the way" (*Problems*
62). Critique is an incomplete response and should proceed "always in
association with practice: . . . practice in the production of alternative
images of the 'same event'; practice in processes of basic editing and
the making of sequences" (62).

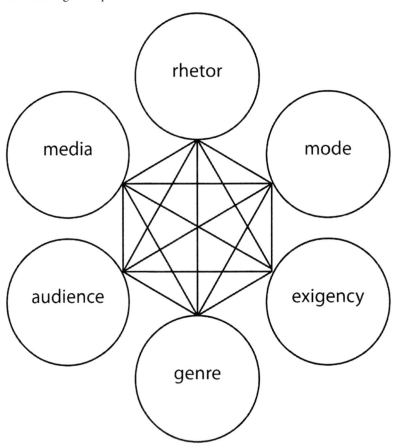

Figure 3. Some kairotic concerns.

We might represent the expanded notion of kairos as a modifica-
tion of the Aristotelian triangle (figure 3).[10] This expansion of kairos
draws attention to an aspect of rhetorical practice that has often been
overlooked: materiality.[11] Modes and media are simultaneously con-

cerns about rhetorical "content" and about infrastructural resources: cables, cameras, storage devices, software, and so on. As we conceive of it, then, kairos is not only a function of social concerns (such as the beliefs and attitudes of the audience) or symbolic concerns (such as the linguistic devices that can best articulate with certain beliefs and attitudes), but is also a function of material considerations, such as the availability of high-definition camcorder and computers with enough processing power to digitize video. In other words, traditional models of rhetorical invention are fundamentally flawed because they fail to account for both the diversity and the materiality of available rhetorical practices.

Kairotic Expansion #2: After the Composition is "Done"

It is also useful to adopt an understanding of kairos that includes what happens after composing is "finished." We would like to illustrate this by introducing two cases: the case of screenwriter Terence Winter and the case of Chinese American novelist Shawn Wong. We should be clear about the nature of these cases. Admittedly, the cases of Winter and Wong are somewhat extraordinary, involving writers embedded in the specialized systems of Hollywood and of literary publishing, respectively. Moreover, these cases do not, at first glance, involve multimodal rhetorics (though, as we'll see, multiple modes, media, and genres all factor into the ultimate success of these writers). Nevertheless, as we explain below, we discern in these cases important lessons for rhetors, teachers, and theorists interested in multimodal public rhetoric.

Case #2: Screenwriter Terence Winter. Terence Winter is currently well-known for his contributions to the *Sopranos* and other critically acclaimed television shows. The unusual path Winter's career followed has been documented in a number of venues, including NPR's *Fresh Air* (Bianculli). In the early nineties, Winter quit his job as a lawyer and moved from New York to Los Angeles to pursue a career in screenwriting. He began teaching himself how to write for TV and film, and finally began sending out completed scripts to "anybody who would agree to read them" (Murphy). Winter discovered, however, that production companies would not seriously consider his scripts because, in his diagnosis, there's a "Catch 22 in Hollywood" in the sense that "you can't get work without an agent and you can't get an agent without work" (Murphy).

So Winter recruited a lawyer friend to serve as his agent, and the two "made up" a "bogus agency" and named it the "Doug Vitanni Agency" (Craddock). They secured a business address through Mail Boxes Etc. and ordered letterhead. Winter himself hand-delivered his manuscripts to appropriate contacts at studios. He identified himself not as the script's author, but as the agency's courier. As he tells it, "I told whoever was sitting behind the desk, I said yeah, hi, I'm the messenger from the agency. This is—these are those scripts you wanted. And the kid behind the desk would say oh, okay, and so at least my scripts now were theoretically in buildings where people could hire me and they would read them because they did come in from an agent" (Bianculli). With the imprimatur of the Doug Vitanni Agency, Winter's work was taken more seriously, and soon he was assigned a show.

Case #3 Shawn Wong's, Homebase. In the introduction to his novel, *Homebase*, Shawn Wong tells the story of how his book came to be published. According to Wong, when *Homebase* was published in 1979, it was "the only Chinese American work of literary fiction in print in America" (x). Indeed, Wong's story is about more than the literary success of one individual. He frames his account as a story about how historically disenfranchised groups devise ways of placing into circulation their own representations of their lived experiences. "I realized one day," Wong writes, "that I was the only Asian American writer I knew in the world and that no teacher in high school or college had ever assigned or even mentioned a book written by an Asian American writer" (xiv).

Wong's story starts when he began to study creative writing at San Francisco State College in 1967. At SFSC, he began tutorials with poet Kay Boyle, who became a friend and mentor. Wong rented a room from Boyle and, through this association, gained access to the rich literary and cultural life of San Francisco (xii-xiii). He met other young Asian American writers as well as more established African American writers like Ishmael Reed and Al Young. "It is no accident," Wong writes, "that my first three books were published by African American publishers. They were the first to recognize the legitimacy of Asian American literature" (xvii). One of those books was *Aiiieeeee! An Anthology of Asian American Writers* (1974), which Wong coedited with

Asian American colleagues Frank Chin, Jeffery Paul Chan, and Lawson Fusao Inada and which was published by Howard University Press. *Aiiieeeee!* contained portions of what would later become *Homebase.*

By the mid 1970s, Wong had finished the manuscript for his novel and was "circulating *Homebase* around to publishers with no success" (xvii). Rejected by major publishers, Wong's book was eventually published by I. Reed Books, Ishmael Reed's independent literary press. "The novel won two literary awards," Wong writes, "and was later published by Plume, a division of Penguin Books" (xvii). Wong concludes:

> The literary history cited here is, of course, not just about one novel, but rather about the dissemination, preservation, and promotion of a whole field of literature. As a young writer, who started writing *Homebase* almost forty years ago, I realized very early on that I was responsible for educating an audience to Asian American writing as well as for writing it. (xvii)

Traditional composition-and-rhetoric frameworks are of limited use in explaining the kairotic struggles of Winter and Wong. It is interesting to think about what support compositionists and rhetoricians might have provided these writers as their writing encountered initial failure and rejection from important sets of readers. Compositionists might have asked Winter and Wong to examine their writing processes. Perhaps you need better brainstorming techniques. Have you tried freewriting? Clustering? Rhetoricians might have drawn attention to the rhetorical situation. Who is your audience? What is your purpose? Perhaps this is not a kairotic moment for you.

The field of composition and rhetoric is primarily focused on the compositions themselves and the processes by which they are created. But Winter's and Wong's problems concerned what happened when the composing process was over and the composition was considered complete. Those who read their works before publication praised them, and, once the works found an audience, both writers met with considerable success. Frameworks that limit themselves to the way a composition can be shaped for a purpose and an audience cannot address the problems that Winter and Wong faced.

The cases of Winter and Wong are suggestive of the important relationship between rhetorical effectiveness and the processes involved in the circulation of the composition. Moreover, these cases demonstrate that rhetorical effectiveness is often a function of the rhetor's ability to navigate complex processes of circulation that are simultaneously material, cultural, and rhetorical.

We might begin to illustrate this by asking why Wong didn't self-publish his novel. Part of the answer is that self-publishing, particularly in the pre-Web, pre-home-computer days of the mid 1970s, was a costly affair, requiring investments in time and money that were typically beyond what most emerging writers could afford. Much of this cost related to the *reproduction* and *distribution* of the composition. In the 1970s, producing multiple copies of a book required substantial investments in raw materials (e.g., paper, ink, chemicals) and equipment (e.g., stat camera, press, plates). Distribution presented yet additional challenges. Once produced, copies of a book needed to be shipped to stores, libraries, and schools where potential readers could access them.

In the case of Winter, the material concerns of reproduction and distribution are not as pronounced, unless we shift our focus from the screenplay to the ultimate goal of the television show or film that was to be produced *from* the screenplay. Once we make that shift, we see all of the problems of self-publishing writ large. If self-publishing a book is resource-intensive, producing a film is doubly so. Even if we limit analysis for a moment to the screenplays as compositions in their own right, however, it is interesting that part of Winter's ultimate success derived from the accomplishment of getting his compositions "in buildings where people could hire me" (Bianculli). Winter's account is, in part, about the way texts travel through geophysical space, about carrying manuscripts bodily to readers.

Problems of circulation, however, are also simultaneously cultural. The cases of Winter and Wong both demonstrate the way writers are required to navigate complex structures of legitimation that will either help or hinder the circulation of their compositions. Winter's screenplays encountered problems because of a clash between two structures of legitimation. Whereas studios required the imprimatur of an agent, agents required evidence of past studio success—"you can't get work without an agent and you can't get an agent without work" (Bianculli). To get past this catch-22, Winter needed to manufacture his own credentials. He found someone to perform the role of agent. He invented an agency. He secured the seals and forms of display that generate and reinforce the ethos of an agency—name, letterhead, business address.

Finally, he delivered his manuscripts to studios in the guise of the agency's courier—a gesture that further reveals the legitimizing structures of Hollywood. The cultural logic associated with unknown writers in Hollywood is the inverse of what typically applies to established writers in most contexts. Once writers are established, their bodily presence lends legitimacy to their composition. We pay money to see a famous writer read from his or her book, but in the cultural system of Hollywood studios, the bodily presence of a nonestablished writer *delegitimizes* the work because it marks it as circulating outside of licensed channels. In terms of how his compositions circulated, Winter was more effective as the delivery boy for the Doug Vitanni Agency than as the documents' author.

We see the operation of legitimizing structures in Wong's case as well. Even if Wong could have afforded the cost of self-publishing, a book published through a "vanity press" is not accorded the same cultural value as one published by Knopf or Random House. Self-published works are not granted ready access to stores, libraries, and schools. Even if Wong had had the resources to ship copies of his book to bookstores (getting them "in the building"), cultural barriers would have halted further progress.

In fact, Wong's account demonstrates his long, incremental advancement through legitimizing structures. He gained the respect of established writers—notably other minority writers whose struggles parallel his own. He formed alliances with other Asian American writers and collaboratively published *Aiiieeeee!* This anthology gained some literary respect and attention for Asian American writing in general, and portions of his novel in particular. The next breakthrough moment came when I. Reed Books published *Homebase*. Though small, I. Reed Books was an established literary press associated with a famous and well-respected writer. This press provided important accoutrements of publication: professional typesetting, full-color cover, perfect binding, a logo, and more. This publication led to additional credentials: literary awards, and ultimately the cachet of a larger press. The material and cultural capital claimed by Penguin Books's Plume imprint—right down to the seal of the flowing P logo—resulted in still wider distribution.

Pierre Bourdieu theorizes legitimizing structures in *The Field of Cultural Production: Essays on Art and Literature*. Bourdieu examines the way objects of "fine art" (like paintings and sculpture) circulate within a complex material-cultural field. His project is nicely summarized by Randal Johnson. Offering a "radical contextualization," says Johnson, Bourdieu explores the relationships between compositions and composers within a "cultural field" that is also "occupied by all the instances of consecration and legitimation which make cultural products what they are (the public, publishers, critics, galleries, academies and so forth)" (9). Cultural fields are themselves located "within the broader field of power" (9). Bourdieu helps us see that a painting is not effective by virtue of its intrinsic properties alone. Rather, its success depends on how it travels through a field of complex relationships between various cultural institutions and structures. The largest barrier Wong faced was that the literary establishment (critics, editors, publishers, award committees, teachers, scholars) was working within larger structures of power that tended to marginalize Asian American writers.

The kairotic struggle, as traditionally conceived, concerns the way a rhetor composes a text to ensure its success in a particular situation. What we are suggesting here in our exploration of the cases of Winter and Wong is that the kairotic struggle—the struggle to exploit the opportunity available to a rhetor at an given moment—extends far beyond the moment when the text is "complete." In a sense, the cases of Winter and Wong show that the real struggle only *begins* once the work is complete. Winter's and Wong's kairotic inventiveness can be seen not only in their compositions, but in the way they negotiated the complex material-cultural fields within which their texts needed to circulate to have any impact on the world. The rhetorical process exceeds the composing process; the rhetor's work is not done when the composition is done. Facilitating the reproduction and distribution of texts introduces new considerations for the rhetor, new assessments of technology and of contexts. It might call for additional acts of composing (the need, for instance, to create the name and letterhead of an agency) and the recruitment of additional collaborators (such as a friend who agrees to perform the role of agent).

CIRCULATION AS A FOCUS OF RHETORICAL THEORY

As we have presented these ideas to others over the past few years, we have encountered some degree of skepticism. On more than one occasion, after pointing out the importance of how texts circulate, we have encountered the flat protest, "but that's not writing!" So let's pursue the matter a bit further.

Trimbur has called for more attention to be paid within the field of composition and rhetoric to circulation. While Trimbur's call has been taken up by several scholars in recent years (see Eyman; Mathieu and George; Ridolfo; Porter, "Recovering"; Shipka), rhetorical theory has yet to confront the full implications of taking circulation into account. Circulation has not yet reached the theoretical richness of other key concepts such as "process" or "audience." To illustrate what it might mean to take circulation seriously as a key theoretical concept, in this section we move circulation from the margins to the center of rhetorical theory, making it a starting point rather than an afterthought.

There is at least one kind of composition whose primary goal is circulation. It's called an address and it appears on the front of envelops and packages. For an address to be considered complete, it only needs to contain the minimum amount of information necessary to arrive at the intended destination. Once it arrives at the destination, it can be discarded. It loses its value. An address is a short composition that enables another composition (the letter, the memo, etc.) to travel to its audience. (It's worth noting, however, that the address can be made to perform a wide variety of rhetorical work. Addresses can contain an organization's logo, can be endowed—via color, typography, and other features—with aesthetic qualities, and can themselves function as a source of legitimation, as when Apple proclaims on its packaging: "Designed by Apple in California.")

Bumper stickers, political buttons, Twitter messages, and sayings are all texts that privilege circulation *almost* to the exclusion of other concerns. A saying, such as a proverb or an aphorism, is an ingenious approach to circulation. The primary vehicle for carrying a saying from place to place is the human body. Rhetors who hope to make effective use of this vessel need to produce compositions that are short and easy to remember. Using a mnemonic device, such as rhyme, is not a bad idea ("A stitch in time saves nine"). Rhetors who hope to exploit the genre of aphorism will need to go even further. According to some, an aphorism is a distinct kind of saying characterized by cleverness or what James Geary calls a "twist": "a good aphorism is like watching a magic trick: First comes surprise, then comes delight, then you start wondering how the hell the magician did it" (16). Composers of aphorisms need to build this surprise, delight, and wonder into their compositions; these qualities will, in turn, incentivize others to repeat the aphorism, facilitating its circulation.

Like a saying, the political slogan printed on a bumper sticker or button is typically short and memorable: "I like Ike." Brevity is encouraged by other considerations of circulation as well. To function as effective vehicles of circulation, messages contained on bumper stickers need to fit on the limited space of car bumpers and need to be printed in type large enough to be read from a distance. Typically, bumper stickers need to be cheaply reproducible, so they can be given away in large quantities. Similarly, buttons need to be lightweight enough to hang on clothing. Like sayings, buttons often rely on the human body for circulation; unlike a saying, a button continually and silently displays its message, which means it can be conveyed in places and at times when talking might not be appropriate. Buttons address strangers and familiars alike, regardless of the social conventions that might prohibit speaking aloud to others; buttons continue to proclaim their message in libraries, restaurants, bus stops, stadiums, concert halls, and classrooms.

If we place circulation at the center of rhetorical theory, the essay or speech cease to be privileged genres; proverbs, aphorisms, buttons, and stickers become preferred options. Our point here is not, of course, that we should stop teaching essays and speeches, but that our theory and pedagogy should richly confront the way the pressures of circulation shape compositions.

Case #4: the DMCVB View-Master Disk. The Detroit Metro Convention & Visitors Bureau (DMCVB) offers an interesting solution to the problem of circulation. Faced with the goal of countering negative perceptions of Detroit (see chapters 7 and 8), the DMCVB proposed, naturally enough, a visual solution: photographs that engagingly capture the vibrant cultural assets of the city. Instead of traditional TV or magazine advertisements, the DMCVB opted for an unusual form of circulation. They had the photos reproduced in the form of a View-Master disk, and mailed these disks, along with View-Masters themselves, to strategically selected audiences.

This seems to violate some of the tendencies we've just been describing. Bumper stickers are short, simple, cheap, easy to reproduce and give away. The View-Master is costly and, compared to a button or sticker, requires a fair amount of bodily investment to access, but in the calculus employed by the DMCVB, important gains offset these liabilities. The View-Master is novel and surprising. It sticks out. The viewing device focuses attention. We place the View-Master to our eyes and the stereoscopic image literally blocks out the rest of the world and occupies our entire field of vision. Finally, the View-Master uniquely supports the DMCVB's goal of shaping perceptions of Detroit in such a way that potential visitors see it as a place of value, a "destination city." The View-Master has long been a vehicle for communicating images of desirable places. Inserting Detroit into the peculiar perceptual-cultural space of the View-Master establishes a metonymic link between Detroit and other locations of desire ("Edgy").

THE CIRCULATION OF MULTIMODAL PUBLIC RHETORIC

Our contention is that *all* successful public rhetoric is successful only if it effectively negotiates the material-cultural challenges of circulation, including challenges related to production, reproduction, and distribution. These circulatory concerns are even more salient and complex in the case of multimodal rhetoric. Jim's FTAA documentary helps to illustrate this.

We have already discussed the media of production Jim used, but a further set of infrastructural factors relates to media of reproduction and distribution. As he weighed his rhetorical options, Jim took into consideration the fact that digital videos can be *reproduced* relatively easily precisely because they are digital. Computers can serve many copies of a file to other users without adding significant cost. Problems of distribution were solved by the Internet and related technologies. When Jim planned his intervention, in a pre-YouTube era, LimeWire's peer-to-peer file-sharing approach allowed more precise searches by those seeking a particular media format and topic. Moreover, peer-to-peer file-sharing provided direct access to content in ways the Web itself (at that time) did not. LimeWire files did not need to be embedded within a website, but were directly accessible through a search restricted to keyword and media format. The point is that for Jim's rhetorical intervention to be successful, he needed to account for complex infrastructures of circulation that were specifically accommodative of multimodality.

These examples of rhetorical circulation introduce another facet of the relationship between composing and distribution. Composers' decisions *anticipate* future considerations of distribution. Processes of circulation *inform* both the material and the symbolic considerations of composing. The moment of circulation *inhabits* the moment of composition. The composer of a political slogan privileges brevity knowing that the slogan is destined for bumper stickers. Similarly, Jim made decisions about his video to keep download time short. Download time increases as the length, quality, and screen-size of the video increase. All of these variables dictate compositional choices. Certain narrative shapes lend themselves more readily to short play times. Certain kinds of visuals (such as shots that rely on subtle detail) work better with uncompressed, high-resolution video. The material dynamics of distribution encourage certain compositional choices.

It may at first glance appear that structures of legitimation are not operational in Jim's kairotic struggle. After all, Jim opted to bypass sanctioned venues of publication. He adopted a mode of distribution that provided a relatively direct link between his own computer and the computer of the end user (via LimeWire). Indeed, Jim's target audience included activists who are suspicious of mainstream media and who value direct access to information outside of official media channels of circulation. Moreover, Jim built ethos into his composition by adopting high production values. Here we might remember the analysis of Zimmermann and Tagg that we introduced in chapter 2. Zimmermann and Tagg demonstrate that the social space of amateurism is equated in our culture with the social space of the nonserious, of kitsch. To ensure that his film would not be dismissed as amateur, Jim took steps to appropriate the conventions of "professional" films. Amateur films are marked by long takes, lack of attention to framing, poor picture and sound quality. Through the use of a high quality camcorder, a non-linear video-editing application, a computer with a relatively fast processor, and an external microphone, Jim was able to produce a film that deployed techniques borrowed from "professional" films, including frequent cutting between shots, careful attention to framing and camera movement, and high audio-visual quality. Again, these considerations of composition *anticipate* the circulatory paths Jim desired for his video. They help it travel through cultural spaces.

Case #5: the WNA Newsletter. A similar dynamic can be seen in the newsletter that circulates in the Westside neighborhood of Lansing, Michigan, where David lives. Four times a year, the Westside Neighborhood Association (WNA) distributes the *Westsider*, a news-

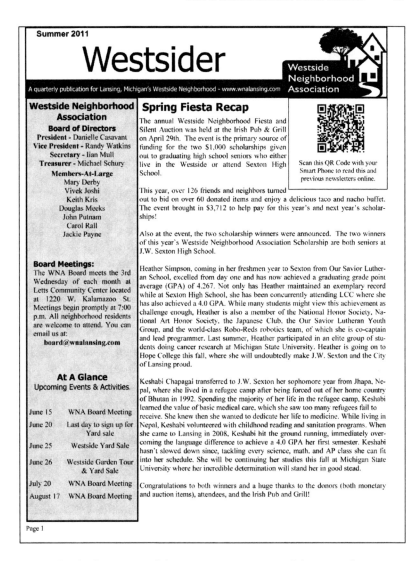

Figure 4. The front page of the Summer 2011 issue of the *Westsider*. © 2011 Westside Neighborhood Association, Lansing, Michigan. Used by permission.

letter for residents (figure 4). The *Westsider* consists of simple textual layouts, simple line drawings, and few, if any, photographs. It is printed on bright, fluorescent-colored paper and hand-delivered to residents—placed prominently into the handles of front doors. Newsletters are immediately visible when residents pull into their driveways. The rhetorical content of the newsletter (few pictures, simple layouts, short

articles) anticipates the method of reproduction (relatively low quality black-and-white copy machine) and distribution (hand-delivery
to residents' homes). It would not be difficult to *produce* a newsletter
that made richer use of color, photographs, and other visuals, but the
WNA's rhetorical task is not accomplished by mere production. The
WNA also needs to *reproduce* the newsletter, to make enough copies
for all residents. Reproducing full-color documents with fine photographic detail is more expensive than reproducing simple black-and-
white documents with line drawings.

The WNA could, of course, forego printing altogether and distribute the newsletter exclusively on the Web, where color and photographs do not incur additional cost; and, in fact, newsletters *are* posted
on the Web. However, the decision to adopt a simpler black-and-white
layout reflects the WNA's assessment that hard copy distribution is
important. Some Westside residents are not regular Internet users, and
even residents who have access to the Internet might not routinely
take the time to visit the WNA's website and download the newsletter.
Hard copy is an important method of distribution in this context. As
residents enter or leave their homes, they immediately encounter the
newsletters stuck in doors. Because these compositions are simple and
brief, consumption is almost complete by the time the newsletters have
been retrieved. Moreover, Michael Warner might draw our attention
to the effect of looking down a block in the neighborhood and seeing
the same fluorescent paper in each door—a bright iteration that makes
the "concatenation of texts" visible and provides a concrete image of
mutual attention, coaxing a public into being (90). Residents are aware
of participating in a shared ritual of textual consumption.

As we were preparing this book for publication, the WNA added
another tool to support the circulation of its newsletter. Issues of the
Westsider now contain QR codes. Readers are invited to "scan the QR
code with your Smart Phone to read this and previous newsletters online" (Westside Neighborhood Association 1). The WNA, then, has
cast a wide net, seeking readers via hardcopies, computers, and hand-
held devices. Moreover, these different forms are mutually reinforcing:
paper sources steer readers to online sources.

Processes of rhetorical invention and composition anticipate processes of reproduction and distribution. We might even take this a
step further and say that reproduction and distribution are partially

constitutive of rhetorical composition. David Graas's *Not a Box*, which we discuss in the introduction to this book, only derives rhetorical meaning when the strategy of distribution (no-waste packaging) is taken into account (figure 1). The D Brand View-Master can shape perceptions of Detroit partly because it makes use of a mechanism of distribution long associated with the presentation of desirable places. In these instances, the mechanism of distribution functions as a feature of the composition, part of what communicates the message.

At first glance we might be tempted to say that Shawn Wong's *Homebase* means the same thing whether it is typed on 8.5" x 11" paper with a manual Smith Corona or typeset between glossy four-color covers by Plume. But that characterization of Wong's case is inaccurate. Wong wanted to introduce Asian American experiences—powerfully captured through the affordances of literary art—into the classrooms, bookstores, libraries, and living rooms that are the traditional domains of Chaucer, Shakespeare, and other "dead white British authors" (xv). Even if a typed manuscript physically arrived in those classrooms, bookstores, and libraries, in another sense it would not have arrived. The "meaning" of Wong's novel could only be fully realized through the successful acquisition of appropriate seals, licensures, and packaging of the literary establishment. Only then could Wong be said to have made progress toward his goal of "the dissemination, preservation, and promotion of a whole field of literature" (xvii).

A final consideration related to distribution concerns the way compositions fuel other compositions. Jim knew that if he made his footage available in a high-quality format, other media producers would be able to appropriate his footage for their own projects—a prospect that itself could potentially further his activist-minded rhetorical goals. Before composing, Jim had to anticipate the ways his film might be appropriated and had to decide whether or not and how to facilitate these processes of *rhetorical recomposition*. We can think about rhetorical compositions as having a kind of momentum (or not) based, *in part*, on preparations that rhetors make. Jim uses the concept of *rhetorical velocity* in chapter 4 to describe how rhetors strategize about the direction, speed, and momentum with which compositions circulate.

The Kairotic Web of Multimodal Composition

The earlier diagram representing the articulation points that comprised Jim's kairotic struggle needs to be updated, then, to include factors related to reproduction, distribution, and recomposition. At a minimum, we would need to add the following points of articulation:

Media of reproduction and distribution: *The media required to get copies of a composition to an audience in the first place.* As a digital composition, Jim's FTAA video was reproduced and distributed via peer-to-peer file-sharing over the Internet, as facilitated by LimeWire. Paper-and-ink documents circulate through combinations of shipping vessels, human and machine sorting mechanisms, etc. Radio content circulates via transmitters, electromagnetic waves, and antennae.

Media of delivery: *The media involved in the presentation of a composition.* Once Jim's video was physically distributed to viewers, viewing it required yet another set of infrastructural resources, such as the application QuickTime. One thing that makes paper-and-ink a useful medium is that it provides its own mechanism of display. Once you hold a book or newspaper in your hands, you typically don't need other infrastructural resources to consume them. Radio shows require a radio receiver, with speakers, volume control, tuner, etc.

Other compositions: *Subsequent compositions that facilitate the rhetorical success of earlier ones.* Winter used letterhead, an agency's name, and a business address to secure readers for his scripts. Wong's *Aiiieeeee!* paved the way for *Homebase.* New issues of the *Westsider* contain QR codes that allow smart phone users to access earlier issues.

Collaborators: *People beyond the composer who facilitate the rhetorical success of a composition.* Winter recruited a friend to serve as agent. Wong published *Homebase* through his ability to recruit the help of Ishmael Reed, who operated I. Reed Books.

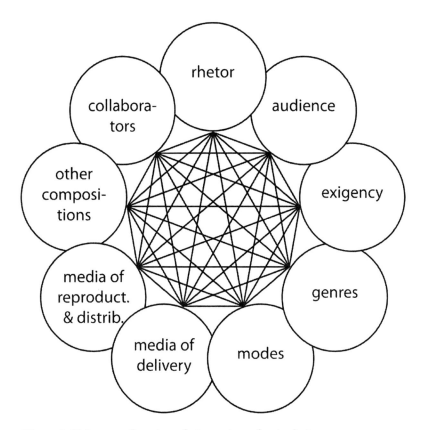

Figure 5. Kairos as a function of nine points of articulation.

We are not claiming that this set of kairotic factors is exhaustive. It would be impossible to list every factor that contributed to kairotic opportunity, every articulation point that enabled kairotic inventiveness. We do claim, however, that this list includes factors that are often overlooked in traditional rhetorical theory and pedagogy. Introducing these articulation points into models of rhetorical practice means introducing additional layers of complexity that need to be accounted for.

Kenneth Burke has represented the situation of human action via the dramatistic pentad. One of the virtues of the pentad is that it allows analysis along "ratios" or pairs of constitutive elements that are read in relation to each other: the act-scene ratio, the agency-agent ratio, and so on. Similarly, we claim that public rhetors can benefit from reading the kairotic articulation points we name in relation to each other. We list nine kairotic factors here, resulting in thirty-six ratios, each one of which performs a heuristic function. For instance, the kairotic struggle includes a reading of *media of reproduction and distribution* in relation to *audience*. Jim chose to distribute his film on-line because the audience he was targeting had access to the Internet and valued it as source of information. The Westside neighborhood chooses hard copy distribution to residents' doors because that's the best way of reaching an audience all located within a few city blocks. Similarly, we can read *media of delivery* in relation to *exigency*. Jim selected video because the problem he planned to address was, in part, a problem emerging from videographic representational practices. The WNA selects ink-and-paper because its primary goal is to communicate a small amount of relatively simple information relevant to the lives of neighborhood residents. The immediacy of paper is suitable for this purpose.

A key characteristic of the kairotic struggle as we envision it is the radical simultaneity of all of these factors, the way they form a web of interdependent relationships that exist all-at-once. As Marilyn M. Cooper observes, "anything that affects one strand of the web vibrates throughout the whole" (370). Or, as Herndl and Licona write in their exploration of Burke's pentad, "[a]gency is the conjunction of *all* the ratios in a rhetorical context" (142, emphasis added). In the case of Jim's FTAA documentary, for instance, if Jim had not had access to LimeWire and the Internet (media of reproduction and distribution), video (medium of delivery) might have been inappropriate *even if* all the other kairotic components (audience, purpose, mode, etc.) had been favorable to video. Rhetorical action is always, to some degree, a compromise that satisfies some criteria better than others.

MULTIMODAL RHETORIC AND THE PUBLIC SPHERE AS MATERIAL-SEMIOTIC-CULTURAL ECOLOGY

The approach we outline here is consonant with the ecological approaches explored by a number of theorists who examine public rhetoric and the public sphere. As we note in chapter 1, the initial model of the public sphere introduced by Habermas has been revised by a number of subsequent theorists. In Habermas's original model, public-sphere discourse is driven by physically copresent individuals engaging in rational-critical debate. Warner troubles this model, emphasizing that publics arise when strangers pay attention to multiple texts circulating through space and time. Warner's model is more like an ecological web of interdependent factors: multiple texts, rhetors, readers, moments and sites of reading, and so on. Other theorists have suggested that we understand rhetorical action as always immersed within complex ecologies (see, for instance, Cooper; Dobrin and Weisser; Edbauer Rice, "Unframing"; Spinuzzi and Zachry; Syverson).[12]

Carolyn D. Rude, for instance, examines the case of a report produced by the Union of Concerned Scientists (UCS). Rude is less interested in the report itself than in the constellation of activities that adhere to its publication. The report doesn't become useful until it functions as a "tool for social action" (279). Activists begin to *use* the report. They take it into the field and draw on its insights. Made available on the organization's website, the report becomes the "seed" of multiple other publications in multiple genres, formats, and media (282). Rude concludes that "plans for dissemination and use" should be considered part of the overall process and that "[t]he writer's responsibility may extend beyond publication. The writer is part of a collaborative team and may not be personally responsible for taking the document into the field, but the writer works with an understanding and vision of a publication within the web of related publications and activities" (286). Similarly, Paula Mathieu and Diana George shift our focus from the single composition and the single author to "networks of collaboration" and "networks of circulation" (145). Mathieu and George write that "[o]ver time we learned that while traditional compositional issues like tone, research, and framing issues are still vital to the process of public writing, equally so is the circulation and physical embodiment of the rhetoric" (146).

Jenny Edbauer Rice offers a compelling reenvisioning of the public sphere as "affective ecology." Edbauer Rice examines a set of rhetorical interventions in Austin that began in a finite way: two local organizations print bumper stickers aimed at protesting unfair practices by city government. This initial action, itself occurring within a complex material-cultural context, connects with other events and happenings in a larger ecology, resulting in myriad and unpredictable rhetorical actions. An original printing of 5,000 is followed by multiple printings, adding up to tens of thousands of stickers. Stickers are joined by t-shirts, tote bags, and mugs. Various organizations appropriate, transform, and resist the message. Drawing on the work of Michael Warner, Margaret A. Syverson, and others, Edbauer Rice offers a model in which the public sphere is not a geophysical place that contains discrete rhetorical objects (authors, texts, venues), but is a highly fluid, always fluctuating sea of "happenings" and "encounters" ("Unframing" 20).

An ecological approach forces us to embrace contingency in the etymological sense of the word: *con-* ("together with") and *tangere* ("to touch") (see *"Com-," "Contingent," "Tangere"*). Rhetoric is what happens when multiple factors come together, become proximate, touch—a convergence that enables some possibilities even as it forecloses others. Embedded in the word contingency are meanings of *affinity* ("[c]lose connexion or affinity of nature"), *chance* as possibility and good fortune ("the being open to the play of chance, or of free will"), and *chance* as something of which one is the victim ("[t]he quality or condition . . . of being at the mercy of accidents") (see "Contingency").[13] In light of the contingent nature of rhetoric, the rhetor is properly conceived not as a "seat of origin" but as a "point of articulation," to borrow a distinction introduced by Dilip Parameshwar Gaonkar (263). The rhetor lies at the juncture of multiple contingencies. Like Gaonkar, we are interested in the way rhetors are positioned within relationships of extant texts and discourses, but the cases we examine above suggest rhetors are also positioned within complex networks of human and nonhuman agents, including collaborators, sites, modes, technologies, and more.

Given the contingent nature of rhetorical action, it is possible to arrive at the conclusion that rhetors have no agency whatsoever. In the diagram we introduce above, kairotic opportunity is the result of thirty-six simultaneous relationships, and it would be easy to add others. The production of an FTAA video could be characterized as a one-in-a-million happening that emerges from the unlikely convergence of an infinite number of factors. But we do not see this radical indeterminacy as inevitable. In the face of contingency, rhetors "simply must muddle along as best we can" (Jasinski 112). One thing is certain: agency is not increased by pretending that rhetorical action transcends contingency, the result of the radically unfettered actions of a rational-autonomous rhetor. We return to this question of agency in chapter 5, drawing on Herndl and Licona's useful exploration of postmodern agency as well as the insights of actor-network theory.

CONCLUSION

In this chapter, we have been concerned with a redefinition of the kairotic struggle. This struggle is traditionally defined in terms of the single rhetor's attempt to fashion a single, word-based composition for a single, stable context. We argue that the potential of multimodal public rhetoric will never be fully realized if this model remains operational. We need to expand the notion of kairos along several lines:

1. The kairotic struggle begins before the rhetor's commitment to a particular mode, medium, genre. It includes the inventiveness of the rhetor in choosing among available possibilities.

2. The kairotic struggle extends beyond the moment when the composition is done to include the complex ways compositions circulate to audiences.

3. Kairos can be understood as the result of a complex web of factors that are radically simultaneous (exert pressure all at once). Some of these factors include audience, purpose, exigency, mode, genre, media of distribution, media of delivery, other compositions, and collaborators.

4. This means that certain material considerations that have traditionally been defined as "nonwriting" factor into the kairotic struggle—things like cameras, the size of hard drives and memory cards, USB cables, computer applications, computer screens, the speed of computer processors, money, shipping containers, cars used to drive texts around, photocopy machines, the shelves where texts are displayed for readers to buy, and more (DeVoss, Cushman, and Grabill 30).

5. This also means that rhetors need to examine the cultural structures that legitimize or delegitimize texts as they circulate; these structures will vary in any given situation. At times the logo of a major press might help a text; at other times it might mark a text as corrupted by the for-profit establishment.

6. Rhetors look forward to and anticipate the nature of circulation that they desire for their compositions. Even though circulation happens after composition, it exerts a pressure on composition.

7. Complexity, uncertainty, instability, and contingency enter into the process at every translation. Cameras fail; computer files get corrupted; editors refuse to look at manuscripts (or,

when they do look at them, apply to them culturally biased standards and reading practices); compositions get blown from door handles by the wind and end up in mud puddles; incredibly compelling videos languish on YouTube because no one knows they're there; and so on.

The full importance of the heuristic that we offer in chapter 2 should now be clearer. Jim's ability to read the kairos of the situation rests upon a complex set of attitudes about rhetorical practice. Jim needed to be open to the *cultural status* of different rhetorical modes and media (the way audiences would value video compared to white papers or other forms), to the *semiotic affordances* of those media (that video allowed a particular kind of critique of representational practices), to the *infrastructural resources* necessary to produce video (the availability of cameras, computers, etc.), and to the way traditional structures of *specialization* can be reconfigured (so that not only did he see himself as the director, camera operator, and editor of his own film, but also its distributor—all roles typically filled by different people in traditional systems of media production).

How does all of this affect teachers, writing assignments, the composition classroom? In chapter 5 we turn our attention to the implications of this expansion of kairos for rhetorical pedagogy. Before we do, however, we would like to explore the concept of *rhetorical velocity* and *rhetorical recomposition* through a careful reading of three practitioner cases.

4 Composing with Rhetorical Velocity: Looking Beyond the Moment of Delivery

Figures 6–8. Thinking about rhetorical velocity. Photographs by Jim Ridolfo.

In the previous chapter we argued that the rhetor's assessment of kairos might be productively expanded to include moments before the rhetor's commitment to words on paper and moments after the composing process is over and the composition is considered complete. Ultimately, this led us to suggest that, if public rhetors are serious about addressing rhetorical exigencies, they must move beyond an understanding of their task as narrowly limited to composing. Rhetors increasingly need to proactively plan for and facilitate the circulation of their compositions. In this chapter, we would like to continue this exploration of rhetorical circulation through a close examination of three cases of rhetorical activism. We show how Jim Ridolfo's concepts of *rhetorical velocity* and *composing for recomposition* can help rhetors come to a deeper understanding of the "rapidity at which information is crafted, delivered, distributed, recomposed, redelivered, redistributed, etc., across physical and virtual networks and spaces" (Ridolfo and DeVoss). If theories of multimodal public rhetoric are to provide any real significance for practitioners, we argue that such theories need to include the possibility of producing rhetorical material for future recomposition: we need to see audience not merely as recipients of rhetorical compositions, but as potential recomposers and redistributors of texts. As DeVoss, Cushman, and Grabill have argued, the timely availability of and access to digital composing infrastructures are extremely significant for new media composers. We argue that rhetors who aim to facilitate rhetorical velocity and recomposition need to consider these same infrastructural concerns—access to resources such as human expertise, software, hardware, and network connectivity—as they relate to *audiences*.

As Adrian Johns points out in *The Nature of the Book*, print culture provides only the illusion of a fixed text, and the digital only makes this illusion more visible. Through the speed of digital circulation and data mining, we're able to see patterns of remix and reuse of texts more quickly (Ridolfo and DeVoss). Trends of reuse and remix, often obscured by physical limitations such as place, geography, and the necessary time required to oscillate between physical texts and places, are patterns made more frequently and easily visible in the digital. We argue that composers will increasingly notice, compose into, and compose around, ideas of recomposition. However, we also acknowledge that for instructors and students alike, thinking about the potential future iterations of a text may be a difficult paradigm shift. This conceptual change poses a challenge to rhetoric and composition studies, where the field has had a habit of equating "the activity of composing with writing itself and to miss altogether the complex delivery systems through which writing circulates" (Trimbur, "Composition" 189–90).

We want our students not only think about the existing visual, aural, textual, tactile, aspects of their own compositions, but we want them to start thinking about the ways their work could be recomposed into other combinations of the visual, aural, textual, and tactile. We want them to think about their composition as a falling Tetris block: Someone else may turn it sideways or upside down and fit it into a new combination. While students may complete their "final" compositions absent of images, sound, and movement, there is an increasing chance that their text may be recomposed, reframed, and remixed to become a part of someone else's future multimodal composition. Ultimately, "kairotic inventiveness" (Walker, "The Body" 49) is enriched through the rhetor's ability to create compositions that anticipate the rhetorical effects of appropriation once the composition is in the pubic domain. Students who learn rhetorically effective ways to "compose for recomposition," we contend, are better equipped and more likely to participate in the public sphere and, in the process, develop rhetorical flexibility in their writing that is not stressed in conventional writing process models. However, considerations of rhetorical velocity and recomposition introduce additional complexities and contingencies into rhetorical practice. Therefore, we explore instances of *negative appropriation* in which rhetorical material is used in ways contrary to the rhetor's original intensions.

A Ripple in the Pond: What Is Rhetorical Velocity?

Rhetorical velocity refers to the way rhetors strategize about the potential recomposition and redistribution of a text. In physics, *velocity* necessarily includes equal consideration of the "speed of an object together with the direction of the motion," making velocity a fitting metaphor for the *change* in the position of a text (Graham, Boardman, and Pearson 8). Rhetorical velocity draws attention to considerations for *how* the text may be recomposed and/or redistributed and the text's potential for becoming actualized in future cycles of recomposition and/or redistribution. In this sense, thinking about rhetorical velocity includes anticipating technical concerns such as the available human and technical resources over *there*, temporal aspects such as *when* and how much time a third party *might have* to recompose/redistribute a text, and rhetorical concerns about what *might motivate* a third party to redistribute and/or recompose the text, or what might give a text future velocity. By inductively strategizing how the rhetorical dominoes may fall, the rhetorician may consider potential speed and distance(s) of her own text, but also the potential speed and destination(s) for future texts composed by third parties.

In their May 2010 interview with the head of the NATO Training Mission Afghanistan and the Combined Security Transition Command, Lieutenant. General William B. Caldwell, IV, Mike Edwards, and Alexis Hart ask the Lt. General about the rhetorical velocity of strategically declassifying and releasing material to the media in a timely manner. They inquire about how he makes sure the information he "put out was sufficiently timely and accessible to make it easy for others to re-use." The Lt. General responded that one of the mandates for his "new command is to try to never produce anything that requires classification" (Caldwell). In other words, Caldwell understands the significance of timeliness in relation to future cycles of distribution/recomposition. If the timeliness and future recomposition of the Department of Defense materials into a third party news story are goals, then it's not rhetorically desirable to produce classified documents. James E. Porter echoes this interpretation of rhetorical velocity when he notes that the concept is about "circulation, but with an eye particularly toward timing (kairos) and 'recomposition'—or the strategy of designing a piece of writing not only for circulation but also for re-use or remixing" ("Recovering" 208). Charles Lowe has recently argued that "rhetorical velocity can help us to draw on delivery . . . as a framework for understanding the rhetorical *effects* of license choice." Lowe posits that the concept may be useful for "thinking about how the choice of either Attribution or Share Alike works as a rhetorical strategy for maximizing the present and future potential reuse of open content toward achieving a sustainable education commons." What the Caldwell interview and Lowe article show are additional concerns for the how timely redistribution of content is not only limited to technology and infrastructure, but also institutional and legal constraints such as intellectual property classifications or license agreements. Both Caldwell and Lowe show how these institutional and legal mechanisms may impact a rhetorician's strategy of delivery and recomposition.

To facilitate recomposition and redistribution, rhetors need to theorize both the intrinsic properties of a text and factors extrinsic to the text. An example of an intrinsic concern might be the rhetorician's choice to release a composition in a particular file format. As Karl Stolley has evangelized in his Lo-Fi Manifesto and elsewhere, file formats (and open file formats in particular) are an important rhetorical choice, particularly when a text's "source code and media elements are available for inspection, revision, and extension outside the scope of any one piece of production software and any one producer," arguing that the broadest possible open file format standards "encourages end-user/reader customization and repurposing." For example, a video delivered to a third party in a proprietary exportable file format such as a Flash Video File (.flv) from YouTube, for instance, will be widely viewable but will require a potential recomposer and redistributor to do additional (perhaps prohibitive) work and possess proprietary software in order to manipulate and/or redistribute the video content. This concern about how prohibitive the file is to access is particularly relevant if the potential recomposer wants to redistribute and/or migrate the content to a platform or file format completely outside of YouTube. In other words, choosing to make the video available in an open file format may have particular rhetorical advantages in terms of future recomposition and/or distribution.

While intrinsic factors are rhetorically important, the file is not distributed into a vacuum. Extrinsic factors may include a text's intellectual property license, another rhetor's motivations to recompose the text, and another rhetor's access to hardware, software, human expertise, time, and money. In other words, extrinsic factors may include the rhetor assessing a third party's behavioral or institutional factors (workflow conventions, infrastructure, availability of human and technical resources, time), legal factors (intellectual property concerns), and/or political factors. Collectively, these considerations help rhetors explore the conditions within which a future rhetor might recompose and/or redistribute a particular text and whether such activity is rhetorically advantageous or desirable. For example, a rhetorician might consider the likeliness of a newspaper to copy and paste boilerplate content directly from a press advisory (Ridolfo and DeVoss). If the rhetor has an established history of delivering press advisories to a reporter at the newspaper in a particular file format and on a certain day, then the rhetor may have a better chance at approximating the text's intrinsic and extrinsic likeliness for future recomposition. In summary, a rhetor thinking about rhetorical velocity may consider any number of intrinsic and extrinsic factors regarding the potential speed, direction, and motion of a text:

- What intrinsic and extrinsic rhetorical factors might motivate or dissuade third parties to recompose and/or redistribute a text?
- What are the technical limitations of any future acts of recomposition, and how might these relate to the time, resources, and motivation of a third party?
- Are distribution and/or certain kinds of recomposition by third parties rhetorically desirable (positive), undesirable (negative), or simply of no concern to the rhetorician (neutral)?

In addition to thinking about a general likeliness for recomposition, the rhetorician may also consider the impact (ripple effects) of these future hypothetical compositions within a specific framework of rhetorical goals and objectives. For example, the rhetor may consider the possibility for undesirable recomposition and/or distribution (negative appropriation). This could be anything from a politician sampling and remixing an embarrassing sound bite from an opponent's television commercial (recomposition and redistribution) to an unsolicited extremist fringe group distributing a more mainstream group's political campaign materials. In the latter case, the fringe group's extremist reputation may then be used by the mainstream's opposition to negatively impact the mainstream's ethos in the eyes of moderate supporters: guilt by (distributive) association. In addition to positive and negative appropriation, there are also acts of appropriation or distribution that are of little consequence to the rhetorician or her goals and objectives (neutral appropriation).

RHETORICAL VELOCITY AS PRACTICE AND ANALYTIC

Rhetors and rhetorical critics come at processes of rhetorical velocity from opposite directions. Rhetors look forward in time to the moment when their compositions will hopefully achieve a kind of circulatory success that will allow for optimal rhetorical impact; however, these broader circulatory achievements are, to some extent, a mystery to rhetors. Rhetors select strategies of production, reproduction, and distribution, but the ultimate effects of these strategies are always to some degree unknowable. The critic, on the other hand, looks backward at rhetorical compositions that are already circulating. The circulatory success of a given composition is often what is most visible to a researcher and might even be responsible for how the researcher discovers a text to begin with. The specific practices of production, reproduction, and distribution that the rhetor embraced may not be visible by the time the critic encounters a text. Researchers interested in rhetorical velocity must do considerable work to understand how original assessment, planning, and decision-making by rhetors shaped subsequent processes of circulation. To the extent that rhetorical theory focuses on the practices of the rhetor, it risks over-emphasizing the roles of strategy and intentionality. To the extent that rhetorical theory focuses on encounters with compositions that are already in broad circulation, it risks reifying rhetorical circulation as a hopelessly mysterious, uncontrollable, ultimately unknowable phenomenon. In this discussion, we hope to walk a fine line between these two extremes; we hope, that is, to explore the roles that rhetor's intentions and strategies play, but also to candidly confront the reality that the way rhetorical compositions circulate is always, to some extent, unpredictable, beyond the control of even the most prepared rhetor.

Why Multimodality and Rhetorical Velocity Together?

While the concept of rhetorical velocity is more easily understood with reference to compositions of a complementary genre and medium (e.g., thinking about a press release being recomposed into a news article or a piece of stock video being cut into another rhetor's film), it's also useful to theorize the potential transitions of texts between different genres and media. In other words, theorizing texts in one genre or medium as potential future building blocks for texts in another genre or media. The website http://sendamessage.nl, for example, allows an individual thousands of miles away to contact and electronically pay a political activist in Israel-Palestine to spray-paint a customized message on the side of the concrete portion of the separation barrier. In addition to the analog composition, sendamessage.nl also promises to compose and e-mail digital images to its customers. While there are a host of ethical issues to unpack in this case example, our purpose here is to introduce the special dynamic that results when the composition of a message oscillates between the digital and the analog to employ multiple genres with limited resources.[14] The authorship of the message is a distributed multi-person process of digital composing, digital delivery, analog recomposing, analog delivery, digital recomposing, and digital delivery. The analog step helps make visible how even a linear, commissioned process of delivery can be multimodal. Because it involves a commissioned act of future delivery, this example stresses the importance of delivery for multimodal rhetorics.

In the next several sections we present three case examples of rhetorical velocity. The first case example focuses on Brad Ward and Twitter, and shows how delivery and multimodality may be theorized together. The second example of a press release and activist campaign demonstrates how rhetorical velocity may be used to theorize how a text may traverse different genres and media. The third case example highlights issues of positive and negative appropriation, or how a text may be recomposed in such a way that its creator finds the act completely undesirable.

Case Example #1: Twitter and #watchitspread

Twitter and Composing for Recomposition (Retweet).

Twitter is a compelling example of a writing platform where one of the primary writing activities is composing with a sense of recomposition. Writers using the microblogging platform compose brief 140 character messages called "tweets," and Twitter users "follow" or "unfollow" each other based on the interest in reading each other's tweets. While one Twitter user has one group of followers, another user could have an entirely different readership. One of the ways Twitter users propagate information between their various spheres of readership is to recompose (retweet) someone else's tweet. As Ben Parr explains:

> To give credit to the original person, users usually put "RT" plus the originator's username at the beginning of the tweet. Here's an example: The Twitter user @benparr tweets: I just heard that Apple is releasing new iPods in July! . . . You [then] retweet by posting **RT @benparr** I just heard that Apple is releasing new iPods in July.

Twitter users also post tweets with accompanying hash tags. These hash tags in turn enable other Twitter users to search and find new users and timely information. For example Twitter-using conference-goers at the 2010 Conference on College Composition and Communication in Louisville, Kentucky, could add the hash tag #cccc2010 to their tweets, allowing participants to aggregate tweets by topic. In addition, the hash tag also provides Twitter researchers with a conversational anchor to potentially help track the proliferation of a message across time and tweet streams. This is the case with Brad J. Ward and #watchitspread.

Brad J. Ward and #watchitspread.

At 1:21 p.m. EST on July 23, 2009, Brad J. Ward, the CEO of the higher education and social media firm Blue Fuego, was conducting an online seminar and tweeted the following request to his over 2,700 twitter followers:

> I am showing a webinar audience how quickly a message can spread on Twitter. Would you please RT? #watchitspread

Ward recalls how he then interactively shared the composing and delivery experience of the #watchitspread demonstration with his webinar audience:

> During the webinar, I shared my screen, let them [the audience] watch me type the message in to Twitter . . . I figured anywhere from 30–60 retweets would be cool enough for the audience to see . . . To my surprise and excitement, there were nearly 750 retweets in the first 30 minutes. Wow! I think the audience was sold on the power of Twitter at that point.

In the next eight hours the #watchitspread message was retweeted over ten thousand times. In addition, several dozen websites discussed the phenomenon. As the daytime July 23, 2009 popularity of the #watchitspread hash tag increased, so too did Ward's visibility in the twittersphere and blogosphere:

> I was ranked #2 on ReTweetRank.com, above everyone on Twitter except @TweetMeme. With RT's definitely playing a role in the algorithm on twitter.grader.com, I bumped up to #796 of 2,844,018 ranked people on Twitter . . . I also picked up about 200 followers in the 24 hours, a nearly 10% increase in followers.

The example of #watchitspread is an ideal case study for rhetorical velocity using the same medium and genre. Ward composed his tweet for recomposition (retweeting) by keeping the character count to 113, leaving room for individuals to add "RT @bradjward" (15 characters), with an additional twelve characters remaining (113 character message + 15 for retweeting + 12 discretionary characters = 140). If for example

Ward's message had been 140 characters in length, potential retweeters would have needed to expend time editing his tweet, resulting in a less likely chance for any successful rhetorical velocity. Because Ward was able to strike a proper balance of characters and composition, many users retweeted his 113-character request verbatim.

As the popularity of the #watchitspread hash tag grew, some Twitter users also began to appropriate the #watchitspread hash tag to propagate their own discussions or promote online advertising. These examples of negative appropriation were relatively harmless in this instance, but they are also a regular, predictable occurrence on Twitter.[15] Ward's #watchitspread example not only made for a successful real-time webinar example, but the broad proliferation of his message across the Twitter and blogosphere helped increase his reputation as a social networking consultant.

This example thus serves as a potentially useful introduction to the concept of how rhetorical velocity functions inside a highly restrictive writing genre and platform. The concept of composing for recomposition is made clear both in terms of the rhetorical situation and the transparency by which we're able to track the proliferation of the #watchitspread hash tag. #watchitspread renders visible processes that are often difficult or impossible to see. We think having instructors and students examine the composition of retweets in class is an effective way to begin to conceptually scaffold toward discussing and analyzing more explicitly multimodal examples of composing for recomposition.

Case Example #2: A WRC Protest and Composing for Cross-Genre Recomposition

The relevance of rhetorical velocity to multimodal public rhetorics is more fully understood through the following example of student activists' uses of cross-genre recomposition.

As part of a national effort by United Students Against Sweatshops (USAS), *Movimiento Estudiantil Xicano De Aztlan* (MEXA) and Students for Economic Justice (SEJ), a local affiliate of USAS, have been working at Michigan State University (MSU) for five years to convince the university to join the Worker Rights Consortium (WRC). On February 24, 2005, over thirty students (including Jim Ridolfo) at MSU "occupied" the first floor of the central administration building, setting up a portable CD player and then dancing for a half hour to salsa music. Within a matter of seconds, the main lobby of the Hannah Administration Building was transformed from a place of university business to a place of protest: students danced, chanted, and held signs. Folks came out of their offices to see what was transpiring. Within minutes the police had arrived, and reporters began snapping photographs and taking notes. As part of a five-year local campaign directly affiliated with a national campaign spearheaded by USAS, as well as the international anti-sweatshop movement, these local student activists staged this particular image event to pressure MSU into joining the WRC. Partly because of strategic media preparation work done beforehand, this image event was covered in three local newspapers, including the *Lansing State Journal,* the widest circulating mid-Michigan paper.[16] This example of rhetorical velocity focuses on the transference of language from the event's press advisory to one of the three resulting news stories.

The Press Advisory

Press advisories are often understood as summary descriptions of a specific event; their potential to effect public discourse, however, is significantly increased when we understand the press advisory as a powerful means for recomposition. In many cases press advisories become as useful as the execution of the event itself for effecting rhetorical purposes. The experienced press advisory writer understands that there is a need on the part of the reporter to write the news story quickly and on time for a deadline. She thinks about how the text of the press advisory may be recomposed by reporters into other genres of writing, such as a print or online newspaper article or the script for evening news broadcasts. This type of writing is often learned through direct first-person experience, but evidence of recomposition can often be found by comparing the text of press advisories and press releases to any corresponding news coverage.

Figure 9. Rhetorical velocity and the press advisory. Photograph by Jim Ridolfo. (Thanks to Maggie Corser for allowing us to photograph her.)

Figure 10. Rhetorical velocity and the press advisory. Photograph by Jim Ridolfo. (Thanks to Maggie Corser for allowing us to photograph her.)

The press advisory for the administration building protest (Figure 11) predicts that the SEJ/MEXA "students will dance vigorously." The advisory was faxed to all of the local media outlets and three news agencies covered the event. The first was from the *Lansing City Pulse*, a weekly print and online newspaper. *The City Pulse* reporter describes the protest dancing as "shake, strut, and salsa," and the news story was carried online March 2, 2005 (Stegmair). The second was from the MSU student newspaper *The State News*, which reported that the protesters "jived, jumped and boogied" (Jarman). The third was the *Lansing State Journal*, which described the event as "vigorous dancing" (*Lansing State Journal*). The *Lansing State Journal*'s use of language from a press advisory for news content may not be indicative of good journalism, but it is not an uncommon occurrence (see Ridolfo and DeVoss). In the example of the *Lansing State Journal*, while the newspaper sent a photographer to the event, they did not send a reporter to take notes. Therefore the "reporter" assigned to write the text for the story had to rely heavily on follow up phone calls and activist-provided boilerplate text. Having a familiarity with this writing circumstance, writers in public relations can anticipate that all or part of their text may be recomposed into other genres of writing, and this is a prime example of composing for recomposition.

RHETORICAL VELOCITY

From the perspective of the reporter, the press advisory may be seen as a useful boilerplate resource for submitting an article on time. Students, however, hoped that this event would draw the for-profit press to the Administration Building, ultimately leading to favorable coverage—in multiple media (print and Web) and modes (text and photographs)—for the WRC campaign. These students anticipating the future appropriation of the February 19 press advisory text can be interpreted in terms of rhetorical velocity. If, for example, the activists' press advisory is recomposed into favorable news coverage, then the activists achieved positive appropriation. However if the activists' press advisory was recomposed (perhaps "flipped") into pejorative anti-WRC content by someone opposed to the campaign, then the activists failed to avoid negative appropriation.

Similar to Twitter, someone may anticipate and trade the potential for some negative appropriation for some degree of positive appropriation. This may be an acceptable trade off, especially if the positive appropriation helps accomplish certain immediate campaign goals or objectives. On the other hand, the longevity and availability of some digital content may mean that a future instance of negative appropriation may be much later and less predictable (see Ridolfo and Rife). A multimodal pedagogy incorporating rhetorical velocity must teach how to weigh these potential benefits and consequences. In addition,

---

FOR IMMEDIATE RELEASE
NEWS ADVISORY
February 22[d], 2005, 9:00 AM

Contact:
Jim Ridolfo, Media Contact
Phone: 517-420-2864
Email: ridolfoj@msu.edu

STUDENTS TO PROTEST INSIDE ADMINISTRATION BUILDING BY DANCING
MSU ADMINISTRATION HAS STILL NOT AGREED TO BASIC RIGHTS FOR WORKERS

East Lansing, MI – On February 24th students will be 'occupying' the first floor of the administration building through dance. Approximately thirty to forty **students will dance vigorously** inside the Michigan State administration building to protest the administration's slow, stalling pace at signing on to a 'code of conduct' that would protect life of the workers who make MSU clothing and apparel overseas.

    When: Thursday, February 24th, 2:00 PM
    Where: MSU Administration Building, 1st floor
    Why: MSU clothing is currently licensed to sweatshops
    What: Thirty students dancing in the main administration lobby,
               during normal business hours

Students at MSU want Michigan State to sign on to an enforceable "code of conduct", a document that will truly be useful in stopping the licensing of the MSU logo to companies that are in direct violation of international standards of human rights. Currently, the administration wants to sign on to a document that 'looks OK on paper', but won't be legally useful in helping to enforce human rights standards and basic rights of human decency. This is what the students and faculty and community members demand.

"We want a strong code of conduct. We won't settle for less," said Tommy Simon, an English sophomore.

"Michigan State has a history of supporting these sorts of issues, as the flagship land grant university we have a history of this type of action and we have an obligation to continue being a leader on labor issues," said Jose Villagran, a MSU student and activist.

Figure 11. The press advisory distributed prior to the SEJ/MEXA protest.

students need to begin to see how the individual bits of their composition may be seen as building blocks for recomposition. This is the case with our final example, where a seemingly benign photograph had the building blocks for a future instance of negative appropriation.

Case Example #3: David Hume Kennerly and Negative Appropriation

In the first two stories we discussed examples where individuals consciously composed for and achieved a positive form of appropriation and recomposition. In this last story we will look at a visual example

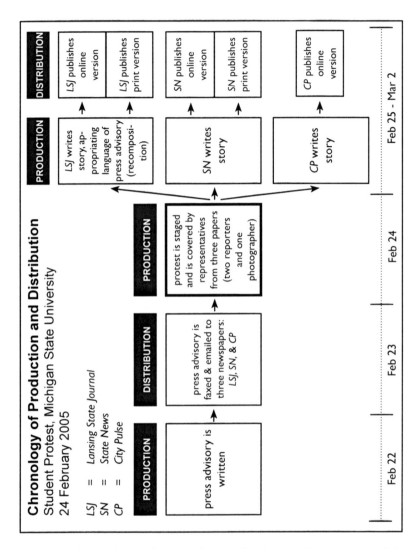

Figure 12. The circulation of a press advisory. This diagram illustrates some of the circulatory events related to the effectiveness of the SEJ/MEXA protest. The protest itself can be seen as the central rhetorical "composition"—a multimodal performance in which students took over MSU's Administration Building, played salsa music, and "danced vigorously." The protestors symbolically substituted action and attention for the inaction and inattention that had until then characterized the MSU administration regarding the issue in question. But the circulation of the protest's message required the help of other rhetorical actions that came both before and after the protest itself, resulting in a complex chain of rhetorical events involving multiple compositions, people, modes, and technologies.

where the composer was not thinking about any sort of future recomposition. However, someone else saw fit to negatively (in the eye of the original composer) recompose his work. We hope this example will serve to illustrate how even when rhetorical velocity is not a primary rhetorical objective, its questions still have a place in our cut-and-paste world.

Figure 13. Changes in the labor of media production. Photographs by Jim Ridolfo.

Figure 14. Changes in the labor of media production. Photographs by Jim Ridolfo.

Negative Appropriation

David Hume Kennerly, a former Pulitzer-prize winning employee of *Newsweek*, photographed Vice President Dick Cheney as he prepared dinner in the kitchen with his family. On the left-hand side of the original photograph are his wife and children. On the right-hand side of the photograph Cheney is depicted sinking a fork and knife into a bloody steak. The photograph of Cheney with his family conveys the image of a helpful family man.

Several years later, however, *Newsweek* (the owner of the stock photo Kennerly shot) cropped the image to exclude Cheney's family. What was left in the frame was just a lone, sinister looking image of the former Vice President sinking his knife and fork into bloody steak. Kennerly perceived this cropping as a form of what we would call negative appropriation:

> The Sept. 14th *Newsweek* cover line—"Is Your Baby Racist?"—should have included a sub-head, "Is Dick Cheney a Butcher?" Featured inside the magazine was a full-page, stand-alone picture of former Vice President Dick Cheney, knife in hand, leaning over a bloody carving board. *Newsweek* used it to illustrate a quote that he made about C.I.A. interrogators. By linking that photo with Mr. Cheney's comment and giving it such prominence, they implied something sinister, macabre, or even evil was going on there. I took that photograph at his daughter Liz's home during a two-day assignment, and was shocked by its usage. The meat on the cutting board wasn't the only thing butchered. In fact, *Newsweek* chose to crop out two-thirds of the original photograph, which showed Mrs. Cheney, both of their daughters, and one of their grandchildren, who were also in the kitchen, getting ready for a simple family dinner. However, *Newsweek*'s objective in running the cropped version was to illustrate its editorial point of view, which could only have been done by shifting the content of the image so that readers just saw what the editors wanted them to see. This radical alteration is photo fakery. *Newsweek*'s choice to run my picture as a political cartoon not only embarrassed and humiliated me and ridiculed the subject of the picture, but it ultimately denigrated my profession.

Kennerly published his above critique in the online Lens Blog of the *New York Times*. Frank J. De Maria, the Vice President of Corporate Communications at *Newsweek* responded to Kennerly:

> We cropped the photograph using editorial judgment to show the most interesting part of it. Is it a picture of the former vice president cutting meat? Yes, it is. Has it been altered? No. Did we use the image to make an editorial point—in

this case, about the former vice president's red-blooded, steak-eating, full-throated defense of his views and values? Yes, we did. (Kennerly)

Kennerly produced a stock photo, and years later a piece of that stock photo was cropped and recomposed with a new caption of accompanying text. This new multimodal composition offered a message substantially different from the one communicated by Kennerly's original photograph. Indeed, as we have tried to illustrate in the above comic, we think media organizations will continue to draw on ever-increasing stockpiles of recomposable footage. We also contend that experiences such as Kennerly's will continue as an all-too-common occurrence in the age of greater textual mobility. We think the example shows that even when one is not composing with a sense of positive recomposition/appropriation, one should still look at the potential particulars of a composition and think about the potential for complex multimodal combinations of negative recomposition.

CONCLUSION: RHETORICAL VELOCITY
AND MULTIMODALITY

We're increasingly posting, publishing, and circulating our compositions in media conducive to composing for recomposition. While the printed word encouraged the illusion of a fixed security, the realities of digital publishing radically undermine any sense of fixity. In a digital context, compositions fluidly emerge from earlier compositions and are recomposed into subsequent compositions. As rhetors increasingly confront the recompositional affordances of digital texts, writing classrooms will need a pedagogical framework for addressing issues pertaining to rhetorical velocity.

Indeed, rhetorical education needs to be substantially transformed if it is to prepare rhetors to confront the complexities of rhetorical velocity. Traditional sites of rhetorical education do not typically address concerns of recomposition outside of discussions of plagiarism, citation practices, and (more recently) copyright law. Teachers perceive their primary role as impressing on students the moral dangers of recomposing outside of prescribed boundaries, but rhetoricians need to see how, in certain contexts, recomposition and/or distribution may be a rhetorical objective. As we have indicated in the second case example, press advisories are written so that they will be recomposed or "plagiarized" by reporters (Ridolfo and DeVoss).

Models of rhetorical invention need to be reconfigured to address issues of rhetorical velocity and recomposition. To be effective, rhetorical decisions need to be informed by rhetors' goals for the way their composition(s) will circulate after they are "finished." On a micro level, the example of #watchitspread demonstrates the way effective composers anticipate the possibilities and constraints associated with circulation, but these anticipatory concerns ripple throughout the composing process. Decisions about modes, media of delivery, media, or reproduction and distribution, the amount and framing of content, all affect the potential for rhetorical velocity and for rhetorical recomposition.

To sum up, the cases we have examined in this chapter suggest that rhetors need to be prepared to confront the challenges associated with the way compositions travel when they are finished. This means asking heuristic questions such as the following:

- Where do I want my composition(s) to go?
- What routes will allow my compositions to reach the destinations I have in mind?
- What human and nonhuman actors might facilitate circulation along these routes?
- What compositional choices might I make to facilitate the kind of circulation I desire?
- What are the key risks and liabilities that result from the circulation of my composition(s)?
- How might my composition(s) be misappropriated (negative recomposition), and what steps might I take to limit such misappropriations?

In this chapter and the two that precede it, we have attempted to outline an expanded understanding of what Jeffrey Walker calls "kairotic inventiveness"—an expansion that involves questions arising before the rhetor commits to words on paper as well as questions that pertain to moments after the composition is complete. This expanded understanding of kairotic inventiveness would be called for even if multimodality were not a consideration, but multimodality intensifies the need for an expanded model because of the complexities multimodality introduces at all stages of the circulatory process, includ-ing invention, production, reproduction, distribution, consumption, redistribution, and recomposition. This expansion has important con-sequences for our understanding of rhetorical agency and pedagogy. We turn to these twin concerns in the next chapter.

5 Challenges for an Ecological Pedagogy of Public Rhetoric: Rhetorical Agency and the Writing Classroom

In the previous three chapters, our goal was to expand our understanding of kairos. We argued, in chapter 2, that accessing new technologies and the rhetorics they enable is no simple affair. Cameras or 3D printers are never simply present to us in all of their kairotic potential. Our ability to see them as options is dependent on our ability to reflect on the cultural and material pressures that dictate our dispositions toward them and to question whether those dispositions are appropriate at this particular moment and place. To see each moment as a moment of crisis—to see the opportunities available at any given point in time—rhetors and those responsible for rhetorical education may find it helpful to engage in critical inquiry along four major axes. This means asking questions about the infrastructural accessibility, the cultural position, the semiotic potentials, and the practices of specialization that pertain to a given rhetorical form.

We shifted to more specific and localized concerns in chapters 3 and 4, focusing on the kairotic struggle of the rhetor within a given context. Specifically, we drew attention to moments of kairotic inventiveness that take place *before* rhetors commit to words on paper as well as moments *after* compositions are complete. We have tried to demonstrate that kairotic invention can be facilitated by reading a set a set of ratios typically overlooked: *mode* ↔ *medium-of-delivery; mode* ↔ *audience; audience* ↔ *medium of delivery*, and so on. We modify Gaonkar's understanding of the rhetor as "point of articulation" to refer to the way rhetors are connected to a complex network of human and nonhuman agents. The *rhetor-as-point-of-articulation* experiences the radical simultaneity of myriad material, cultural, and semiotic factors that enable and constrain rhetorical action. Rhetorical invention and rhetorical practice are distributed across this complex network.

If we're right about the need to revise our understanding of rhetorical invention and rhetorical practice, what implications do these revisions have for rhetorical pedagogy? In this chapter, we turn to the challenges that rhetorical educators face as they prepare students for the role of *rhetor-as-point-of-articulation*. Before we get to those challenges, however, we find it necessary to address considerations of rhetorical agency. In the model we outline in the previous three chapters, rhetorical action feels more like emergence (the result of many confluent elements) than the strategic action of a rational autonomous subject. In light of this, it is tempting to conclude that rhetorical education is obsolete. If rhetorical action results from the convergence of so many different elements beyond the rhetor's control, what is the point of teaching rhetors in the first place? We begin, therefore, with a discussion of rhetorical agency.

WHO'S TO BLAME?: THE PROBLEM OF AGENCY IN ECOLOGICAL CONTEXTS

The ancient concept of kairos reminds us that rhetoric is an intensely situated activity and that many situational components are beyond the control of the rhetor. Nevertheless, many traditional models of rhetorical practice rely on an understanding of rhetorical agency as a relatively straightforward and unproblematic affair. In this view, rhetors exploit kairotic opportunity by the skillful deployment of rhetorical devices in the speeches they compose and deliver. As Gaonkar puts it, while traditional rhetoric "recognize[s] the situational constraints, including the specificity of the audience addressed, they are, in the last instance, so many items in the rhetor's design. The agency of rhetoric is always reducible to the conscious and strategic thinking of the rhetor" (275).

An ecological understanding of rhetorical practice, however, seriously complicates this notion of agency. "In a complex system," Syverson writes, "it can be difficult to determine the extent of individual responsibility or agency" (200). Similarly, Warner's discussion of the public sphere is saturated with uncertainty about the role of intentionality, planning, and strategy. Warner complicates models of rhetorical action as a "localized exchange" comprised of "a speech event involving speaker and addressee" (90). Instead, he emphasizes the "concatenation of texts through time" (90). Publics are "essentially intertextual, frameworks for understanding texts against an organized background of the circulation of other texts"—and this background itself is of "infinite complexity" (16). In a move that seems to explode models of rhetorical context cherished by writing teachers, Warner asks, "For whom does one write or speak? Where is one's public? These questions can never be answered in advance, since language addressed to a public must circulate among strangers" (128). Texts and their circulatory paths are already overdetermined because "[e]very sentence is populated with the voices of others, living and dead, and is carried to whatever destination it has not by the force of intention or address but by the channels laid down in discourse" (128). It is fair to say that Warner's project is about revealing the problems and contingencies that characterize publics as complex systems.[17]

It would be a mistake, however, to conclude from this emphasis on complexity that Warner's conception of publics and counterpublics is nihilistic, lacking any opportunity for what Felski calls (in her exploration of a feminist "counter-public sphere") "goal-oriented political struggles based upon common interests" (167, 169). Alongside the language of contingency and indeterminacy in Warner's writing, is a discourse of possibility, hope, and opportunity. A "counterpublic," Warner writes "enables a horizon of opinion and exchange; its exchanges remain distinct from authority and can have a critical relation to power" (56). Moreover, a counterpublic "can work to elaborate new worlds of culture and social relations" and can enable "active participation in collective world making" (57). Indeed, some reviewers have emphasized a utopian dimension in Warner's vision. In Jessica Blaustein's reading of Warner, for instance, a salient point is that "if publics are not merely reflective of pregiven social forms, but rather constitutive of sociality itself, then there are no better tools for generating new social forms" (172). Blaustein observes that "[t]his refreshingly utopian impulse frames each of Warner's chapters" (172). She subtitles her review "A Handbook for Alternative World-Making," encouraging a reading of Warner as a guide for praxis.

Our own analysis admittedly focuses more concretely on rhetors and the decisions with which they are faced, but as figure 5 shows, in our expanded definition of kairos, we are forced to catalogue a set of articulation points that quickly result in a level of complexity that can feel overwhelming. If rhetorical action is the result of the felicitous alignment of thirty-six ratios (and actually there are many more than that!), a successful rhetorical act seems more like winning the lottery than a result of conscious strategy.

Our argument, then, rests on a delicate balance. On the one hand, we argue that rhetorical action is characterized by a surprising degree of complexity that emerges from the interplay of elements that have often been overlooked. On the other hand, we find it essential to preserve some understanding of rhetorical agency. Indeed, without something like the concept of agency, there is little reason for composition and rhetoric, as a field, to exist. As Cheryl Geisler notes, the need for pedagogy is at stake in discussions of agency, for "only if we can assent to the role of the rhetor in producing efficacious action can we as a discipline have a mission to educate such rhetors to have agency" (13).

To shed light on what we have in mind by this delicate balance between control and contingency, we turn to insights that emerge in postmodernism-inflected conversations about the relationships between subjectivity, discourse, and ideology. To gain a better understanding of the role nonhuman "actants" (such as technologies and spaces) play in models of human agency, we supplement postmodern understandings with those provided by actor-network theory (ANT).

RHETORICAL AGENCY RECONSIDERED

Rhetorical agency has become the focus of considerable theoretical attention in recent years.[18] For our purposes, a useful starting point is provided by Herndl and Licona's "Shifting Agency: Agency, *Kairos*, and the Possibility of Social Action." Herndl and Licona begin with a "theoretical stalemate" between two opposing models of agency that was introduced to the field by John Clifford (136). On one side of the stalemate lies a "naïve humanism" that posits "autonomous, rational actors" (cf. Habermas). On the other side of the stalemate is "the poststructural subject" posited by Louis Althusser, Michel Foucault, and others (136). In privileging this model, Clifford ultimately represents subjectivity as (in Herndl and Licona's words) "a nonporous, inflexible category into which subjects are interpellated by ideology and determined by discourse" (136).

However, as Herndl and Licona observe, many of us feel "that neither of these formulations explains the rhetorical and social phenomena we experience" (136). To move past this stalemate, Herndl and Licona begin with Anthony Giddens's relocation of agency from "the intentions people have in doing things" to "their capability of doing those things in the first place" (qtd. in Herndl and Licona 137). From there, they move to Susan Bordo's assertion that agency "is in fact not 'held' at all; rather people and groups are positioned differently within it" (qtd. in Herndl and Licona 137). In this view "agency exists at the intersection of a network of semiotic, material, and yes, intentional elements and relational practices" (137). This is consonant with Burke's pentad in which "agency is the conjunction of all the ratios" (142). Herndl and Licona (echoing Paul Smith) conclude that agency "exceeds the subject" (142). That is, agency is not contained within a single unified human subject, but is the function of our relational position within a multifactorial matrix. Herndl and Licona are ultimately drawn to the concept of kairos because it forces us "away from the individual and toward the opportunity itself" (156). "We could push this theoretical formulation of kairos further," they continue, "and read agency as the momentary conjunction of multiple material, semiotic, and situational conditions of possibility" (156). Herndl and Licona thus gracefully negotiate the extremes of the "theoretical stalemate" they set out to address, theorizing an understanding of agency that neither reinscribes a romantic or naïve understanding of the rational autonomous subject nor succumbs to fatalistic readings of Foucault and other poststructuralists.

Herndl and Licona's assertion that agency as positioned "at the intersection of a network of semiotic, material, and yes, intentional elements and relational practices" is consonant with a model of agency provided by actor-network theorists (137). What ANT adds, however, is a more detailed account of the role *material* elements (nonhuman actants) play. A full explication of ANT is beyond the scope of our discussion. Instead, we offer a close reading of two important works that illustrate ANT's contributions to understanding agency.

Latour's often-cited "Where Are the Missing Masses? The Sociology of a Few Mundane Artifacts," examines the way technologies operate in our daily lives, using everyday examples such as doors and seatbelts. Latour's title refers to a metaphor derived from astrophysics. The movement of galaxies in relation to each other leads astronomers to infer the existence of "dark matter"—"missing masses" that are not visible but that nevertheless seem to be exerting a substantial force on the universe. Latour claims that sociologists, like astronomers, sense the operation of invisible forces: "[w]hen adding up social ties, all does not balance. . . . Something is missing" (152). Latour demonstrates that "the missing masses of our society are to be found among the nonhuman mechanisms" (169).

Latour focuses on the role of technologies in achieving social and moral goals, or what he calls "programs of action" (152). One such program is ensuring that motorists wear seatbelts. Traditional models of moral behavior would explain seatbelt wearing in terms of laws, societal norms, and the "conscience" of the individual, but Latour demonstrates that this program is enforced by a network of human and nonhuman actors. In a humorous passage, Latour describes his quest to break the law and drive down the road at speed without wearing his seatbelt. This is impossible because the car has built-in devices that enforce seatbelt wearing: a flashing message and an alarm. Latour claims to have gone to the extreme of paying mechanics to disable these devices. Anticipating such actions, subsequent cars are equipped with automatic seatbelts. "I cannot be bad anymore," Latour writes, "I plus the car, plus the dozens of patented engineers, plus the police are making me be moral" (152).

It becomes interesting to ask in this situation, as Latour does, "Where is the morality?" (152). The final output is a moral one: Latour wears his seatbelt. However, morality does not seem to be located, as in modernist accounts of human agency, *in* Latour; it does not lie in his will or intentions. Neither does morality seem to be located, as some postmodern conceptions would have it, in the interpellation of the subject by discourse. Somehow, the culture's attempt to inscribe the ideology of seatbelt wearing seems to have failed in the case of Latour: left to his own devices, he refuses to "click it." What works is something different from either individual will or discursive pressure: a network of human and nonhuman agents.

Importantly, "programs of action" are never absolute. Latour pushes against the network; the network pushes back. Latour can engage in various practices to circumvent the network: he can ignore the alarm or pay mechanics to disable it. These attempts can in turn be addressed through further translations, such as automatic seatbelts. Latour offers a particular understanding of the "kairotic struggle" that we have been exploring throughout this book, a version that pays due respect to the role played by nonhuman agents.

Latour goes one step further, suggesting that a machine is like a text: just as an author anticipates the expectations and practices of readers, a machine-builder anticipates the expectations and practices of users. No one group (authors or readers, machine builders or users) has complete power: "[t]here might be an enormous gap between the prescribed user and the user-in-the-flesh" (161). An author might write a book that goes completely unread. An engineer might build a machine that goes completely unused. At the other extreme, however, are "occasions" when "the gap between the two may be nil: the prescribed user is so well anticipated, so carefully nested inside the scenes, so exactly dovetailed, that it does what is expected" (161).

In short, Latour's network of human and nonhuman actors can be designed. Programs of action are precisely attempts by humans to recruit a set of resources to achieve a particular result. They are like rhetorical compositions, constructed in anticipation of an end user in a particular context. In fact, Latour reinforces this link between programs of action and rhetoric by using his own written text as a mini program of action. He ends an early section with the mysterious aside: "This little point having been made, let me go on with the story (we will understand later why I do not really need your permission to go on and why, nevertheless, you are free not to go on, although only *relatively* so)" (155). Within the program of action comprised of Latour's text, we are only "relatively" free.

In "On the Methods of Long-Distance Control: Vessels, Navigation and the Portuguese Route to India," John Law focuses not on everyday technologies that populate our daily routines but on the large-scale networks involved in late fifteenth-century Portuguese imperialism, asking how it was possible "to arrange matters so that a small number of people in Lisbon might influence events half-way round the world" (235). Achieving this required the orchestration of a complex network of human and nonhuman agents:

> Seamen, merchants, masters, envoys, it was necessary to keep all of these in line and to make use of their efforts. . . . And such compliance was not only required from the human components of the system. It was also expected from its inanimate parts—from the hulls and sails that made up the vessels and the environments in which those vessels sailed. (240)

Any understanding of how colonization worked needs "to develop a form of analysis capable of handling the social, the technological, and the natural and the rest with equal facility" and to account for "the way in which these are fitted together" (235). Such an account would need to address new technologies of ship design (new sails and hulls), new navigation equipment (astrolabes and quadrants) and techniques (steering by astronomical observation), new ways of condensing knowledge (tabularly presented data), and training techniques (drills, manuals).

We might jump to the conclusion that agency was lacking in this highly complex and distributed system. Power seems to be hopelessly emergent, a happy accident that results from the chance configuration of a million radically simultaneous factors, but this is not the story John Law tells. His account of Portuguese expansion is disturbingly full of the shrewdness and intentionality of human actors. The decisive moment in his account occurs in 1484, when "King John II convened a commission and charged it with finding a method for navigating outside European waters" (247). This commission recruited an ensemble of experts—men who possessed deep knowledge of astronomy, cartography, geography, and more. This commission "was responsible for one of the earliest successful practical applications of scientific knowledge to practice: the *Regimento do Astrolabio et do Quadrante*. . . . [I]t's importance is beyond question" (248).

Herndl and Licona, Latour, and Law all explore the way agency "exceeds the subject," is distributed across complex networks of human and nonhuman actors, including people, discourses, and technologies. But none of these theorists excludes the roles of education, planning, intention, or design. Herndl and Licona conclude with a reference to the usefulness of their model for rhetorical praxis, noting that "[i]n some practical sense . . . it might help rhetors better gauge the opportunities for efficacious action and better position themselves in the relational practices that configure the conditions for action in the world" (151). Similarly, John Law writes that "there is more than a hint of Machiavelli in the [ANT] method, and the author of *The Prince* is cited approvingly by several actor-network theorists for his merciless analysis of the tactics and strategies of power" ("Notes" 6). Law writes that "[o]rganisation is an achievement, a process, a consequence, a set of resistances overcome, a precarious effect. Its components—the hierarchies, organisational arrangements, power relations, and flows of information—are the uncertain consequences of the ordering of heterogeneous materials. So it is that actor-network theory . . . demystifies" ("Notes" 8). We particularly like the word "choreograph" as the verb for negotiating complex networks. In her application of ANT theory to infertility clinics, Charis Cussins uses "ontological choreography" to capture the "coordinated action of many ontologically heterogeneous [human and nonhuman] actors in the service of a long-range self" (600). The complex push-and-pull relationships of actors in networks is neatly summarized by Bryn Williams-Jones and Janice E. Graham:

> Every actor in a network is essentially independent and capable of resistance or accommodation. . . . Each actor (whether a person, group, company, machine, nation) has its own diverse set of interests, thus a network's stability will result from the continual translation of interests. Between humans, translation is analogous to negotiation of common interests; between humans and non-humans, the interaction will be through design of scripts. . . . Policies, behaviours, motivations, and goals are translated from one actor to another; and actors are themselves translated and changed in their interactions with others. (275)

In short, agency does not evaporate, but is distributed across a fragile and complex dance among multiple and ontologically disparate actors.

So how does this relate to a theory and pedagogy of multimodal rhetoric? In the model of multimodal rhetoric we are exploring here, success is a function of multiple composers, multiple audiences, multiple compositions, multiple technologies, multiple channels of circulation—the convergence of many heterogeneous elements. Nevertheless, agency does not evaporate. The preparedness, planning, anticipation, and design of multiple rhetors working in concert can never amount to anything close to absolute freedom, and all rhetorical action is contingent on many factors beyond the control of the various human actors involved. As the case of "Cotton Patch" illustrates, rhetoric can fail to happen altogether when the task of choreography becomes too great. It does not follow, however, that rhetors have no agency.

What is absolutely certain is that we do not increase our agency by pretending that it exists apart from a complex network of human and nonhuman agents. Yet this is precisely what most rhetorical pedagogies do, as we demonstrate in the following section. What we propose is that multimodal pedagogy should foreground the reality that "agency exceeds the subject," should provide students with opportunities to feel, practice, and reflect on their role as *rhetors-as-points-of-articulation*.

AN ECOLOGY OF KAIROS IN THE WRITING CLASSROOM

The role of education is emphasized in the accounts of agency we have just explored. While all of these accounts emphasize that the final outcome is the "precarious" effect of networks, all hold out hope that networks can be "ordered," "designed," "choreographed," "coordinated," and "negotiated." Indeed, networks depend on human agents who are capable of articulating with nonhuman agents. In the case of Portuguese sailors, this means that human actors need to be educated. The network demands the development of educational aids (such as manuals) and techniques that prepare human agents to function appropriately. We, obviously, do not endorse strategies that treat agents as mechanistic tools in networks of power. Instead, we emphasize the importance of critical reflection and tactical resistance. The important point here, however, is that acknowledging the complexity of networks only underscores the role of education; it does not diminish it.

As others have observed, rhetoric is not an end in and of itself, but a means to address an exigency (see Bitzer; Dias, et al.). This is most salient in the dynamics of *public* rhetoric: public rhetors engage in rhetorical action in order to address something beyond themselves: a policy, a belief, a perception, an attitude. Because rhetoric is a means to an end, public rhetors conceive of their task broadly. They consider multiple modes. They anticipate channels of distribution. They do what is necessary to get the job done. This might mean (as in the case of Terrence Winter) inventing a literary agency or (as in the case of the Westside Neighborhood Association) hand-delivering newsletters to the front doors of members of the audience. Moreover, the fact that writing is a means to an end informs the entire rhetorical process from invention to the ways rhetors involve themselves in the circulation of their own compositions.

In the composition classroom, however, the case is very different. In the classroom, rhetoric (usually writing) is not a means to address a public exigency, but a performance to be assessed by the teacher. This changes everything. The presence of the teacher alters—sometimes intentionally, sometimes by default—the dynamics of rhetorical practice in fundamental ways. Suddenly, the focus is not on using rhetoric to solve a problem; instead, the focus is on using rhetoric as an end in and of itself (Dias, et al.; Freedman, Adam, and Smart). Because of this, students in a classroom typically do not get to experience the complex processes of rhetorical invention we have been describing in this book.

To put it as bluntly as possible: assignments that begin with the teacher's directive "write a paper" are already broken. In public contexts, rhetors make choices about modes, media, and genres based on their relationship to a multifactorial web, including exigency, audience, and infrastructural resources. In classroom contexts, the teacher dictates mode, medium, and genre. By eliding substantial parts of the kairotic struggle, classroom pedagogy curtails the rhetorical and ultimately the civic agency of public rhetors.

Many new media assignments are broken in the same way. An assignment that begins "make a video" or "make a website" is just as limiting as an assignment that begins "write a paper" because it does not allow the rhetor to select modes, media, and genres, and therefore does not allow the rhetor to engage in the complex processes of invention that are informed by the radically simultaneous constellation of factors such as available infrastructural resources, audience, exigency, etc. In short, it does not allow rhetors to experience the richness of *rhetor-as-point-of-articulation*. It presents an impoverished version of the kairotic struggle and of rhetorical invention.

Opportunities for making decisions about reproduction and distribution in the traditional writing classroom are even more limited than opportunities for assessing modes and media. In the traditional writing classroom, as Trimbur points out, delivery is reduced to "an afterthought at best" ("Composition" 190). In contrast to this reduction, Trimbur suggests that delivery be linked to public-sphere participation, arguing that delivery "must be seen . . . as ethical and political— a democratic aspiration to devise delivery systems that circulate ideas, information, opinions, and knowledge and thereby expand the public forums in which people can deliberate on the issues of the day" (190).[19]

In public contexts beyond the classroom, rhetors are deeply mindful of the challenges of reproduction and distribution because those are the processes that allow their compositions to have an impact on the world (see McComiskey, *Teaching* 37). As Warner says, a public is called into being when multiple texts capture the attention of multiple strangers dispersed in space and time. Rhetors, therefore, seek out strategies of reproduction and distribution that will allow their texts to be multiplied, to reach strangers, to capture attention, and to persist over time. These strategies of reproduction and distribution both inform the composing process itself and constitute additional rhetorical actions that remain to be performed after the composition is done. The rhetorical process exceeds the composing process.

In the classroom, the only audience that counts is not comprised of strangers dispersed in space and time, but of classmates and a teacher who are geophysically co-present. As Trimbur notes, reproduction means printing out a few copies of a three-page paper for peer response; distribution means handing the paper to the teacher (195). In some ways, new technologies, as they are integrated into the writing classroom, work to mask the challenges of reproduction and distribution rather than foreground them. Students no longer have to worry about the cost of paper and ink (often very real concerns for public rhetors), but simply email their papers to their instructors.

In a sense, then, public contexts beyond the classroom are always *kairotically rich.* That is, they always ask rhetors to engage in processes of invention, production, and distribution that are informed by a complex network of human and nonhuman agents. But in the composition classroom, it becomes difficult to preserve this richness.[20] The process of rhetorical invention is reduced to a caricature of what actually happens in the world beyond the classroom. The kairotic struggle and the opportunity for kairotic inventiveness fail to happen.

This is not to say that rhetors ever have perfect knowledge of situational factors. As Warner and others point out, knowledge is always imperfect. Rhetors can never be certain that a given mode or medium will elicit attention, or that a given distribution method will safely deliver a composition to its intended audience. (David sometimes throws the WNA's newsletter in the trash without reading it.) The composition classroom should help students make meaningful decisions *in the face of* uncertainty and indeterminacy.

Table 2. Comparison of classroom and public contexts.

Traditional Writing Class	Public Contexts
Writing is produced in order to receive a grade from a teacher.	Rhetorical action is aimed at bringing about some change in the world.
Audience is frequently unspecified.	Concerns for audience inform rhetorical choices at all levels.
Audience, when specified, is singular.	Audience is a complex mixture of different groups and individuals who sometimes have conflicting needs and values.
It is assumed that alphabetic text is the primary or even exclusive mode of communication.	It is assumed that composers will choose the mode, medium, and genre that will be most effective within the rhetorical situation that invited the response to begin with.
Rhetorical compositions circulate through the unproblematic gesture of handing a paper to the teacher.	The circulation of rhetorical compositions is an important challenge that informs the composing process at all levels and continues to require attention after the composition is "finished."
Composing is a cognitive-cultural-symbolic activity in which material concerns are incidental.	While it certainly entails cognitive-cultural-symbolic components, composing also involves actively negotiating complex constellations of material resources and constraints, including time, space, money, technologies of production, reproduction, and distribution, institutional structures, and more.
The chief unit of activity is the single composer.	The labor of rhetorical production is distributed across a variety of producers, technologies, and sites.
The chief unit for measuring rhetorical output is the single composition.	Rhetors see their task as participating in an orchestrated effort that involves multiple compositions spanning multiple modes and media.
A composition is "done" once it has been composed.	Rhetors anticipate the ways their compositions may be recomposed by future rhetors.

CURRENT APPROACHES TO TEACHING PUBLIC RHETORIC

Innovative scholar-practitioners like Bruce McComiskey and Jody Shipka have presented approaches designed to address some of the problems we raise here. McComiskey outlines a sophisticated pedagogy of public rhetoric in *Teaching Composition as Social Process*. As an advocate of a "post-process" approach, McComiskey rightly observes that traditional process-oriented pedagogies tend to elide the issue of "where essays go when they are finished—and to what effect" (20). Public rhetors are ultimately concerned not with their rhetorical compositions in and of themselves, but with the "impact" their compositions have on the world (37).

Accordingly, McComiskey shifts our attention to the broader "cycle of cultural production, contextual distribution, and critical consumption," a model of textual circulation that McComiskey adapts from Richard Johnson and other theorists working within a cultural studies framework (24). McComiskey asks his students to critique cultural artifacts using this cycle as a "heuristic" in order to help "students understand both writing and culture as dialectic social processes through which they can derive a degree of agency" (25). McComiskey's students perform sophisticated critiques of advertisements, for example, examining the ways they encode cultural values (cultural production), the venues in which they are presented (contextualized distribution), and the way audiences interact with such artifacts (critical consumption) (25–29).

Importantly, McComiskey does not stop with classroom critique. Mindful that "critical consumption alone does not, in and of itself, lead to social reform" (32), McComiskey has students intervene in cycles of textual circulation: "For example, students might decide to write a letter to IBM executives explaining that their advertisements encourage husbands and fathers to neglect their families" (37). Students select their target audience strategically, in order to maximize the "potential impact" (37) of their "practical letters" (42).

McComiskey's approach has certain limitations, however. The kairotic inventiveness of McComiskey's students operates within narrow parameters—parameters that do not emerge from the totality of the rhetorical context, but instead are dictated from above by the teacher. McComiskey dictates the mode (writing), media (ink and paper), and genre (letter) students need to use. None of these constraints are derived from the rhetorical context itself. In McComiskey's account, there is no reference to why a written letter would be better, for instance, than a sit-in protest, a viral video, or a merchandise campaign comprised of t-shirts, coffee mugs, and bumper stickers.

Aware of the potentials of multimodal rhetoric, McComiskey describes an assignment sequence that asks students to produce a college "viewbook"—a book that represents the people and spaces of a school through textual and visual resources. McComiskey's students begin with a "critical discourse analysis" of an extant viewbook of their choosing and then "analyze and critique the cultural values represented in the viewbook" that they have selected (91). This analysis lays a foundation for creating their own viewbooks, allowing students to "construct your own cultural values, social values, and ideal identities" (97). Again, we admire this approach for the thoughtful way that it progresses from critical analysis to production and for the way that multimodal rhetoric is viewed as a tool for shaping cultural values and identities (a focus we take up in chapter 7). There are certainly times when teachers will want students to experience certain genres of composing, and the viewbook is clearly a genre selected to address a set of learning goals that McComiskey has explicitly articulated and that we ourselves agree with.

But important kairotic concerns are left out when assignments are framed in this way. In the viewbook assignment, students are not given a chance to assess and select from other possible modes and genres that might work better in this context. (What if members of the target audience find viewbooks boring?) Moreover, students are not given the opportunity to inquire into the way processes of reproduction, distribution, and circulation might shape their assessment of the efficacy of viewbooks. How much will it cost to make multiple copies of a viewbook? How many copies are required to achieve the rhetorical goals in this situation? What other forms of distribution (e.g., a PDF version distributed via the Web) might be worth examining? Are there legitimating structures that should be taken into account (e.g., a viewbook distributed at a local record store or coffee shop frequented by members of the target audience might be better received than one that comes unsolicited in the mail)?

More recently, Jody Shipka has offered a useful framework "geared toward increasing students' rhetorical, material, and methodological flexibility" (285–86). As Shipka observes, "assignments that predetermine goals and narrowly limit the materials, methodologies, and technologies that students employ in service of those goals . . . per-petuate arhetorical, mechanical, one-sided views of production" (285). The framework that Shipka offers, however, does not foreground as-sessments of mode that are informed by exigency, purpose, and audi-ence or the concerns of reproduction and distribution. Shipka adopts an essentially expressivist approach in which students select modes and media in order to represent their feelings and experiences. For instance, asked to produce a composition based on the *OED*, one of Shipka's students experiences "physical and intellectual punishment . . . while sitting in front of the computer looking for usable *OED* data online" (297). To express this frustration, he produces a video tailored to "bore the socks off" his audience (297). Likewise, another student, confessing "that she was extremely frustrated for the first part of the semester," sees the *OED* assignment as "her opportunity to articulate that frustration through a piece that was intentionally designed" to instill frustration in her audience. The framework Shipka offers is lim-ited by her expressivist approach. As Warner observes, engaging with a public means moving beyond the self to engage with strangers dis-persed in time and space.

Shipka, drawing on Trimbur, rightly points out the importance of integrating concerns of circulation into our pedagogies, but again her framework needs to be transformed and extended if it is to ef-fectively serve public rhetoric. One student, for instance, produces an intricate composition comprised in part by a set of specialized mirrors. Although this is clearly an imaginative approach to the problem of de-livery, it does not seem to be informed by a broader understanding of circulation as a process that extends beyond the classroom—by essen-tial questions such as, *How could this intricate composition be effectively reproduced so that a sufficient number of copies could be made to address the exigency for which it was intended? How could these multiple copies be distributed to their intended audience? What are the costs involved in reproduction and distribution? How do the benefits of this approach weigh against competing approaches that might be easier to distribute?*

So What Would You Do If You're So Smart?

The problems with traditional pedagogy that we explore here are not easily solved. In an ideal world, we would ask students to form small non-profit organizations, construct a mission statement, and then give them a budget of $10,000 to operationalize their mission through rhetorical action. This would allow them palpable experience with the challenges faced by *rhetors-as-points-of-articulation*. Such an approach would differ from service-learning approaches in which students perform relatively circumscribed tasks for community partners whose missions are constructed independently of students. In the approach we imagine, students would be in the driver's seat—would control mission, resources, planning, and implementation. Rhetoric would become necessary to achieve the mission of the organization—*to get the job done.*

Unfortunately, we have not found a way to implement this approach within the writing classroom.[21] It requires too much money and time, and involves too many risks. In chapter 9, we explore a specific pedagogical approach that addresses many (though not all!) of the concerns we identify here. For now, we limit ourselves to outlining guiding principles for a pedagogy informed by ecologies of kairos.

The pedagogy we imagine would invite students to experience the richness and challenge of *rhetors-as-points-of-articulation*, would invite them to experience kairos as a moment that begins before the commitment to words on paper and extends after the composition is done, to include processes of reproduction, distribution, and recomposition. At least some of the invitations to compose would be left open enough for students to go through processes of rhetorical invention informed by the thirty-six ratios outlined in chapter 3. This means that rhetorical contexts would include enough information for students to make educated guesses about what modes, media, and genres would best articulate with a particular audience and exigency.

In this approach, the role of nonhuman agents (technologies, spaces, money) would not be elided, but would be placed front and center. Here we align ourselves with a growing realization in the field that we cannot afford to adopt what Christina Haas and Christine M. Neuwirth call a "computers are not our job" attitude (325). As Edbauer Rice warns, we cannot indulge our sense that technological considerations are "*beneath* us" ("Rhetoric's" 372). It is still common to hear compositionists remark that the 'technology should not get in the way of writing.' This attitude is obsolete. Technology is always "in the way," in the sense that all communication is enabled and constrained by technologies at multiple stages of circulation, and multimodal rhetoric tends to involve rather more considerations of technology.

Writing teachers need to adopt what Stuart A. Selber describes as a "professionally responsible" approach to computer literacy ("Reimagining" 470). Noting that "students reach technological impasses when they lack the computer-based expertise needed to solve a writing or communication problem," Selber suggests that "a functionally literate student resolves technological impasses confidently and strategically" (493). Rather than treating modes, media, and the technological complications associated with them as incidental, such an approach would ask students to see all rhetorical action as inextricably linked to "infrastructural" resources (DeVoss, Cushman, and Grabill) and would encourage students learn, assess, choreograph, and critique these resources. Indeed, as Edbauer Rice suggests, technologies should be seen as occasions for the deployment of rhetorical imagination. "The potential for production," writes Edbauer Rice, "lies in the ability for writer-users to imagine what can be done with these tools. This takes two skills: knowing how to imagine rhetorically and knowing how to use the equipment" ("Rhetoric's" 378). In the pedagogy we have in mind, inventorying, managing, assessing, learning-to-use, and imagining *through* infrastructural resources would be central activities.

As we integrate multimodal rhetoric into our own pedagogies, we find ourselves increasingly devoting class time to composing in technology-rich spaces, such as multiliteracy centers and humanities computing labs (see, for instance, Trimbur, "Multiliteracies"; R. J. Selfe). Composing becomes a class activity in which the instructor, knowledgeable classmates, and specialized media experts (such as students who staff the lab) are proximate and provide just-in-time support.

To sum up, the pedagogy we imagine would have the following characteristics:

1. It would give students opportunities to write within kairotically rich settings—settings that provide ample information about audience, exigency, purpose, and other contextual factors that make rhetorical decisions intelligible.
2. It would give students opportunities to select modes, media, and technologies of production, reproduction, and distribution strategically, based on their understanding of these kairotically rich settings.
3. It would involve students in critically reflective discussions about different semiotic options and how they might articu-

late with a constellation of kairotic factors such as exigency and audience (i.e., students might explore through critical discussion how a video and a white paper might accomplish different things within a particular context).

4. It would ask students to be attentive not just to production, but to the broader process of circulation—to how public rhetors individually and in collaboration with others strategize about the way their rhetorical compositions will travel through material-cultural contexts to reach intended audiences and address exigencies.

5. It would ask students to be attentive not just to a single composition, but the way an exigency might be addressed by multiple compositions in multiple media.

6. It would ask students to participate in complex forms of collaboration: not just coauthored essays, but multifaceted projects in which larger groups work together to organize a campaign of compositions.

7. It would ask students to confront the materiality of rhetoric, offering extensive experience negotiating complex constellations of technologies, spaces, money, institutional structures, and other resources that enable and constrain multimodal composing.

8. It would provide experience in sophisticated forms of assessment of rhetorical effectiveness, including inquiry into how well compositions circulated, found their audiences, and into how intended and unintended audiences received those compositions. In short, it would ask students to attempt to discern the impact of their rhetorical actions.

THE OTHER FUNCTION OF RHETORICAL EDUCATION

Rhetorical education has a dual function. On the one hand, it exposes learners to various rhetorical practices and resources, facilitating their maturation as rhetors. At the same time, rhetorical education inscribes learner's subjectivities. It normalizes certain things while marginalizing others. It suggests certain ways of seeing the world and discourages other ways. It shapes the way we think about ourselves. It shapes who we are. Moreover, this is inescapable. There is no neutral way to teach rhetoric that does not touch the subjectivities of those involved. The question is, *What kind of subjectivities do we want to encourage?*

Susan Miller famously explores a related set of issues in *Textual Carnivals*. Miller shows that composition has historically been complicit in fostering in students a "passive subjectivity" (185). This can be traced back to the use of literature as what Terry Eagleton calls a "moral technology" whose "task . . . is to produce an historically peculiar form of human subject who is sensitive, receptive, imaginative and so on . . . *about nothing in particular*" (qtd. in S. Miller 91). Composition carries on the tradition of creating such passive subjects through its "emphasis on intransitive *processes*" (97). "The composition student," Miller writes, "is expected to experience processes, activities, strategies, multiple perspectives, peer groups, and evaluations that have no articulated relation to actual results from a piece of writing" (100). In many ways, the pedagogical approach of McComiskey that we outlined earlier, with its emphasis on the "potential impact" of student compositions, can be seen as an attempt to avoid the problems Miller identifies.

We want to focus here on a set of problems that are related to those identified by Miller. Composition classrooms continue to prompt student rhetorical action through assignments that dictate an alphabetic, paper-based response. What kind of subjectivity is produced by this practice? It seems to us that if students are required to take writing classes, and required in those writing classes to face every rhetorical exigency with writing and are never allowed to consider alternative rhetorical responses, they will learn to see responses other than writing as marginalized, irrelevant, and/or off-limits. The institution of first-year writing as a narrowly word-focused endeavor functions to produce individuals who see writing as a mainstream, inevitable, and privileged form of rhetorical action and who see alternative forms, such as music, video, and animation, as somehow "other": marginalized, nonserious, unimportant, ineffective. As it is typically configured, first-year writing produces *writers*, as distinct from *multimodal public rhetors*. Why not produce a film in response to this exigency? Because I am not a *filmmaker*. That is not who I am. That is not part of my identity. That's what students who major in film and video do, those folks in that other building down the road, the one with all those cameras and computers.

In the pedagogy we envision, students would be habituated to think of themselves as producers of culture, as potential users, at any moment, of the full range of semiotic and material tools available. Videos, music, game elements, stencils, 3D plastic prototypes, die-cut paper sculptures—nothing would be "off limits" per se, but would instead be assessed in relation to the concerns of kairos. The point is, this is not simply a function of *what I can do* but also of *who I am*. When students encounter a 3D printer, do they perceive a new possibility or do they conclude, *I am not an industrial designer; this is of no use to me?* To some extent, the answer to this question will be dictated by what structures of rhetorical education have trained students to think is "normal" or "natural."

PART III

The Challenges and Possibilities of Multimodal Semiosis

6 A Fabricated Confession: Multimodality, Ethics, and Pedagogy

In May 2002, nearly twenty-seven years after the original crime had been committed, the trial of Michael Skakel began in a Connecticut courtroom. Skakel was accused of killing Martha Moxley, his neighbor at the time of her death in 1975. The trial received a substantial amount of media coverage, partly for the tabloid interest generated by Skakel's relation to the Kennedy family, but also because of the unusual role multimodal digital rhetoric played in the prosecution's case. As legal scholars Brian Carney and Neal Feigenson describe it, the "prosecution worked with visual communication consultants to design a customized, comprehensive visual toolbox on CD-ROM that included over 100 crime scene and autopsy photographs, documents, diagrams, and digitized audio and video recordings." The prosecution's closing argument included a particularly striking use of media: a presentation that combined crime-scene photographs with tape recordings of Michael Skakel's own voice. A photograph of Martha's corpse is shown on screen while Skakel recounts, "I was like 'Oh my God, did they see me last night?'" This juxtaposition of photographs and Skakel's own words seems to amount to a confession; Skakel clearly alludes to having committed an act that he does not want to be discovered. The photograph of the corpse seems to name that act. Skakel's words, however, are taken out of their original context; they come from his conversation with a ghostwriter hired to write his biography. In the original context, Skakel recounts being afraid of having been seen masturbating outside the Moxley residence the night before.

Legal commentators and scholars continue to debate whether this use of multimodal rhetoric was appropriate or not. In one interview, Christopher Morano, a member of the prosecution's team, claims

"[t]hat's the way that people see things in real life. When they watch
the evening news, they're going to see a person talking. And while that
person's talking, they're going to be seeing some video about what the
person's talking about. This is what people are comfortable with now,
and that is why this is what has to be brought into the courtroom"
(Orson, "Multimedia in the Courtroom"). But NPR's Diane Orson,
paraphrasing legal scholar Todd Fernow, reports that "the rules for
presenting evidence aren't geared for the powerful impact visual images can have on jurors' emotions" (Orson, "Multimedia Display"). In
their appeal, Skakel's lawyers call the prosecution's multimodal presentation a "made-for-conviction movie that literally fabricated a confession" (Santos, et al. 67).

In the Skakel case we are confronted with another example of rhetorical action that emerges from a complex network of human and
nonhuman actors. Human actors include the ghostwriter who made
the original recordings of Skakel's voice, the photographers who took
pictures of the crime scene, the media workers at the consulting firm
employed by the prosecution, and the prosecuting attorneys themselves. Human actors also include numerous stakeholders charged
with interpreting the prosecution's presentation. The defense attorneys, the trial judge, and subsequent appellate judges were charged
with adjudicating whether the composition conformed to the rules for
evidence. Members of the jury needed to assess the argument embedded in the composition to discern how it factored into the determina-
tion of Skakel's guilt or innocence. Nonhuman actors—technologies
and semiotic resources—include visual and aural/oral representations
captured, assembled, and presented via tape recorders, cameras, photographic paper, scanners, electronic display screens, audio speakers,
software interfaces, CD-ROM storage media, and more.

Surrounding all of these things are more intangible factors. The
rules of evidence, themselves a kind of composition produced over
time by numerous rhetorical actors, govern what practices of persuasion are allowable in this context. But these parameters do not exist
in a cultural vacuum. In some complex way, they reflect the mores of
the surrounding culture, society's notions of fairness and justice. Over
and above these notions of fairness and justice are additional cultural
norms, values, expectations, and practices that shape the production of
discourse in this context. When Morano claims, "That's the way that
people see things in real life," he points to everyday practices of rhe-

torical consumption by members of the jury—individuals immersed in a culture that is saturated with the multimodal rhetorics of TV, film, and the Web. The implication is that rhetorical practices valued outside the courtroom ought to be valued inside it as well.

We are interested in examining the Skakel case in this context for several reasons. Before we list these, however, it is important to state what we are *not* interested in. First, we are not interested in defending Michael Skakel. Skakel's guilt or innocence is for others to judge and is of no concern to us here. Similarly, we are not interested in arguing that Skakel was treated unfairly and are not interested in assigning moral blame to the prosecutors or media consultants who contributed to the development of the multimedia composition used in the closing argument. We are not legal scholars and are not qualified to make judgments about whether or not the multimedia presentation conforms to rules of evidence.

For us, the prosecution's multimodal presentation is an opportunity to examine the way multimodality and materiality alter the dynamics of rhetorical ethics. Accordingly, we are interested in several key points of articulation within the broader network of human and nonhuman actors that engendered the prosecution's presentation: the specific semiotic resources involved (e.g., spoken words, photographs, and design elements) and specific technologies involved (e.g., tape recorders, cameras, and electronic displays), and the way all of these things articulate with broader models of rhetorical ethics. Our basic argument is that current models of rhetorical ethics need to be revised to account for the distinctive processes of multimodal semiosis.

At the same time, the Skakel case demonstrates the way ethical considerations are altered by complex processes of reproduction, distribution, and recomposition. The "fabricated confession" can be understood as an example of what we identify in chapter 4 as "negative appropriation." Media components, particularly the recording of Skakel's interview with the ghostwriter, were taken out of their original contexts and placed into new ones, resulting in meanings and effects very different from the ones their original creators intended. The altered understanding of rhetorical ethics we explore here has important implications for rhetorical pedagogy. Near the end of this chapter, therefore, we build on the insights learned from the Skakel case to make suggestions about the kind of pedagogical practices that might facilitate ethical use of multimodal public rhetoric.

McComiskey draws attention to the transformed nature of rhetorical ethics in the context of multimodality, noting that Arthur Asa Berger contends, "[t]hose who create images and symbols must think about the moral implications of what they do. . . . To the extent that seeing is believing, we must make sure that the images we create do not generate beliefs that are individually or socially destructive" (qtd. in McComiskey, "Visual" 199; see also Kellner 98). McComiskey himself, eager to respond to detractors of visual rhetoric, contends that "modes and technologies . . . cannot be described as ethical or unethical; only their users and the uses to which they are put can be described in this way" ("Visual" 198). Nevertheless, as Porter writes, "there is no neutral technology because all technologies are always already invested with a category bias; they are always socially and culturally situated . . ., constructed out of specific historical circumstances and reflecting the biases of that context" (*Rhetorical* 67). To ethically practice multimodal rhetoric, we need to account for a confluence of material, cultural, and semiotic concerns. In the multimodal presentation used by the prosecution in the Skakel case, ethical considerations are inextricably linked to aural and visual semiotic resources, tape recorders and cameras, photographs and audio speakers. The ethical is bound up in the material.

We might be tempted to characterize the multimodal presentation used by the prosecution in the Skakel case as a successful negotiation of the kairotic struggle. Working within a complex network of constraints and possibilities, the prosecution was able produce a rhetorical composition that appears to have been singularly successful. Michael Skakel was convicted, and many observers agree that the multimodal composition played a key role. As we noted in our discussion of the concept in chapter 1, however, kairos is not reducible to rhetorical efficacy. It dictates not just an effective response but also an ethical one. This chapter, then, continues our quest to develop a multimodal public rhetoric based on kairos by exploring the ways modes, media, and technologies introduce distinctive challenges to the ethical rhetor.

RHETORICAL ETHICS IN THE PUBLIC SPHERE

Noting that "argumentation" is the "chief cognitive activity by which a democracy . . . functions," Richard Fulkerson and attempts to outline a pedagogy in which argument is seen

> in a larger, less militant . . . context—one in which the goal
> is not victory but a good decision, one in which all arguers
> are at risk of needing to alter their views, one in which a par-
> ticipant takes seriously and fairly the views different from his
> or her own. . . . It is crucial that students learn to participate
> effectively in argumentation as a cooperative, dialectical ex-
> change and a search for mutually acceptable (and contingent)
> answers. (16–17)

In his emphasis on cooperation, respect for difference, and openness to
change, Fulkerson outlines a particular model for public sphere activity that we might call the *cooperative-rational* model. While theorists
who subscribe to this model may not agree on every detail, they share
a concern for what Habermas calls "the cooperative search for truth"
(*Moral* 88–89). We can find echoes of this model in Edward P. J.
Corbett's trope of the "open hand," which corresponds to "the kind
of persuasive discourse that seeks to carry its point by reasoned, sustained, conciliatory discussion of the issues" (288).

    In the cooperative-rational model, the role of affect tends to be lim-
ited to feelings of civic friendship and cooperation. As in Habermas's
original model of the public sphere, "the authority of the better argument" is privileged over persuasive tactics aimed at stirring emotion
or capturing attention (36). In this view, the "better argument" offers
hope for achieving results that are fairer to stakeholders than results
based on the authority of social status, verbal trickery, or deception.
Articulating, respecting, and scrutinizing different perspectives is important in this model because it helps to ensure that the "better argument" will prevail. As Iris Marion Young explains,

> through public deliberation citizens transform their prefer-
> ences according to public-minded ends, and reason together
> about the nature of those ends and the best means to real-
> ize them. In free and open dialogue others test and challenge
> these assertions and reasons. Participants are careful to sort
> out good reasons from bad reasons, valid arguments from in-
> valid. The interlocutors properly discount bad reasons and
> speeches that are not well argued, and they ignore or discount
> rhetorical flourishes and emotional outbursts ("Communica-
> tion" 121).

In this passage, Young sketches a picture of public exchange in which participants calmly, patiently, and methodically scrutinize their own and each others' perspectives.

To ensure that the better argument prevails, those who advocate a cooperative-rational approach devote much attention to establishing ground rules for appropriate discursive interaction. Fulkerson, for instance, ends *Teaching the Argument in Writing* by reviewing a set of nine guidelines that he takes from Trudy Govier (136–38). These characteristics include "well reasoned arguments" that use "relatively neutral" language and that are transparent about their own shortcomings (qtd. in Fulkerson 136–38). Several of these guidelines pertain to the goal of explicitly recognizing the existence of perspectives, facts, and arguments that might lead to conclusions different from the one endorsed by the speaker. Because the point is not to win the argument, but to reach a good decision, arguers reveal the logic behind their reasoning so that it may be subjected to critical scrutiny.

Indeed, an abiding preoccupation for Habermas is to articulate the various norms for discursive interaction that will be conducive to the "goal of reaching a rationally motivated agreement" (*Moral* 88). Some of these rules pertain to the logical consistency of the discourse itself, such as "[n]o speaker may contradict himself" and "[d]ifferent speakers may not use the same expression with different meanings" (qtd. in Habermas 87). Other rules pertain to the goal of entering into good-faith arrangements that respect all participants, such as "[e]very speaker may assert only what he really believes" and "[e]veryone is allowed to question any assertion whatever" (qtd. in Habermas 88–89). As Thomas McCarthy notes, Habermas "builds the moment of empathy *into* the procedure of coming to a reasoned agreement" (ix).

In our discussion of the public sphere in chapter 1, we allude to a critique of Habermas's narrow focus on rational-critical debate and align ourselves with those who call for a more capacious understanding of public rhetoric that includes poetic world making. In arguing for this more capacious model, however, we do not mean to dismiss the role that reasoned, conciliatory argument might play in some contexts. A kairotic approach demands that we discern what is "fitting" (i.e., both efficacious and ethical) in a given context. In many contexts, rhetors might choose to adopt a conciliatory approach in which they transparently outline claims, evidence, and warrants and listen respectfully to the responses of others.

We align ourselves, therefore, with other scholars in the field who recognize the legitimacy of multiple forms of rhetorical exchange in the public sphere. Corbett, for instance, does not rule out the possibility that close-fisted rhetoric is appropriate in some contexts. In an eloquent passage that evinces a kairotic approach, Corbett concludes that the "open hand and the closed fist have the same basic skeletal structure. If rhetoric is, as Aristotle defined it, 'a discovery of all the available means of persuasion,' let us be prepared to open and close that hand as the occasion demands (Corbett 296). Similarly, Dennis A. Lynch, Diana George, and Marilyn M. Cooper argue for an inclusive model of rhetoric that balances "confrontational and cooperative perspectives, a multifaceted process that includes moments of conflict and agonistic positioning as well as moments of understanding and communication" (63).

In the next chapter, we turn to a model of public rhetoric that emphasizes "poesis," a model that preserves a role for the rich possibilities of affect, desire, and the imagination. In the present chapter, we explore the Skakel case as an opportunity to examine the challenges associated with a conciliatory, reasoned approach. We do not see these approaches as mutually exclusive; each is valuable in the right context. The Skakel case reveals, however, that using multimodal rhetoric in ways consistent with the cooperative-rational approach is no simple or straightforward matter.

THE DISTINCTIVE CHARACTERISTICS OF MULTIMODAL SEMIOSIS

Before we turn to the specifics of the Skakel case, it will be useful to examine some of the more general insights about the way the material form of a rhetorical composition alters the terms of communication. The tradition of critical semiotics stemming from Roland Barthes is a good starting point. For Barthes, photographs and other forms of iconic rhetoric are understood to be especially deceptive in their tendency to masquerade as transparent and authoritative representations of reality. Photography theorist Victor Burgin alludes to this tendency in a famous passage:

> More than any other textual system, the photograph presents itself as "an offer you can't refuse." The characteristics of the photographic apparatus position the subject in such a way that

> the object photographed serves to conceal the textuality of the photograph itself—substituting passive receptivity for active (critical) *reading*. (146)

Rather than reveal itself as a rhetorical artifact, a photograph tends to assert itself as a given, a transparent window on reality, as natural, objective, neutral, authoritative, true, and real. Virtually every inquiry into how photographs mean is forced to confront this tendency at some point. Barthes's own observation is that "the denoted image naturalizes the symbolic message, it innocents the semantic artifice of connotation . . ." (45).

As Paul Messaris points out, a photograph's pretense of objectivity stems from its status as both an "index" and an "icon" (xii-xvii). As an index, in the Piercean sense, a photograph derives authority from the fact that it seems to be caused by the thing it represents. Light reflects off an object, enters the lens, and causes a photochemical reaction with the film that results in what Susan Sontag calls a "trace" of the real (154). As an icon, a photograph derives authority because our process of decoding it seems to be coequal with our process of decoding the world itself. Even Umberto Eco, who denies that a photograph is in any way an "analogue" of reality, concedes that "we perceive the image as a message referred to a given code, but this is the normal perceptive code which presides over our every act of cognition" (33, 32).

Film—particularly in the documentary tradition—shares the iconicity and indexicality of the still photograph. Visual anthropologist Jay Ruby observes that

> the filmic illusion of reality is an extremely dangerous one, for it gives the people who control the image industry too much power. The majority of Americans . . . receive information about the outside world from the images produced by film, television, and photography. If the lie that pictures always tell the truth is perpetuated . . ., then an industry that has the potential to symbolically recreate the world in its own image continues to wield far too much power. (149)

Photographs and film as media and modes are not neutral; some rhetorical goals are more easily achieved than others as a result of the material realities of iconic media and the way they are constructed within Western cultures. Whereas deliberative rhetoric reveals its strategies in order to facilitate cooperative dialogue, photographs and documentary films often conceal their rhetorical nature, pretend, in fact, not to be rhetorical objects at all. Whereas open deliberative rhetoric reveals the status of any authorities it cites so that participants in the dialogue can critically assess them, photographs and film tend to assert themselves as authoritative, as mechanical reproductions of reality that cannot lie. As "offers you can't refuse," the photograph and film are the opposite of cooperative rhetoric.

Photographic authority, however, is a tendency, not an inevitability. Michael J. Shapiro observes that "photography plays a politically radical role when it opens up forms of questions about power and authority which are closed or silenced within the most frequently circulated and authoritative discursive practices" (130). Self-reflexivity is one strategy for achieving this alternate possibility in which photographs *denaturalize* reality, revealing rather than masking hidden assumptions. "To be reflexive, in terms of a work of anthropology," Ruby explains, "is to insist that anthropologists systematically and rigorously reveal their methods and themselves as the instrument of data generation and reflect upon how the medium through which they transmit their work predisposes readers/viewers to construct the meaning of the work in certain ways" (152). Reflexivity, for Ruby, is essential: "the maker of images has the moral obligation to reveal the covert—never to appear to produce an objective mirror by which the world can see its 'true' image" (140). Ruby outlines a variety of rhetorical strategies for achieving reflexivity, including filmic techniques that remind audiences of the camera's operation. Filmmakers can eschew the "voice of god" narrator and instead foreground uncertainty (for example, by including discussions in which those involved in the production of the film argue about what has happened). They can include multiple retellings of a single event from different perspectives and with different frames so that audiences are made aware of the contingency of meaning (Ruby 115–35). Wysocki suggests making something like Ruby's concept of reflexivity an integral part of our definition of new media.[22]

A FABRICATED CONFESSION

With the preceding discussion of filmic and the photographic rhetoric in mind, we can begin to unpack the processes of semiosis operating in the multimodal presentation used by the prosecution in the Skakel trial. The feeling on the part of the defense that the prosecution introduced a "fabricated confession" results from a number of concomitant factors:

The indexical and iconic nature of the semiotic resources. As both indexical and iconic signs, the photographs of Martha Moxley's corpse assert themselves as neutral and authoritative. The audio recordings are indexical as well, the result of a tape recorder mechanically converting sound waves that travel through the microphone into information encoded on magnetic tape. These raw materials of evidence appear to be unquestionable, to offer us unmediated and transparent access to reality. They seem to dispense with confounding factors, like human bias and flawed memory, and present themselves as objective, neutral, innocent.

Synchresis: the linking of semiotic resources. Taken separately, the photographs and audio clips do not constitute a confession. The apparent confession results precisely from the syncing of the two semiotic resources. To understand this, we need to look carefully at the composition itself. Here is the prosecution's representation of it:

> [Screen 1] "And I woke up, went to sleep, then I woke up to Mrs. Moxley saying 'Michael, have, have you seen Martha?' [SE 5, photo of Martha Moxley is shown] I'm like, 'What?' And I was like still high from the night before, a little drunk, then I was like 'What?'"

> [Screen 2] "I was like 'Oh my God, did they see me last night?' And I'm like, I don't know, I'm like and I remember just having a feeling of panic." [SE 16 photo of the victim's body under the tree is shown].

> [Screen 3] "like 'Oh shit.' You know, Like my worry of what I went to bed with, like may . . . , I don't know, you know what I mean I just had, I had a feeling of panic." [SE 17 photo of the victim's body under the tree]. (Connecticut v. Michael Skakel)

Useful, here, is film theorist Michel Chion's concept of "synchresis": "the forging of an immediate and necessary relationship between something one sees and something one hears" (5). Synchresis brings about "[t]he spontaneous and irresistible mental fusion, completely free of any logic, that happens between a sound and a visual when these occur at exactly the same time" (xviii-xix). Synchresis, then, names an affordance that pertains precisely to multimodality. It rests on our ability to receive information through two separate channels simultaneously and our ability to fuse or synthesize that information into a single message. The power of the closing argument in the Ska-kel trial lies in this mental fusion, which itself is the result of material and cultural realities. The work of synchresis in this instance is to galvanize into a single, coherent text two artifacts that were originally contextually separated: the police photographs of 1975 and the audio recordings of 1997. As Feigenson and Sherwin point out, the multi-modal presentation "elides" the twenty-two years separating the two forms of evidence.

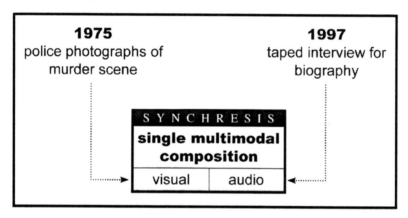

Figure 15. The function of synchresis in the "fabricated confession."

Coherence, here, is not merely a textual nicety, but is essential to the evidentiary role of the composition. The disparate textual artifacts seem to be pieces in a larger puzzle. More than merely placed next to each other, they seem to fit together, to be made for each other. As in a jigsaw puzzle, when these pieces are placed together, a larger picture emerges—a picture that is not suggested by either of the pieces sepa-rately, but that nevertheless feels inevitable. The audience appears to have been given a privileged view, borrowing the perspective of omni-science. Again, this privileged perspective is founded, in part, by the nature of artifacts as indexical signs, of innocent and authoritative re-cordings of reality. An almost arithmetical logic seems to be at work—

photographs + audio recording = guilt—where photographs and audio recordings have the neutrality and objectivity of numbers.

Genre and culturally conditioned meaning-making practices. Synchresis is accomplished, in part, by the learned meaning-making practices of audiences, as prosecutor Christopher Morano knows: "When they watch the evening news, they're going to see a person talking. And while that person's talking, they're going to be seeing some video about what the person's talking about. This is what people are comfortable with now, and that is why this is what has to be brought into the courtroom" (Orson, "Multimedia in the Courtroom"). This "comfort" is the result of our daily experience with multimodal rhetoric in film, television, and other media. As Morano suggests, the particular genre evoked by the prosecution's multimodal composition is the television news story. This genre implicitly tells us how to "read" the presentation—how to construct meaning from the disparate parts being integrated through synchresis. Moreover, because the defining characteristic of a TV newscast genre—what separates it from the sitcoms and dramas that come before and after it—is its commitment to reporting the "truth." By evoking this genre, the prosecution's composition further establishes its ethos and further mobilizes the audience's trust.

The tacit nature of the message. Carney and Feigenson explain that the prosecution's multimodal presentation communicates the "prosecution's theory of the case." If this is so, we might paraphrase the message communicated by the multimodal presentation as follows: *We contend that 'Did they see me last night?' should be interpreted to mean 'Did they see me kill Martha Moxley last night?' We contend that Skakel's sense of 'panic' should be interpreted as his fear of being discovered as the killer.* But nothing like this is communicated explicitly through the aural-visual presentation by the prosecution. It seems more accurate to say that the indexical and iconic nature of the discrete semiotic elements deployed, the evocation of the TV newscast genre, and the operations of synchresis all conspire to erase parts of the message that mark it as a claim (something that requires supporting evidence) rather than a simple statement of fact. The tacit nature of the message means that there are no discursive markers (such as "we contend") that indicate this is an assertion nor are there discursive markers (such as "should be interpreted to mean") that would indicate the interpretive work necessary to arrive at this conclusion. "This is our assertion of what happened" becomes simply "This is what happened." (For discussions of the tacit nature of visual rhetoric, see Burke 86–87; Hill 36–37; Feigenson and Sherwin).

The role of affect. In "The Psychology of Rhetorical Images," Charles A. Hill explores the contributions cognitive psychology can make in understanding how images persuade. Following Arjun Chaudhuri and Ross Buck, Hill writes that, "[p]sychological studies have confirmed the common assumption that, in general terms, images tend to elicit more emotional responses while print messages tend to elicit more analytical responses" (30). Likewise, Feigenson and Sherwin write that "pictures, more so than words, convey meaning through associational logic which operates in large part subconsciously, through its emotional appeal" (298). An account of the ethical implications of the multimodal composition used in the Skakel trial needs to confront the role emotion plays. Emotion is not, in and of it self, unethical. The question is whether a reliance on emotion as persuasive strategy undermines the process of critique when such a process is warranted. In the Skakel case, we would need to inquire into the emotional responses generated by the images of Moxley's corpse and by Skakel's admission of panic.

As our citations above indicate, Feigenson has examined the use of multimodal rhetoric in the Skakel trial (and in the courtroom more generally) in a series of articles and presentations coauthored with others. In an early article, Carney and Feigenson conclude that the prosecution's multimodal presentation "exemplifies the highly persuasive yet entirely proper use of the technology" and that its "impact on the jurors was profound." From an evidentiary perspective, however, Carney and Feigenson maintain that the multimodal presentation was not fundamentally different from more traditional presentations, such as holding up hardcopy versions of the photographs. "The only difference," they contend, "is that the interactive multimedia system allowed [the prosecution] to juxtapose words and images more smoothly, preventing the jurors from being distracted from the content of his argument: that Michael Skakel was guilty of murdering Martha Moxley."

We are not legal scholars, and our purpose here is not to establish whether or not the use of this multimodal presentation was legally appropriate. Instead, we aim to raise more general issues about the ethical implications of multimodal semiosis. Considered within this larger context, what Carney and Feigenson fail to confront is precisely the semiotic work accomplished by synchresis. Synchresis names the process by which separate semiotic elements (in this case images and spoken words) that involve separate modalities add up to a semiotic whole that is greater than the sum of its parts. An explanation of the ethics involved needs to examine whether the semiosis that results from synchresis itself is ethical. Carney and Feigenson's analysis focuses on those parts in isolation from each other; since those parts had been entered into evidence already, their use in the presentation is proper. Synchresis, however, names an effect derived from the *relationship between* elements.

Later articles that Feigenson has coauthored with other scholars seem to complicate the earlier conclusion that the prosecution's multimodal presentation was appropriate. Feigenson and Sherwin explore the tacit nature of visual rhetoric:

> Lawyers want to (and do) communicate implicitly for all sorts of reasons: to comply with legal rules and/or discourse conventions that forbid saying those things explicitly, to build the kind of solidarity with their audiences that only unspoken understandings can produce, to generate new meanings via Gricean implicature, but most importantly, because audiences can sometimes be persuaded most effectively when key steps in their thinking remain implicit to them. . . . [V]isual representations can create these kinds of implicit meanings very differently, and in some ways better, than (spoken) words alone can. (295–96)

Feigenson and Sherwin conclude that "when the emotional underpinnings of judgment remain outside of awareness, they are less susceptible to effective critique and counter-argument" (309).

The multimodal presentation used by the prosecution in the Skakel trial, then, is strikingly at odds with the cooperative-rational system of ethics described earlier. The cooperative-rational system of rhetorical ethics is founded on the principle that the reasoning involved in an argument be exposed for public scrutiny. The multimedia presentation used in the Skakel case, however, manipulates the technologies and semiotic resources involved so that "key steps" in its logic remain "implicit." Those interested in public rhetoric should be concerned about the ethical implications of relying on approaches that seek to resist critique and counter-argument. Indeed, distinctions between ethical persuasion and propaganda often rely on whether or not the tactics of persuasion are made clear. For instance, Michael J. Sproule writes that one of the distinguishing characteristics of propaganda is that its conclusions are "packaged to conceal both their persuasive purpose and lack of supporting reasons" (qtd. in Jowett and O'Donnell 3).

Some have suggested that the Skakel case reveals that the courts are not ready for multimodal rhetoric (see Feigenson and Dunn; Orson, "Multimedia Display"). The rules established for the presentation of evidence and arguments were designed for word-based rhetoric and therefore are not able to address the special ethical issues raised by multimodality. Our point here, however, is that the failure of the legal system to adequately confront the peculiar complexities of multimodal rhetoric echoes a more general failure in the wider culture. Technology and practice change more rapidly than our ability to theorize the implications of those changes. In moments of open deliberation with other citizens in the public sphere, we have all been trained, to some degree, to abide by certain ethical principles: We avoid deliberately misleading interlocutors, *ad hominem* attacks, inflammatory language, and so on; but, these rules do not take into account the peculiarities of multimodality.

360 Degrees: Using Multimodality to Facilitate Perspective Taking

The website *360degrees* (figure 16) illustrates an alternative set of multimodal rhetorical strategies, illustrating the kind of self-reflexivity described by Ruby, Shapiro, and Wysocki ("Opening"). We see this site as more aligned with the ethical values of cooperative-rational rhetoric.

The self-announced purpose of this site is to "challenge your perceptions about who is in prison today and why" ("About"). The title of the site, alluding to a circle, foregrounds the importance of taking a holistic view, one that encompasses a variety of perspectives. The trope of the circle is visually reinforced by a number of design elements. The site's menu, for instance, is a series of floating circles labeled "Timeline," "Stories," "Dialogue," etc. The section of the site labeled "Stories" includes seven cases of incarceration. These cases are not represented by a single authoritative voice, but by a collection of

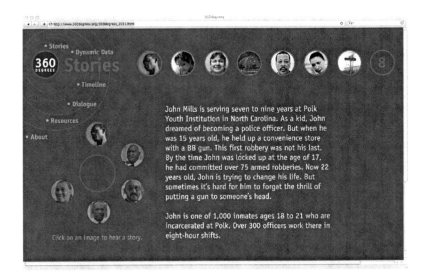

Figure 16. Screen capture of the 360degrees website. © 2001, courtesy Picture Projects, 360degrees.org.

voices, including the individual who was incarcerated, representatives of the criminal justice system (judges, prosecutors, guards, juvenile program workers), victims, and relatives of victims and convicts. These individuals are represented visually by still photos. Each photo (itself framed as a circle) is positioned around a larger circle, providing an image of round-table dialogue. Clicking on one of the circles calls up an audio recording of a monologue in which the individual voices his or her understanding of the case. These audio recordings are accompanied by a video in which a camera films a 360-degree circuit of a physical space relevant to the person talking (e.g., a prison cell, an office, a bedroom).

360degrees uses the figure of the circle to foreground the idea of perspective, to communicate that these issues and cases cannot be reduced to a single authoritative view. Moreover, by adopting a prominent metaphor that is iterated in words, design elements, and video, the website foregrounds the act of representation itself. By making its key metaphors explicit and by continually drawing attention to them, the website points to its own rhetoricity.

BROADER CONCERNS OF MULTIMODAL RHETORICAL ETHICS

In the previous sections we attempt to introduce a set of ethical issues pertaining to the distinctive ways multimodal semiosis occurs, arguing that multimodal semiosis often masks the underlying reasoning involved and is therefore at odds with a particular system of rhetorical ethics. But this is only one set of ethical issues that rhetors need to confront as they use multimodal public rhetoric. Scholars working in a variety of fields have introduced other issues as well. Visual anthropology explores issues related to representing cultural difference, and technical communication theorists like Sam Dragga, Nancy Allen, and Donna S. Kienzler demonstrate that rhetorical choices related to the visual presentation of information have ethical implications. Rhetorical education can benefit from integrating the insights of these discussions.

Another group of scholars explore the ethics of rhetorical recomposition—the ethical considerations that pertain to appropriating and remixing media elements produced by others. Remixing has emerged as a common and often powerful strategy of composing in recent years.[23] To some degree, a culture of remix is facilitated by new technologies that make it easy to combine different media elements. Once music, photographs, and other elements are digitized, they can easily be modified and spliced. Applications for graphics editing, sound editing, digital animation, and digital video all enable composers to combine multiple media elements created by others into new, remixed compositions. A presentation like the one used by the prosecution in the Skakel trial—which creates a new composition by combining photographs and audio recordings created by separate individuals working in disparate contexts—is easy, from a technical standpoint.

The appropriation of media elements is often fraught with cultural implications and complexities. For instance, 2 Live Crew was sued for using the distinctive bass line from Roy Orbison's "Oh, Pretty Woman." In considering this case, the courts had to confront the complex issue of whether or not 2 Live Crew's track could be considered a form of "social commentary" and thereby make a claim for protection under fair use. Oscar Brand, an expert witness for the defense, testified that rap music, as a form of Black cultural expression, "make[s] fun of the 'white-bread' originals and the establishment. . . ." He explained that "this anti-establishment singing group is trying to show how bland and banal the Orbison song seems to them. It's just one of many examples of their derisive approach to 'white-centered' popular music" (Acuff-Rose Music, Inc. v. Campbell). In this case, the ethics of remix turn, to some degree, on our understanding of how minority cultures use remix to critique the dominant culture.[24]

Something close to the converse of this dynamic occurs when the cultural assets of historically disenfranchised groups are exploited. For instance, in a track called "Return to Innocence," the Germany-based group Enigma used a sample of the aboriginal Taiwanese "Jubilant Drinking Song" performed by a farmer named Kuo Ying-nan, then in his seventies. An account of this incident by Timothy D. Taylor reveals that this act of appropriation introduces a number of complex ethical issues. It is unclear, for instance, whether Kuo knew he was being recorded when he originally performed the song for various European audiences. According to Taylor, Enigma did not consult Kuo before incorporating his performance into their track. Enigma licensed the song from a third party for a small fee, no portion of which apparently went to Kuo. This case raises ethical questions that must be candidly confronted by a remix culture: Who wins and who loses when forms of cultural expression are appropriated? How do asymmetries of power (such as those that exist between a chart-toping European pop band and a seventy-something Taiwanese farmer) factor into processes of appropriation? What practices are required to respect and compensate the original producers of media materials, especially when those producers are separated through barriers of distance and culture?

Agency, Ethics, and Pedagogy

Even as the cases discussed above call attention to a host of ethical issues, they simultaneously demonstrate the reality that these ethical considerations are distributed across a network of human and nonhuman agents, many of which are beyond the control of a single rhetor. In the Skakel trial, the prosecution's multimedia presentation emerged from the confluence of multiple producers, multiple technologies, and multiple semiotic resources against a backdrop of overlapping and competing systems of cultural conventions and practices. Raising similar issues is the case of "Cotton Patch," a living-newspaper theatrical vignette that critiques New Deal policy and that we discuss in the introduction to this book. In that case, director Joseph Losey concluded that the coordination of the multiple contingencies involved was not possible. The vagaries of script, props, actors, and intertextual expectations could not be effectively orchestrated. The result of this failure was the potential endorsement of racial stereotypes. In light of this, the only ethical course of action was to abandon the rhetorical project entirely, to cut "Cotton Patch" from the show.

Isolating any single component of the larger network reveals the failure of agency and a corresponding failure to effect an ethical outcome. Kuo had little control over how Enigma used his voice. The ghostwriter who made the original recordings of Michael Skakel could not have foreseen their use by the prosecution in a murder trial. David Hume Kennerly was powerless to constrain the way *Newsweek* used his photograph of Dick Cheney. Moreover, even if we assume that composers *desire* an ethical outcome, other parts of the network potentially confound that goal. What we show in our analysis of the prosecutor's presentation in the Skakel trial is that it is difficult to account for all of the myriad factors that bear upon ethical considerations.

Given the way agency and ethics are distributed across so many different points of articulation, it would be tempting to give up on the goal of achieving an ethical outcome. But this conclusion runs counter to the conclusions of many theorists who attempt to confront the dynamics of complex systems. As we argued in the previous chapter, Herndl and Licona, Latour, and Law reconfigure, but do not reject the possibility of human intention, planning, and design. Each component of the system is a potential entry-point for unpredictability, but is also a point that can be revised to improve the overall system.

Importantly, all of these thinkers preserve a place for education. Rhetors may only be part of a larger network, but they are an important part; and what Herndl and Licona, Latour, and Law demonstrate is that the way individual actors function within larger networks is shaped, in part, by the way they have been prepared by previous experiences, including educational experiences, broadly conceived. For sailors to function in networks of Portuguese colonization, Lisbon had to devise new educational techniques. Likewise, we contend that education has a role to play in facilitating the ethical use of multimodal rhetoric.

As a starting point, teachers can foreground rhetorical-ethical analysis in the classrooms and can reveal how considerations of ethics intersect with the material-cultural concerns of mode and medium. Students can critically interrogate examples of multimodal public rhetoric that are carefully selected to introduce fundamental ethical concerns. Many of the cases we discuss in this book, including the appropriation of Kennerly's photo of Cheney, the multimodal composition used in Skakel trial, and Enigma's "Return to Innocence," can prompt critical reflection about the ethics of multimodal rhetoric. The web abounds with other examples. For instance, Eric Blumrich's "Grand Theft America" (GTA), a short digital composition that explores the 2000 Florida election scandal, is a remix composition that combines music, photographs, animations, and alphabetic text to create a complex political message. Many viewers see GTA as an effective use of multimodality to capture attention and raise awareness about an important set of issues. Other viewers point out that Blumrich uses media in ways that challenge traditional understanding of rhetorical ethics.

In "The Ethics of Delivery," Sam Dragga provides a number of hypothetical cases that are useful for prompting critical exploration of visual ethics (see especially 83–84). One case concerns an organization that, hoping to send a welcoming message to candidates with disabilities, has an employee pose as a wheelchair user for a photograph placed on recruitment materials. Another case concerns an organization that manipulates color to maximize representations of profit and minimize representations of loss. Dragga includes a scale for assessing the ethicality of each scenario, providing a useful starting point for critical discussion. In "Doctoring Diversity: Race and Photoshop," Lisa Wade explores a number of instances in which organizations attempt to create an image of racial and ethnic diversity by digitally altering photographs used in publicity materials. For instance, the cover of a University of Wisconsin recruitment booklet features a photograph of students attending a football game. The original photograph contained only white students, so the brochure's designers digitally inserted the face of Diallo Shabazz, a black student who had never attended the game.

Critiquing cases like these can help students build a conceptual foundation for assessing the ethical dimensions of their own multimodal compositions. Critique provides an opportunity to develop an analytically precise vocabulary—including concepts like *icon, index, synchresis,* and *reflexivity*—which can be applied to their own work. Moreover, critical analysis can be used to generate a set of heuristic questions that students can use to explore the ethicality of their compositions:

- What media, modes, genres, and technologies are recruited in your composition?
- What attitudes, beliefs, and values will target audiences bring to those media, modes, genres, and technologies? How do those dispositions encourage or discourage critical scrutiny?
- How do the various technologies and semiotic resources that you use *work together* to achieve an effect and communicate a message? How easy is it for audience members to discern the way this message is produced? Does this context warrant taking steps to help your audience scrutinize your argument?
- What are the histories of the media components (e.g., music, photographs) used in your composition? Who was involved in their creation? What were the original goals of those who contributed to their production? How does your use of the materials articulate with those goals? What structures of power are associated with the composition and recomposition of these media components? Who gains and who loses based on your recomposition of them?

CONCLUSION

Our fundamental point in this chapter has been that multimodality raises new and complex considerations for rhetorical ethics. We began by exploring a particular ethical framework, the "cooperative-conciliatory" model, that is commonly invoked in discussions of the public sphere. The prosecution's multimodal presentation in the Skakel trial suggests to us that processes of multimodal semiosis raise distinctive challenges for rhetors who wish to embrace this model of rhetorical ethics. However, we do not agree with those who hold that this model should govern all public-rhetorical action. Instead, following Corbett and others, we suggest that this model should be embraced strategically, when it is kairotically appropriate. This is consistent with a rhetorical ethics that, as Porter puts it, functions as "a critical inquiry" that "necessarily leads toward a standpoint about what is good or desirable *for a given situation*" (*Rhetorical* 68, emphasis added). In the next chapter, we examine other forms of rhetorical action that activate a broader understanding of the public sphere as fundamentally based on *poesis*.

7 Public Rhetoric as the Production of Culture

Ethnic minorities, women, gays, third- and fourth-world people, the very rich, and the very poor are telling the middle-class, middle-aged straight white males who dominate the industry that the mass-mediated pictures of the Other are false. Many wish to control . . . the ways in which they are imaged by others.

—Jay Ruby

The activist is suspicious of exhortations to deliberate, because he believes that in the real world of politics, where structural inequalities influence both procedures and outcomes, democratic processes that appear to conform to norms of deliberation are usually biased toward more powerful agents.

—Iris Marion Young

A few years ago, a website for a neighborhood organization featured a rudimentary slideshow. The first image shows an African American woman standing in front of a simple Cape Cod home. Subsequent images show 1920s-era brick Tudors, green grass, neatly trimmed shrubs, tree-lined streets, sunlit parks, and neighborhood events (Grandmont Rosedale Development Corporation). At first glance, a simple visual composition of this kind may seem uninteresting. Indeed, it hardly seems rhetorical at all. Placed on the margins of the webpage, it appears to be a bit of visual ornamentation or "window dressing." The pictures in the slideshow convey what we would expect of any neighborhood: people, houses, parks.

We contend, however, that this slideshow performs important rhetorical work and constitutes an important form of public-sphere participation. Grandmont-Rosedale is a neighborhood in northwest Detroit. The GRDC slideshow counters mainstream media depictions that characterize Detroit as empty of people, meaning, order, and cultural value. Relying on this trope of emptiness, many mainstream media accounts of Detroit focus on the city's shrinking population. These accounts are strewn with images of so-called "green ghettos," burned-out homes, and empty streets. In recent years, Detroit has become famous for the "ruin porn" generated by photographers who flock from across the globe to gawk at spectacular pre-war skyscrapers that are now abandoned and deteriorating. Too often, the soundtrack for these images is characterized by sounds of sirens and gunshots or, perhaps even worse, by a deep silence that feels jarring and unnatural for an urban core, a silence that signals the absence of productive human activity. Based on the way the dominant culture constructs the city, many outsiders conclude, categorically, that Detroit is a scary place with "nothing of any real value to offer" (Pritzlaff).[25]

Images of Detroit's emptiness tell part of the story—but only part. Detroit's population *is* shrinking, and the city contains its share of abandoned buildings and vacant lots. Despite its shrinking population, however, Detroit (as of the 2010 census) is the eighteenth largest city in the nation. At over 700,000 residents, Detroit is larger than Boston, Pittsburg, Seattle, and many other brand name cities. It is not empty. Measured by almost any set of metrics one cares to apply, Detroit is an extremely rich location of culture.

One manifestation of the emptiness trope is the claim that Detroit is a "food desert"—a space devoid of high quality food, like fresh produce, which residents of other locations take for granted. In a recent series of articles and blog entries, Detroit writer James D. Griffioen meticulously critiques this claim. Griffioen profiles several of his favorite locally-owned grocery stores and documents the high-quality produce they make available. His articles include abundant photographs showing brightly-colored and neatly-stacked apples, pears, tangerines, and other fresh fruits and vegetables. Google maps embedded in his articles provide a different kind of visual evidence. Googling "supermarket" causes the map to light up with orange dots, making visible the prevalence of food in the city (Griffioen, "But Where Do

You Shop?," "Honey Bee Market," "Yes There Are Grocery Stores in Detroit").

Griffioen's efforts stand in contrast to the mainstream, for-profit, conglomerated media, which use all of the affordances of multimodality in order to represent the city in the ways that best serve their interests. Films, TV shows, Web essays, and news stories combine images, sounds, and words to rehearse a narrative of emptiness and silence because this is the most convenient way to package the city for consumption by outsiders. Ruin porn, like regular porn, sells. Indeed, the aptness of the phrase "ruin porn" derives from the way it captures the fascination—the can't-look-away response—that images of Detroit's emptiness evoke in commercialized venues of consumption.

The traditional strategy for confronting mainstream representational practices in the composition classroom is to ask students to write written critiques of films, TV shows, and other popular-culture forms. Such critiques can expose the way the values, desires, and assumptions of the dominant culture are encoded into the multimodal content of these forms. We believe written critique can be powerful, but it is only a partial solution at best.

The GRDC and Griffioen demonstrate a more efficacious response. They leverage the multimodal power of the Web to introduce an alternate set of codes—different images, sounds, words. They combine writing, photographs, and video to richly capture the cultural assets of Detroit. They choreograph a diversity of semiotic resources to fundamentally reshape perception, attitude, and identity. As such, they help answer a key question: *Why would we want to use multimodal public rhetoric in the first place?*

To see these rhetorical activities as legitimate forms of public-sphere participation, however, we need to revise the rigid and narrow model of the liberal bourgeois public sphere introduced by Habermas. In this chapter, we explore post-Habermasian models of the public sphere outlined by Michael Warner, Houston A. Baker, Jr., Scott Welsh, and others—models that describe a public sphere based on "poetic world making" rather than on rational-critical debate alone (Warner 114). In these models, the product of the public sphere is not just public opinion, but a fundamental transformation of the metaphors, ideographs, narratives, and god-terms that govern consciousness and identity. Rhetors become producers of culture itself. We see this post-Habermasian understanding of the public sphere as offering the best chance for realizing the full potential of multimodal public rhetoric.

POST-HABERMASIAN MODELS OF THE PUBLIC SPHERE

We could explain the GRDC's multimodal rhetoric in terms of "rational argument." The GRDC's slideshow offers visual evidence that empirically refutes the false claims spread by mainstream media. Undoubtedly, such a description captures some of what is going on here, but this is far from a complete account of the cultural work performed by the GRDC's rhetoric. The images provided by the slideshow have a function that extends well beyond their evidentiary one. The GRDC images operate metonymically, referencing objects (neatly-trimmed shrubs, well-kept lawns, and historic brick homes) that are associated in our culture with the orderly, familiar, comfortable, and charming—the cultural schemas that form the very basis of American identity. The smiling woman standing in front of her home does more than simply proclaim that people live in Detroit. Any table from the US census could do that. At the very least, the photograph of a particular Detroit resident helps to establish that Detroiters are more than abstractions, more than numbers. They are real individuals with real lives and real stories. We might even say that the photograph of this Detroiter facilitates processes of identification, in the Burkean sense of the word. American audiences will recognize in this image of home and homeowner a familiar narrative of American life. A smiling woman standing in front of a standard brick home bridges the gap between viewers (situated in their various cultural locations) and Detroit. For certain audiences, Detroit is transformed from the nation's Other to a familiar site of everyday human activity, one as worthy of empathy as the next neighborhood over.

The GRDC materials rely on narrative, metonymy, pathos, embodiment, and identification more than on rational-critical argument. To see them as legitimate forms of public-sphere participation, we need to broaden our understanding of the public sphere. Warner, perhaps, puts it most succinctly and powerfully when he writes that a "public is poetic world making" (114). In traditional models, publics "exist to deliberate and then to decide" (115). For Warner, however, "the perception of public discourse as conversation obscures the importance of the poetic functions of both language and corporeal expressivity in giving a particular shape to publics" (115). Indeed, in Warner's view, the radical potential of publics is linked precisely to the ability of groups to introduce their own forms of expressivity—their own styles, forms, and practices of semiotic exchange. Counterpublics "might not be organized by the hierarchy of faculties that elevates rational-critical reflection as the self-image of humanity; they might depend more heavily on performance spaces than on print" (123). A "queer public," for instance, "might be one that throws shade, prances, disses, acts up, carries on, longs, fantasizes, throws fits, mourns, 'reads'" (124).

Warner is not alone in sketching a model of the public sphere based on poesis. In his contribution to *The Black Public Sphere*, Houston A. Baker, Jr., outlines a broadly similar model, using the examples of Martin Luther King, Jr., and other civil rights activists. Following Fraser, Baker calls attention to "revised notions of how human interactive modes—other than reason alone—bear on publicity" (14). He draws attention to the roles of "wishes," "desires," and "fantasies" (14–15). Following Arjun Appadurai, he invokes the role of the "imagination" (15–17). Baker notes that King drew on "the language of the black church and its traditions in their full emotional and metaphorical brilliance" (22). "Music," "spectacle," and "performance" function as tools for establishing a public and achieving the goals of the civil rights movement (19–22). "Radically new forms of visibility," writes Baker, help to focus "attention" on issues of equality and justice (33–34).[26]

Scott Welsh draws our attention to the way public sphere activity can address not just issues of common concern, but the "background culture" that determines how we frame, perceive, and feel about those issues to begin with. In Welsh's model, the proper function of the public sphere is "not . . . to change interlocutors' minds, one by one . . . but to effect a shift in prevailing relationships between and meanings of key cultural-political terms, events, or narratives.[. . .] [B]ackground culture becomes the 'source' *and* 'goal' of effective political speech governing meanings of a political collectivity" (690). Similarly, DeLuca begins his exploration of the "image event" by rejecting narrow models of public rhetoric as "civil, reasoned, verbal discourse" (14). Instead, rhetoric is "the mobilization of signs for the articulation of identities, ideologies, consciousnesses, communities, publics, and cultures" (17). He demonstrates that social movements deploy the visual, spectacular, and performative rhetoric of "image events" to "contest social norms and deconstruct the established naming of the world" (59). The "unorthodox rhetoric" of the image event "reconstitutes the identity of the dominant culture by challenging and transforming mainstream society's key discourses and ideographs" (16).

Warner, Baker, Welsh, DeLuca, and others provide an understanding of the public sphere that is markedly different from the Habermasian one.[27] In place of rational deliberation, this post-Habermasian public sphere embraces all of the possibilities associated with poetic world making. As such, it embraces the whole range of human experience, including desire, affect, and the body. It does not limit itself to generating "public opinion," but targets the very foundations of culture itself, including identity and consciousness.

PUBLIC RHETORIC AND POESIS

Some compositionists and rhetoricians might object that a model of the public sphere based on poetic world making steers us away from the proper concerns of composition and rhetoric. In this section, we want to construct a conceptual bridge between the tradition of rhetoric and the model of the public sphere founded on poesis.

Historically, two binary oppositions have been invoked to define rhetoric. On the one hand, at least since Plato's *Gorgias*, rhetoric has been contrasted with dialectic. In the most extreme characterization, dialectic seeks to uncover universal truths by employing the mechanics of logic. There is little room for affect, trope, or narrative, as these things merely obfuscate. From the perspective of dialectic, rhetoric is a form of trickery, a way of facilitating persuasion that relies on nonrational strategies of persuasion such as emotional appeals, verbal devices, and deception. Some deliberative models of the public sphere can be characterized as arhetorical in the sense that they privilege a form of discourse in which the basic tools of rhetoric (such as appeals to pathos) are considered off limits. "Deliberative theorists," Ivie writes, "would exclude rhetoric from the political realm altogether " ("Rhetorical" 277).

At the other end of the spectrum from dialectic is poetics, the realm of aesthetics and the imagination. Seen from this perspective, the problem with rhetoric is not that it obscures the rational, but that it is too crudely functional. According to James A. Berlin, "English studies was founded on a set of hierarchical binary oppositions in which literary texts were given idealized status approaching the sacred. Against

these privileged works, rhetorical texts and their production were por-
trayed as embodiments of the fallen realms of science and commerce
and politics . . ." (xiv). Rhetoric, in this view, is a vulgarly pragmatic
endeavor that places the beautiful in service of the practical, the transcendent in service of the everyday.

There are good historical and theoretical reasons, however, to reject
both the rhetoric-dialectic and the rhetoric-poetic binaries. G. Thomas Goodnight, among others, sees rhetoric and dialectic as mutually
sustaining. Noting that a "complete disjunction between dialectical
and rhetorical argument can only demean both enterprises," Goodnight explains that if we posit dialectic as "the only valid form of communicative reasoning, then rhetorical argument would appear at its
best as defective discussion and at its worst as the use of psychologi-
cal and social force in the service of conformity" (332). On the other
hand, privileging rhetoric to the exclusion of dialectic would result
in a construction of dialectic as "so much hair splitting and carping
apologetics" (332).

More important for our purposes in this chapter are rhetorical scholars who trouble the distinction between rhetoric and poetics (see, for
instance, Berlin; Gentili; S. Miller, *Trust*; and Walker, *Rhetoric*). Berlin
reminds us that in ancient Greece both rhetoric and poetry were linked
to the political life of the community, and "in medieval Europe, even
poetic production was included in rhetorical instruction in the lower
schools" (xii-xiii, xvi). Even a cursory examination of current conversations in rhetorical theory reveals an abiding concern with what poetics
and rhetoric have in common. Consider the roles that narrative, metaphor, depiction, presence, and pathos play in rhetoric, not just as labels
to be used for critical analysis but also as tools that should be taught to
and used by public rhetors. Walter R. Fisher writes that "[t]he ground
for determining meaning, validity, reason, rationality, and truth must
be a narrative context" (3).[28] He further contends that

> [t]he narrative paradigm *challenges* the notions that human
> communication—if it is to be considered rhetorical—must be
> an *argumentative* form, that *reason* is to be attributed only to
> discourse marked by clearly identifiable modes of inference
> and/or implication, and that the norms for evaluation of rhe-
> torical communication must be *rational* standards taken es-
> sentially from *informal* or *formal logic*. (2, emphasis added)

Robert L. Ivie opens a discussion of the role that metaphor plays in rhetorical practices surrounding US-USSR relations with the statement, "I begin with the premise that metaphor is at the base of rhetorical invention" ("Metaphor" 166). Ivie draws on I. A. Richards, Kenneth Burke, and others in order to explain that the rhetorical work of metaphor is about focusing attention and imaginative transformation. Borrowing the language of Max Black, Ivie observes that the "vehicle" of a metaphor "and its 'system of associated commonplaces' organize our view of the tenor much like a filter determines which particles will be selected out and a mold defines a final shape (Black 73–75)" ("Metaphor" 166).

Michael Osborn argues that "depiction" is a "master-term of modern rhetoric" (80). But this challenges the model of rhetoric as "as a study primarily of rational calculations" or a set of practices "in which speakers devise complex arguments and proofs to defend well-considered positions" (97). As Michael Leff and Andrew Sachs observe, for Osborn "the more primitive force of image-generation controls things—not only absorbing much of the function of argumentation but also forming the base from which argument proceeds" (253).

Alan G. Gross offers several explorations of Chïam Perelman's notion of "presence" as the foundation of rhetoric. "But," Gross writes, "despite its apparent utility, there is a fundamental problem with any sort of presence in Perelman's system, indeed in any rhetorical system that insists that persuasion is basically rational, basically an activity of reasonable human beings in search of a consensus founded on the force of the better argument" (18). The problem is that an emphasis on presence means that the "strongest agents remain imagination and the emotions" (qtd. in Gross 18).

Pathos itself has long been a vexed but inescapable concern of rhetorical theory. Laura R. Micciche observes that "[i]n academic as well as popular culture, emotions raise suspicion because they are said to cloud judgment and manipulate reason. Indeed, emotion is regularly cast as reason's spoiler, by everyone from Nietzsche to Donald Trump" (1). For Micciche, however, emotion is "a valuable rhetorical resource" that "contributes to meaning-making, judgment formation, and communication" (1). Likewise, Mark Robertson Armstrong, synthesizing a wide range of rhetorical theorists, notes six uses of emotion in deliberative rhetoric. For Armstrong emotions

1. "make certain features of the deliberative situation salient";
2. "form part of deliberative judgment";
3. foster "engagement";
4. "are crucial determinants in motivation";
5. "participate in and form a part of the aesthetic dimensions of our lives"
6. "express attitudes" and therefore are a key component "to consider when assessing the character of . . . [intentional] action" (9–11).

What's notable about these accounts is not just their insistence that devices and appeals commonly associated with poesis are also the domain of rhetoric, but that, in exploring those devices and appeals, there is a need to call attention to the endangerment of rhetoric's presumed commitment to the goal of "consensus founded on the force of the better argument" (Gross 18)—the goal, in other words, that links rhetoric to the Habermasian model of public sphere based on rational-critical debate. That rhetorical practice exceeds practices of dialectic, that it activates human subjectivity much more broadly and deeply, that it mobilizes the imagination, the emotions, and the body—this is rhetoric's peculiar public secret. Anyone who has encountered Aristotle's logos, ethos, and pathos knows it, and yet those who reference this dimension of rhetoric feel compelled to adopt a defensive attitude. Despite the fact that Habermas and other strict deliberationists have been thoroughly critiqued, the rational-critical model apparently continues to dominate.

How does this relate to multimodality? We tried to suggest, in our exploration of the GRDC materials, that many multimodal forms do not conform to what we might think of as "public rhetoric" if we, by design or default, embrace the rational-deliberationist model of rhetoric too rigidly. Videos, animations, photographs, brochures, posters, stencils, podcasts, and other multimodal compositions might not, at first glance, look like rhetoric at all or might look like the "bad" version of rhetoric as trickery or propaganda. Many effective multimodal compositions rely on narrative, metaphor, depiction, presence, and pathos. Moreover, they do not necessarily embrace the rational-critical value of making explicit their argumentative logics. We can only understand these forms, as legitimate public-rhetorical forms, if we are mindful of a larger tradition of rhetoric, a tradition consonant with the post-Habermasian models of the public sphere provided by Warner and others.

There may be contexts in which we would want to temporarily and deliberately forbear from using some of the affordances of multimodal rhetoric in order to achieve specific goals. In the previous chapter, we proposed that the Skakel case demonstrated some of the dangers of relying on multimodal rhetoric in the courtroom, where there is a need to critically scrutinize the logics by which a defendant's guilt or innocence is determined. But the situation is very different in the case of Detroit, which is marked by vast asymmetries of power. Those who live in Detroit will need to recruit all available means of persuasion if they are to counter the "ruin porn" produced by commercialized, mainstream media. In the next section we turn to the cultural work performed by rhetoric as poetic world making. We examine the way rhetoric, so conceived, articulates with the goals of transforming constructions of race, class, gender, and place that are circulated by the dominant culture.

THE CULTURAL WORK OF MULTIMODALITY

The potential power that you possess as a writer is based on this ability to put images of the world you see, and ideas about these images, into other people's heads.

—Wayne C. Booth and Marshall W. Gregory 10

But none of these can compete with the rhetorical power mobilized in a single Hollywood movie or magazine ad, whose complex interweaving of image and text . . . dominate the living patterns and imaginations of millions of North Americans.

—Jeff Rice and Marcel O'Gorman

We might productively begin with the obvious statement that everyday human experience is intensely multimodal. We are continuously absorbing information through multiple senses simultaneously. We know our worlds through sights, sounds, tastes, smells, and tactile sensations. A corollary to this is that human culture is multimodal. The substance of culture takes the form of codes and expressions that activate the full range of human experience. We have TV shows and paintings, graffiti and poems, music and dance, and so on. It is difficult to conceive of culture as unimodal or even as privileging a single mode, such as alphabetic text. As Iedema observes, "our human predisposition towards multimodal meaning making, and our own multi-semiotic development or ontogenesis, requires attention to more than one semiotic than just language-in-use" (33).

Those who control cultural forms control consciousness itself. As Enzensberger observes, while "all of us . . . like to think that we reign supreme in our own consciousness, that we are masters of what our minds accept or reject" our consciousness is actually the product of a "consciousness industry" in which mass media play a privileged role (3, 95). The consciousness industry is intensively multimodal, encoding cultural categories such as race, class, and gender into the languages of film, TV, music, and other cultural forms.

We can see this clearly in constructions of race. In "Morphologies: Race as a Visual Technology," Jennifer A. González writes that "[s]kin color, hair color, and eye color become marking devices for those who seek to situate the genetic history of humans within the narrow confines of phenotype. Race has always been a profoundly visual rhetoric . . ." (380). According to González, photographic technologies have been particularly implicated because "a conceptual parallel exists between the 'truth effects' of photography and what might be called the 'truth effects' of race. Both kinds of 'truth effects' naturalize ideological systems by making them visible and, apparently, self-evident" (379–80). Similarly, in *Colored Pictures: Race and Visual Representation*, Michael D. Harris contends that "[r]acial discourses, though discourses of power, ultimately rely on the visual in the sense that the visible body must be used by those in power to represent nonvisual realities that differentiate insiders from outsiders" (2).

Likewise, scholars call attention to the way multimodal compositions use aural markers to construct race. For instance, in *English with an Accent: Language, Ideology, and Discrimination in the United States*, linguist Rosina Lippi-Green explores the way "[f]ilm uses language variation and accent to draw character quickly, building on established preconceived notions associated with specific regional loyalties, ethnic, racial, or economic alliances" (81). Through her analysis of twenty-four Disney films, Lippi-Green demonstrates that "[w]hat children learn form the entertainment industry is to be comfortable with *same* and to be wary about *other*, and that language is the prime and ready diagnostic for this division between what is approachable and what is best left alone. For adults, those childhood lessons are reviewed daily" (103).

We've focused on race here, but we could make the same argument for any cultural category. The tools by which race, class, gender, place, and other key cultural categories are established and maintained are intensely multimodal. The foundations for framing our experience of the world are maintained through the mobilization of a vast array of cultural tools: images, maps, charts, diagrams, paintings, drawings, animations, performances, moving images, music, noise, gesture, clothes, furniture, and more. A system of rhetorical education that only addresses words equips citizens to participate in only a small fraction of the rhetorical practices that matter. Such a system cedes culture itself to mainstream commercial media. When we ask who owns multimodal rhetoric, we are really asking, *Who owns culture? Who owns consciousness?*

FROM CRITIQUE TO CULTURAL PRODUCTION: LESSONS FOR THE COMPOSITION CLASSROOM

Recognizing the legitimacy of a public sphere based on poesis has important implications for rhetorical education, broadly conceived, and for first-year composition in particular. If poesis is a legitimate paradigm for public rhetoric, teachers who have students make music, podcasts, narrative films and animations, digital photo essays, and the like are not merely creating "fun" assignments for students or opportunities for "self expression" and "creativity." Framed properly, these assignments can help prepare students to be full and active participants in the various and overlapping publics and counterpublics within which they are situated.

The *Semiotics and the Media* website, produced collaboratively by Thomas Streeter and his students, illustrates this point. In their Web essay "This Is Not Sex: A Web Essay on the Male Gaze, Fashion Advertising, and the Pose," Streeter and his students re-stage a series of magazine advertisements, substituting men where women are depicted in the originals. The men mimic the poses and facial expressions of the original women models. The result is visually jarring precisely because visual codes associated with specific cultural constructions of women—codes we normally take for granted—are graphically brought to our attention in the restagings. As the Web essay proclaims, "Most viewers find the images of the men odd or laughable. But the images of the women seem charming and attractive" (Streeter, et al.). The visual restagings found in "This Is Not Sex" differ from traditional critique in that they act directly on the cultural codes themselves, destabilizing and disrupting them by applying to men visual conventions that the dominant culture associates with women.

We see ourselves as building on a tradition of composition aimed at preparing students to transform the dominant culture by directly changing the way culture is encoded into the multimodal semiosis of music, film, radio, TV, and the Web. In *Rhetorics, Poetics, and Cultures: Refiguring College English Studies*, Berlin draws on cultural studies and critical pedagogy to outline an approach in which students critique TV shows such as *Family Ties* and *Roseanne* and then produce their own TV shows. As we discussed in the chapter 5, Bruce McComiskey outlines a similar approach in *Teaching Composition as a Social Process*. McComiskey's students critique the way student identities are encoded into the multimodal rhetorics of viewbooks and then produce their own viewbooks, encoded in ways that reflect their own identities and lived experiences.

More recently compositionists have recommended pedagogical reforms based on their analysis of Web-based rhetorics. Gail E. Hawisher and Patricia A. Sullivan observe that "as women have more control over writing their own visualizations online, we see some women representing themselves complexly in creative, rhetorically effective ways" (288). They warn that "as inhabitants of this [visually saturated] world—as women, as English professionals, and as teachers—we cannot afford to ignore the visual. We do so at our own peril" (289). Dànielle DeVoss and Cynthia L. Selfe write that

> We are witnessing the emergence of new spaces for identity formation and display, spaces where women are rewriting conventional narratives of the public-private divide, the unified subject, and cyberspace as a male domain. New media and new realms have invited new rhetorical positionings for the creative souls working in these spaces, and as teachers of composition, we need to help students explore, develop, and communicate more effectively in them. (46)

One compelling attempt to translate the goal of poetic world making into a curricular vision is the plan for liberal education outlined by Kurt Spellmeyer in *Arts of Living: Reinventing the Humanities for the Twenty-First Century*. Spellmeyer critiques models that limit the possibility and responsibility of cultural production to an elite few—"gifted" artists like James Joyce. Instead, Spellmeyer champions the capacities of "amateurs" (222) and "ordinary citizens" (7). In this view, the role of the humanities is to facilitate "[o]ur direct involvement in the making of culture" (7). Spellmeyer notes that

> People as widely different as the Balinese, the Navajo, and the pre-Meiji Japanese have regarded the making of art not as the purview of a chosen few, but as a normal part of any life well lived. For these people, the hyperspecialization of the humanities in our society might seem as bizarre as appointing one person in every thousand to experience emotions or to see colors on behalf of everyone else. Clearly, no one can feel emotions or see colors on my behalf, and by the same token, the creativity of others cannot substitute for my own creativity. (7–8)

In a similar vein, Bruno Gentili emphasizes the communal function of Greek poetry. "An essentially practical art," Gentili writes, Greek poetry "was closely linked to the realities of social and political life, and to the actual behavior of individuals within a community" (qtd. in Bettini vii). Not a written text consumed in private, a Greek poem was "a solo or choral performance, to the accompaniment of a musical instrument, before an audience" (qtd. in Bettini vii). As a multimodal form of communication involving multiple producers working in concert, poetry in this context was social, political, and practical. Like rhetoric.

Here, of course, we are not talking narrowly about "poetry" but about "poesis" as a broader paradigm of symbolic exchange. What we've tried to establish in this chapter is that post-Habermasian models of the public sphere introduced by Warner and others, contemporary models of public rhetoric introduced by Ivie and others, historical explorations of ancient and medieval cultural forms by Gentili and others, and even broad visions for liberal education by Spellmeyer and others all provide a foundation for locating forms of poesis precisely in the center of the social and political life of society. We see this conception of poesis as the best chance for facilitating a robust tradition of multimodal rhetoric. The multimodal compositions produced by the GRDC, which we explored at the beginning of this chapter, illustrate some of the potentials of this tradition. Teachers who provide opportunities for students to explore—through both analysis and production—the social potential of narrative films, photo essays, "living newspaper" vignettes, digital animations, and poetry can claim a coherent and well-established theoretical foundation for doing so.

PART IV

Practice and Pedagogy: A Synthesis

8 Case Study: The D Brand

"Notown" —title of a 2009 article by Daniel Okrent about Detroit in *Time.*

In the previous chapter we began with a brief discussion of two instances of multimodal public rhetoric—Web compositions produced by the Grandmont Rosedale Development Corporation and by Detroit blogger James D. Griffioen—aimed at countering representational practices that construct Detroit as scary, empty, and valueless. Detroit is interesting, in the context of this book, because it is a striking example of why a public rhetoric based on multimodal poesis is necessary. Detroit's marginalization is encoded into the metaphors, narratives, and images of the dominant culture. These metaphors, narratives, and images can and should be critiqued, but critique is not enough. We need new metaphors, new narratives, and new images. In this chapter, we turn to the case of the D Brand, a sustained attempt to transform Detroit's "image." The case of the D Brand will allow us to synthesize our discussion of public rhetoric as "poetic world making" (Warner) with the ecological approach we explore in chapters 3–5.

We should state at the outset that we realize turning to the case of the D Brand as a model of public rhetoric might be considered by some readers a blasphemous move. The D Brand is not a grass-roots organization. It's a non-profit organization, to be sure, but it's inextricably linked to concentrations of capital. "[T]o be clear about one thing," writes one representative of the DMCVB, "[o]ur tourism brand was developed expressly to promote tourism, pure and simple, beginning with a certain type of visitor for whom we think our 'product' is especially relevant and appealing" (Townsend). Accordingly, the rhetorical practices associated with the D Brand reflect the pressures and exigencies of marketing; this is not the grand style oratory of Cicero and is certainly not the eloquent and convicting rhetoric of justice and equality used by Martin Luther King, Jr. Embracing the DMCVB might seem to some like selling out. We contend, however, that public rhetors have a lot to learn from the case of the D Brand. Moreover, the D Brand offers a special opportunity for examining public rhetoric because the DMCVB provides access to a variety of materials that are typically not available for critical analysis. In addition to the many different kinds of rhetorical compositions themselves (logos, videos, photographs, Web materials, etc.), we examine interviews with and articles by the initiative's developers as well as supporting materials such as goal statements, market research, media kits, and brand guidelines—all of which are publically available for analysis.

Vibrant, Urban, and Real: Changing the Detroit Narrative

> At the outset of my career if someone had told me that I would be spending a lot of time developing and managing brands, I would not have known what to say. I left college infected with the political bug. . . . Since then I've worked on Capitol Hill . . . and founded a coalition of economically endangered inner ring suburbs. . . . Not long ago it dawned on me that I'd been working on brands in one way or another for nearly 20 years.
>
> —Jim Townsend

The D Brand campaign began with a set of clear rhetorical objectives, including the following:

- Develop a platform for clear, consistent and compelling communications with value that can inform a broad range of initiatives and extend beyond any one individual campaign.
- Provide a means for positively shaping tourist perceptions of Detroit over the long-term.
- Create a coherent, compelling story that brings together the suburbs and the city. (La Brecque, "Metro" 8)

As a first step toward meeting these objectives, the D Brand, like students in the approaches of Berlin and McComiskey that we discuss in earlier chapters, performed a sophisticated analysis of the cultural context before embarking on their own rhetorical intervention. Project developers gathered information through surveys, focus groups, interviews, and more (La Brecque, "Metro" 6–7). This research facilitated an understanding of Detroit's cultural assets as well as the negative perceptions of the city held by outsiders, including perceptions that "Detroit is dangerous and crime-ridden," "Detroit is a city beset by racial tension," and "Detroit is another industrial has-been" (La Brecque, "Metro" 21–23).

These negative perceptions are not completely unfounded, but they sketch a narrow, incomplete picture of Detroit. Detroit has many material, cultural, and historical assets that are unacknowledged by totalizing myths that construct the city as empty. The dominant culture, abetted by commercialized mass media, relentlessly circulates accounts of depopulation, disinvestment, and disorder in Detroit. The D Brand mounts a counter-offensive aimed at transforming this "background culture" (Welsh). Adopting a capacious understanding of the available means of persuasion, the DMCVB embraces the task of cultural production, broadly conceived. It seeks to destabilize and transform the codes of the dominant culture by placing into circulation new metaphors, new narratives, and new images.

A television spot called "Blind Date," for instance, parodies suburban banality. A white woman waits for her blind date at a restaurant that, at first glance, appears upscale and romantic, with white tablecloths and glowing candles. But when the date shows up, he turns out to be tacky and boring. He picks his teeth and slurps his pasta. The woman intermittently looks at her smart phone, which is receiving live video feeds from friends at iconic Detroit locations: in front of *The Thinker* (a sculpture by Rodin located outside the Detroit Institute of Arts), the outdoor amphitheater at Hart Plaza (a forty-acre, outdoor plaza in the city's civic center), and along the Detroit River (with a nighttime glimpse of Detroit's skyline reflected in the surface of the water). The video feeds from Detroit show images of assets that are difficult to find in the suburbs: skyscrapers, iconic public sculptures, the Detroit River, large outdoor concert venues. Kinetic camera movements capture racially diverse crowds listening to live music. In contrast, the restaurant, with its elevator music and muted colors, feels static, boring, and socially isolated. "Blind Date" creates a contrast between a suburban milieu that is tacky and lifeless with Detroit cultural environment that is—to borrow terms from the D Brand "back story," which we discuss in a moment—"vibrant," "urban," and "real" ("Inspiring" 9).

Compositions like "Blind Date" can, of course, be analyzed in terms of rational-critical argument. The visual evidence they provide refutes claims that Detroit is culturally empty. The rhetorical work of such compositions, however, cannot be fully accounted for in rational-critical terms. If the goal were merely rational argument, a written account that named Detroit's cultural assets would be sufficient. Compositions like "Blind Date," on the other hand, engage in poetic world making. The D Brand is ultimately designed to "change the Detroit narrative, to change the storyline that attaches to Detroit in people's mind both locally and globally" (qtd. in Ramsey). Accordingly, the disparate components of the D Brand all support a specific "story" about Detroit that counters the negative stories circulating in the dominant discourse. This story is explicitly codified in the D Brand "back story," a short description meant to help media workers conceptualize the initiative on a fundamental level:

> A lot of us are restless. We're looking for something that's harder to find all the time: Places with a soul all their own. Cities that know what it means to be urban. Places where we can plug into what's really going on. ("Inspiring" 38)

The D Brand is an instance of "applied storytelling" (also the name of one of the firms that contributed to the brand's development).

The D Brand does not pretend that Detroit is just like the suburbs, a rhetorical move that would be both futile and false. Instead, the dominant culture's ideographs and images are turned against itself. Alleged liabilities are recast as assets. Detroit is not scary, violent, and empty, but is "vibrant," "urban," and "real" ("Inspiring" 9). It has "soul," "imagination," and "power," is where you can plug into "what's really going on" ("Inspiring" 8, 38). In contrast to Detroit, other places are not comfortable, safe, and friendly, so much as they are sterile, static, and dull.

Like the "Blind Date" TV spot, the various components of the D Brand embody this back story. Other TV spots, photographs, and print materials all depict various cultural assets in Detroit using dynamic angles, bright colors, and high production values. One of the more interesting components of the initiative is a set of conceptual maps that chart Detroit space as culturally engaging. These maps are stylized, rendering the complex shape of Detroit's literal roads and borders in solid colors, regularized shapes, and clean lines. They break the vast space of metro Detroit (undifferentiated and overwhelming to outsiders) into districts and subdistricts with unique identities. This stylization performs important cultural work. Mainstream media depicts geophysical space below 8 Mile Road (the northern border of the city) as a blank frontier—a wild, lawless, disorderly space. The D Brand's conceptual maps replace images of chaos with images of geometric order, replace images of a scary unknown with colorful representations of cultural assets.

It Has to Come from a Thousand Different Places: The Ecological Approach of the D Brand

The D Brand adopts an ecological approach to public rhetoric that illustrates many of the ideas we explored in chapters 2–5. Kairos is not merely the function of shaping a single verbal performance for a single audience, but is a function of how multiple compositions produced through the labor of multiple actors can be coordinated across time and space to address a set of related rhetorical exigencies. Even more broadly, in addition to producing and distributing specific rhetorical compositions, the D Brand lays the groundwork for felicitous emergence. "Nobody invented the D Brand," Eric La Brecque writes, "You might say it was distilled from all the perceptions and experiences that hundreds of people and dozens of organizations shared over the course of many months" ("Creating" 1).

As we discuss above, the D Brand is a multifaceted campaign. It places into circulation a "concatenation of texts through time" (Warner 90), recruiting multiple semiotic modes (aural, visual, written, tactile), multiple media (print, TV, Web), and multiple genres (conceptual maps, logos, brochures, TV advertisements, photographs, webpages, and more). Unifying thematic elements (the back story) and formal elements (logos, color schemes, type faces, and visual styles) are applied across these different components, creating coherence and solidarity. In Warner's terms, these unifying elements create an "intertextual environment of citation," linking multiple compositions together in the consciousness of an emerging public (97).

The D Brand seeks out opportunities at all stages of circulation, including opportunities related to production, reproduction, distribution, and recomposition. Media of distribution, for instance, are interconnected and mutually leveraging. Print materials point readers to the website, and the website provides access to many different media components, including digitized versions of print materials and TV spots.

The D Brand appreciates opportunities afforded by rhetorical recomposition. As Jim Townsend explains, "[i]t takes a lot to change the basic buzz about a place. It can't come from one place; it has to come from a thousand different places. It doesn't mean adopting the same words and pictures, but they need to be moving in the same direction" (qtd. in Ramsey). Therefore, the DMCVB's approach is designed to be applicable across multiple contexts and organizations: "we secured the goodwill of many individuals along the way by making a commitment to arrive at insights that could help the region as a whole tell a compelling story for other purposes, too, such as economic development, employee recruitment, and a more positive media portrayal" (Townsend). The DMCVB explicitly welcomes the participation of collaborators, including those involved with "economic development or community enrichment" who might use the resources of the D Brand to "help attract companies, talent and investment into our region—and to foster civic pride" ("Inspiring" 1).

To facilitate the goal of rhetorical recomposition, the D Brand provides a wide range of intellectual and semiotic resources for others to use. For instance, the D Brand makes available a range of media components: the D Brand logo, B roll video footage, and an archive of photographs "available free of charge for editorial usage and the positive promotion of metro Detroit . . ." (Detroit Metro Convention & Visitors Bureau).

In addition to these raw materials, the D Brand provides a broader set of conceptual resources to guide future rhetorical production. A booklet, for instance, spells out the "Detroit brand guidelines." Available for download from the DMCVB website, the booklet presents the conceptual basis for the D Brand campaign, including both short and long versions of the D Brand Back Story ("Inspiring"). The booklet also contains practical recommendations for using logos, maps, photographs, color schemes, and typography. Through such conceptual materials, the D Brand attempts to build a shared understanding of rhetorical work among likeminded stakeholders and lays the groundwork for a larger rhetorical effort. The DMCVB distributed their materials to approximately two hundred organizations (Whitesall 10). Moreover, the D Brand proactively negotiates structures of legitimation by encouraging respected institutions, such the Henry Ford Museum, the Detroit Tigers baseball team, and others to integrate the D Brand materials into their communication initiatives (Henderson 17; Whitesall 10). Association with well-known organizations helps to establish the ethos of the brand.

A cynical reading of the D Brand's approach to rhetorical velocity and rhetorical recomposition would characterize it as a crass attempt to recruit an army of free sales representatives. Indeed, the D Brand is candid about its own self-interest. What keeps the effort from becoming merely profit-oriented is the DMCVB's attempt to involve numerous stakeholders from the beginning, an attempt to arrive at a shared understanding of the work that includes its own self-interests, but is not limited to them. From this initial networking, the D Brand developed not a script that others should repeat, but a flexible set of topoi that could be adapted and applied by others: "[w]e're not trying to say something that precise, we're trying to create a tone and a feeling about Detroit" (qtd. in Ramsey).

Bazerman offers a decentered understanding of kairos that is useful in this context. Bazerman observes that "the simple vision of the single rhetor acting against a coherent socially ordered audience lulls us into attributing a fixity to the shifting sands of society" (175). In place of this simplistic understanding, Bazerman recommends that kairos be assessed from a more "distant standpoint, viewing all participants, their conceptual frameworks, and the relationships and transactions among them from the separate standpoint of an analytical observer" (174). This analytic perspective ultimately leads to practical understandings applied by rhetors. Indeed, Bazerman claims that his goal

> is to give deeper guidance to both rhetor and audience, who are all potential rhetors. Indeed, though audiences may be temporarily mute and standing still, they will not be for long. They too will act and speak. . . . All are users of language, alternately as receivers and producers. The mutual interplay of all their actions creates the evanescent yet compelling atmosphere of society. (174)

This vision of kairos, then, requires "*kairotic* coordination," which, done effectively, "can lead to the kinds of shared orientations to and shared participations within mutually recognized moments" (184). The D Brand can be seen as an example of this decentered understanding of kairos. The DMCVB developed a rhetorical initiative based on extensive conversation with stakeholders. "Kairotic coordination" emerged from these conversations, creating a zone of "shared orientations" and "participations." Stakeholders who consume the rhetorical resources associated with the D Brand one day might use them to produce their own resources the next.

We should stress that we do not intend this analysis to be a ringing endorsement of the D Brand. Indeed, some of the D Brand's materials adopt problematic constructions of race, as when a traditional Asian family dinner is presented as boring in contrast to Detroit's exciting cultural scene ("Meet the Parents"). Moreover, repackaging Detroit as "vibrant," "urban," and "real" risks catering to an established white practice of exoticizing urban spaces as thrilling frontiers. As we said at the beginning of this chapter, the DMCVB is closely linked to concentrations of capital and the rhetorical practices it adopts are inflected by that reality. Like all rhetorical actions, the D Brand should be subjected to rigorous critical scrutiny, and its practices of representation should be interrogated through the lens of a situated rhetorical ethics.

LESSONS FOR THE COMPOSITION CLASSROOM

Faced with a formidable cultural exigency—widespread, negative perceptions of Detroit—the DMCVB deploys multimodal rhetoric as a form of cultural production enabled by a complex network of human and nonhuman actors. Kairotic opportunity is not understood in terms of what can be accomplished by a single rhetor who engages in a single, virtuosic performance, but as what can happen when an expansive constellation of factors are negotiated, coordinated, choreographed. The D Brand seeks not just to produce and circulate many and diverse rhetorical compositions itself, but to lay a broad foundation for felicitous emergence. It recruits the participation of multiple actors through "kairotic coordination" (Bazerman 184).

It seems to us that current structures of rhetorical education are not well suited to preparing students to engage in an approach like that of the D Brand. Most assignments, grading and assessment practices, model texts, and models of the composing process are designed to prompt and reward discrete alphabetic performances by single composers. These performances are valued for making transparent the logic of their argument, for thoroughly developing ideas, and for conforming to conventions of academic prose. Few of the D Brand's compositions would be considered valuable according to such criteria. Almost any single composition would be seen as incomplete and underdeveloped, precisely because the D Brand has accurately concluded that its rhetorical goals cannot be achieved through any single composition. Indeed, much of the D Brand's most important rhetorical work results in elements that most writing teachers would not even recognize as "compositions"—raw materials (such as photos, logos, typefaces, and guidelines) that *other composers* can use to make their own compositions. It's as if a student decided that instead of writing an essay, she was merely going to create a set of resources that would help *other* students write essays. To value the rhetorical actions of the D Brand, teachers would need to develop a grading rubric that gave credit for (1) the use of unifying elements across multiple compositions to establish an intertextual network; (2) the facilitation of rhetorical recomposition through the development of raw materials that others might find useful and through the careful selection of distribution channels (such as a Web-based image archive); (3) the development of a shared understanding of rhetorical work through conversations with stakeholders and through the development of flexible guidelines and topoi; and (4) the circulation of a new set of cultural codes in order to counteract the codes of the dominant culture (which were themselves originally understood through extensive research undertaken at the beginning of the rhetorical initiative).

Again, our point here is not to uncritically endorse the D Brand, but is instead to explore a model of public rhetoric in which rhetorical action is recast as the choreographing of multiple modes, multiple rhetors, multiple media, multiple technologies, multiple genres, multiple compositions—a model that, moreover, pays due attention not just to composing, but to the broad arc of circulation, including the way compositions are produced, reproduced, distributed, consumed, and recomposed. What would the composition classroom look like if it adopted such a model of public rhetoric? In the following chapter, we attempt to sketch a portrait of a reconfigured composition classroom.

9 Multimodal Public Rhetoric in the Composition Classroom

We contend that realizing the full social potential of multimodal public rhetoric would require broad transformations. We have tried to demonstrate in the preceding chapters that multimodality is inextricably linked to broader cultural practices and attitudes; these attitudes are formed and reformed at all age levels, in both school and nonschool settings. Schools, libraries, community media centers, community arts centers, and alternative educational institutions are all potentially sites of transformation. As compositionists, of course, we are most immediately concerned with the ways that sites of higher education can support critically reflective practices of multimodal public rhetoric by working across curricular and cocurricular structures. Writing centers, humanities computing labs, living and learning communities, virtual game environments, and other structures potentially have a role to play. In this chapter, however, we focus on the kinds of transformations that could be implemented within the confines of a single FYC course. We briefly review ongoing conversations in the field about possibilities and challenges related to teaching public rhetoric and then describe one approach that attempts to address some of the pedagogical challenges explored in this book.

ACTIVIST RHETORS IN THE COMPOSITION CLASSROOM

Lloyd Bitzer famously observes that "a work of rhetoric is pragmatic; it comes into existence for the sake of something beyond itself; it functions ultimately to produce action or change in the world; it performs some task. In short, rhetoric is a mode of altering reality. . . ." (3–4). Many of the concerns we take up in the previous pages follow from rhetoric's pragmatic imperative. Why should rhetors consider other modes and media before committing to words on paper?

Because other modes and media might address the rhetorical exigency more effectively than words alone can. Why should rhetors concern themselves with processes of reproduction and distribution? Because rhetorical compositions can only address exigencies if they get to an audience and they can only get to an audience if they are reproduced and distributed.

Helping students perceive and use rhetoric as a tool for intervening in the world, however, is not necessarily an easy task. Too often, the university classroom in general, and the writing classroom in particular, reinforce passive-analytical- rather than practice-activist-oriented dispositions. This point is made by Elizabeth Ervin, who begins her exploration of teaching public rhetoric in the composition classroom by reviewing research by Paul Rogat Loeb that suggests universities "mostly provide models of political detachment" (qtd. in Ervin 384). Rogat quotes a Michigan student who observes, "It seems like we're supposed to be aware, but we're not really supposed to act" (qtd. in Ervin 384). As we mention in chapter 5, Susan Miller explores the ways composition courses based on literature appreciation potentially create passive subjects (*Textual*). Courses that take a cultural studies approach, in which students explore the political implications of popular texts, are not necessarily better. Susan Wells claims that such an approach leads to "a self-reflexive practice directed at critique and self-consciousness rather than intervention or agency" (334). Similarly, Ervin worries that an approach characterized by cultural critique alone "might convey tacit support for a voyeuristic relationship between students and their world, in which reading, analyzing, discussing, and writing in composition class are equivalent to intervening, acting, and participating in the 'real world'" (385). More recently, Douglas D. Hesse observes that the field remains characterized by having "students write *about* the civic sphere, not *in* it" (350).

Some approaches to teaching public rhetoric attempt to position the composition classroom as a micro public sphere, a place of rhetorical deliberation among citizens. In this model, rhetoric is ostensibly used by students to deliberate with each other about social issues of common concern. This raises a new set of problems. Eberly claims that "the classroom cannot be a public space; the power of the teacher as well as the teacher's and students' subjectivities relative to the institution keep the classroom from ever being truly public" ("Rhetoric" 292). Janice M. Lauer, Elizabeth Ervin, and Susan Wells all question the efficacy of this approach on similar grounds. Lauer, perhaps, sums up the problem best in a series of pointed rhetorical questions. Noting that some compositionists advocate a construction of the "class as public community," Lauer asks

> Is this a representative public community? Would students under any other circumstances write to each other about issues? Does this captive group have a stake in these issues? Is there a textual record with conventions and expectations for evidence that can be studied? Will these groups prepare or motivate students to write in their future public worlds? Will writing within a community of peers empower students to participate as citizens in broader public communities? (68)

Lauer's question, "Would students under any circumstances write to each other about issues?" is particularly relevant to the argument we have been making in this book. As Warner says, a public is a relationship created by texts circulating among strangers through time. In this book we have been particularly interested in the way public rhetors' processes of rhetorical invention are informed by considerations of circulation. A classroom, however, is characterized by highly specialized and constrained conditions of circulation. A classroom is not comprised of strangers separated in time and space, but classmates who are geophysically copresent, which means processes of circulation in classroom settings are much simpler than most public settings. Indeed, in the writing classroom, there is arguably no need for any form of writing at all. If your public meets every Monday and Tuesday at 10:00 a.m., why not just talk to them? All of the complexities related to selection of modes and media of production, reproduction, and distribution—the concerns of chapters 2–5—are elided in the simplified context of a "public" consisting of twenty-five students who sit next to each other in a classroom. If students address each other through writing, they are likely doing so because the teacher told them to, rather than because their own rich assessment of the context led to the conclusion that writing was a kairotically felicitous response.

Rather than limit classroom rhetoric to critique or insular deliberation, several scholar-teachers recommend having students use rhetoric as a tool for addressing problems that students care about in the world outside the classroom. Eberly, across a series of articles, has advocated "returning to rhetoric's origins in democratic praxis" ("Rhetoric" 290).

"[T]eaching the praxis of rhetoric as a productive and practical art," Eberly suggests, "can be a radically democratic act" ("Rhetoric" 290). She envisions classrooms as "protopublic spheres" that "emphasize letters to the editor, newsgroups, on-campus events, and other venues where citizen critics might be published and where citizen criticism might be performed" ("Rhetoric" 293). In a similar vein, Ervin begins her discussion of how to facilitate "civic participation" in the composition course by recounting her own actions as a public rhetor, including writing a letter to the editor of her local newspaper (382). "Civic involvement . . . doesn't just happen," Ervin insists, "it requires models of such behavior and structured opportunities for participating in it" (384).

Embodying the goal of teaching rhetoric as a productive art that can address exigencies beyond the classroom, pedagogies described by Berlin, McComiskey, Eberly, and others ask students to *begin* with critique, but they do not stop there. Berlin asks students to examine the way culture is encoded in TV shows like *Roseanne* and *Family Ties*. McComiskey asks students to look at the way college viewbooks encode student subjectivities. Eberly asks students to examine discourses associated with the 1966 Tower shootings at the University of Texas at Austin. Critique is important in these pedagogies, not as an end it itself, but because it informs future rhetorical actions. After analyzing the cultural codes and discourses, students are invited to transform them through rhetorical action. In these pedagogies, critique functions as a politicizing force, a way for the classroom community to explore social issues beyond the classroom to determine if there are, in fact, exigencies that students might conceivably care about. It is notable that the approaches outlined by Berlin, McComiskey, and Eberly are based around cultural material that is relevant to students' lives. Berlin and McComiskey both ask students to examine the way they are being encoded in multimodal cultural forms (such as TV shows and viewbooks). Eberly asks students to explore a historic event that continues to inform life on their campus. These explorations raise issues that students potentially care about—or come to care about through lively analysis and critique. They ask students to consider their actual and possible roles within various and overlapping publics and counterpublics.

Asking students to produce public rhetoric aimed at exigencies outside the classroom has two pedagogical functions. First, and most obviously, it provides students with experiences that hopefully help them mature as rhetorical practitioners. As Eberly observes, "classrooms understood as protopublic spaces allow teachers and students to engage in education as the praxis of public life, widely defined" ("From *Writers*" 175). The classroom builds on the rich rhetorical experiences and practices that students already possess, helping them expand existing and develop new heuristics, processes, and capacities. This function of a pedagogy of rhetorical praxis pertains to the question *What can I do?*

The second function of a pedagogy of rhetorical praxis is that it reinforces particular kinds of subjectivities and habits that form the preconditions for public participation. This function pertains to the question of *Who am I?* Eberly claims that the pedagogy she outlines forms the basis for "processes of public-oriented subjectivity-formation" ("Rhetoric" 292–93). Elsewhere, Eberly builds on Richard Sennett's "theory of public subjectivity that offers writers a means of thinking about how they might construct *ethe*—invent and present themselves—in different publics or at different points in a public's process of forming, acting, disintegrating" ("From *Writers*" 169). Finally, Eberly is "suggesting that these rhetorical practices can form collective habits, these habits can be experienced as pleasurable, and these shared rhetorical practices can sustain publics and counterpublics—on campus and beyond campus" ("Rhetoric" 294). The composition classroom is one site where society models and reinforces the kind of rhetorical practices it values. In that sense, the classroom is not just a place for teaching skills, techniques, and processes, but is a place for nurturing a set of understandings about the social world we live in (or want to live in) and the kinds of social practices—including rhetorical practices—that sustain it. We see this subjectivity-forming, habit-forming role of the composition classroom as crucial to realizing the full potential of multimodal public rhetoric. When teachers ask students to map rhetorical options for addressing public exigencies, they are simultaneously normalizing a social practice and encouraging students to see themselves as potentially involved in shaping the surrounding culture.

In the pedagogical approach we describe below, we attempt to build on the work of Berlin, McComiskey, Wells, Eberly, Shipka, and others. We find that we need to adapt these approaches, however, in order to adequately prepare students to confront the challenges of poetic world making within rhetorical ecologies.

TEACHING THE PRODUCTION OF CULTURE
IN RHETORICAL ECOLOGIES

In this book we have examined a process of rhetorical invention that is different from the one emphasized in most composition classrooms. Traditional models of the composing process emphasize strategies for single rhetors to generate single, word-based compositions that are then submitted to the teacher for a grade. The process of rhetorical invention that we outline positions rhetors as a point of articulation within a complex network of radically simultaneous human and nonhuman actors. In this approach, rhetors begin their assessment of kairos before they commit to words. They assess modes and media of production, reproduction, and distribution in relation to audience, purpose, and exigency. Their understanding of how their compositions will be reproduced and distributed informs compositional choices. Considerations of infrastructural resources are foregrounded; rhetors assess the technologies, competencies, and forms of capital available to them, including possibilities for collaborating with others. Collaboration might take many different forms. Rhetors might seek help as they learn new interfaces, might borrow equipment and software, might enlist others to help distribute compositions, and might enlist others to engage in future forms of recomposition.

After outlining this distributed and ecological approach to rhetorical invention, composition, and circulation, we turned our attention to the dynamics of multimodal rhetoric itself, suggesting that rhetors who wish to preserve the model of public rhetoric based on rational-critical argument face a set of challenges that are distinctive to multimodality. We further suggested that public rhetors have good reason for considering options that fall outside of the rational-critical model and aligned ourselves with theorists like Michael Warner who advocate a public sphere based on poesis. In the remainder of this chapter, we describe one approach that attempts to prepare students to engage in poetic world making in rhetorical ecologies. This approach is based on David's experiences with teaching a section of FYC in Michigan State University's Residential College in the Arts and Humanities (RCAH). The RCAH is small college at MSU with its own dean, tenure-system faculty, and major. The RCAH has an interdisciplinary curriculum that invites students to engage in historical and critical inquiry, a variety of forms of cultural production, and civic engagement. The course we explore here, RCAH 112 "Writing, Research, and Technologies," is a core course in the RCAH major and is the second in a two-course sequence that fulfills MSU's fist-year writing requirement. All students enrolled in the course are RCAH majors.

In the approach to teaching this course we describe here, the basic assignment sequence follows a pattern similar to the ones outlined by Berlin and McComiskey: students begin with analytical critique and then devise rhetorical interventions aimed at bringing about social change. The course begins by thematizing "the production of culture," which serves as the subtitle for David's course. The syllabus opens with a passage from Kurt Spellmeyer that alludes to the role of the humanities in facilitating "[o]ur direct involvement in the making of culture" and champions the role of the "ordinary person" (7). Course readings invite students to continue exploring this theme. Students read the first chapter of Enzensberger's *The Consciousness Industry: On Literature, Politics and the Media*, which explores the role of various media and cultural institutions in shaping our perceptions, attitudes, and beliefs. Selections from Dick Hebdige's *Subculture: The Meaning of Style* explore how subcultures adopt resistant rhetorical practices to critique and transform the dominant culture. Selections from Neil A. Gershenfeld's *Fab: The Coming Revolution on Your Desktop—From Personal Computers to Personal Fabrication* explore the way emergent technologies allow nonspecialists to produce three-dimensional products, expanding our understanding of what forms of cultural production are available at any given moment.

In this approach, students are invited to interrogate many different kinds of rhetorical practices, including academic critique, socially conscious art, and nonprofit branding and advertising. Collections like *Graphic Agitation* and *Graphic Agitation 2* (McQuiston), *Design Anarchy* (Lasn), and especially *The Design of Dissent* (Glaser and Ilic) provide examples of graphic design used to address social exigencies that foster rich classroom discussion and quicken students to the possibilities of visual activism. Online materials such as "Grand Theft America" (Blumrich), "The Meatrix" (GRACE and Free Range Studios) and "reBurger" (The Yes Men) provide examples of the possibilities associated with digital video and digital animation. To explore the way a broad, multifaceted, ecological approach can address rhetorical exigencies, students examine the D Brand and other campaigns, such as those presented on the Ad Council website. These multifaceted campaigns provide modes for thinking about the coordination of multiple modes; multiple media of production, reproduction, and distribution; multiple compositions and genres; and multiple collaborators.

To see how rigorous academic critique can help foster understanding of cultural semiosis, students explore five articles from academic journals, each of which focuses on a different form of cultural production. Articles were selected from *The Journal of Popular Culture* and *American Quarterly*—journals that invite an interdisciplinary approach to the study of contemporary American culture. In "Belly Dancing: Arab-face Orientalist Feminism, and U.S. Empire," Sunaina Maira explores the recent popularity of belly dancing in U.S. contexts. Maira ultimately concludes that "belly dancing performances are entangled with the imperial engagements that link the United States and the Middle East and reveal a deeper politics of imperialism, racialization, and feminism in this moment of U.S. empire" (318). In "Selling American Diversity and Muslim American Identity through Nonprofit Advertising Post-9/11," Evelyn Alsultany explores efforts by the Ad Council and others aimed at counteracting attitudes of intolerance toward Arabs and Muslims that emerged in the wake of the 9/11 attacks. Alsultany argues that "in an effort to deconstruct the binary opposition between American citizen and Arab Muslim terrorist, these PSAs reproduced restrictive representations of diversity" (595–96). Other articles explored the way sexual values are dramatized in the TV show *Sex and the City* (Cramer) and the way ethnicity is constructed in American restaurants (Gvion and Trostler).

The first major writing assignment in the course is loosely patterned after these academic journal articles (see Appendix A for a copy of the assignment sequence). Students write a Cultural Problem Analysis (CPA) in which they identify a problem, explore what other scholars in the humanities and social sciences have written about the problem, and then identify a set of cultural artifacts (such as films, TV shows, songs, etc.) that they can analyze themselves with the aim of contributing to a deeper understanding of the problem. CPAs both fulfill the institutional requirement that the course prepare students to engage in sophisticated, research-based analysis of the kind they will be asked to do in future courses, but also lays a foundation for other forms of rhetorical production.

After completing their CPAs, students develop a Plan for Rhetorical Intervention. Plans are a chance for students to formally design

and present a broad, multifaceted campaign after the pattern of the
D Brand and the Ad Council campaigns examined earlier. Plans ask
students to precisely frame their rhetorical context. What problem are
they addressing? What audiences are they targeting? Where are these
audiences located? What do they value? Students have some degree
of freedom in selecting a scale for their Plans. Students might, for instance, attempt to address an exigency that is particular to the living
and learning community of the RCAH, might select an exigency embedded in the greater Lansing community, or might focus on a broad,
national issue. The point is to frame the Plan with enough detail so
that relevant possibilities and constraints are clear.

Plans call for students to present a detailed overview of the kind
of campaign that would be appropriate for the context as they have
framed it. Students explain what modes, genres, and media of production, reproduction, and distribution would be appropriate. They look
at the diagram of how Jim's press advisory circulated (figure 12) and
design their own maps in anticipation of how they expect their own
compositions to travel. Plans are typically much broader and more involved than what students can actually accomplish in a sixteen-week
course. Their purpose is to provide a space for students to think formally about rhetorical ecologies—about the way kairotic opportunity
is distributed across networks of human and nonhuman agents, about
the way multiple compositions in multiple genres can work together
across space and time as they circulate through material-cultural contexts, about future possibilities of recomposition, and more.

Finally, students create an Intervention Showcase for a public open
house called Public Knowledge. Inspired, in part, by Eastern Michigan University's Celebration of Student Writing (see Adler-Kassner and
Estrem) and similar events at other institutions, Public Knowledge is a
forum in which students present their work to peers, faculty, staff, and
community members. In developing their Showcases, students select
some combination of rhetorical components from their Plans that they
could realistically complete in time to present at the open house. The
format for the Showcase is modeled after the kind of displays found
in many professional contexts, such as conventions. Students critically examine different models, from simple "science fair" displays to
complex mixed-media installations designed by large corporations for
trade shows. The basic goal of the Showcase is to communicate a sense

of the larger Plan for the proposed rhetorical intervention in such a way as to make it compelling to the public audience of the open house.

The Public Knowledge open house is a two-hour event at the end of the semester. Students in all sections of "Writing, Research, and Technologies" participate in the event in some fashion. Past events have featured a very wide range of student performances and compositions, including break dancing, soap-box speeches, graffiti installations, videos, paintings, games, puppet shows, and many forms of mixed-media installations. Faculty who teach the different sections of the course work together to organize the event, attending to considerations of space, technology, food, setup, and more. Faculty invest considerable effort in publicizing the event in the College, across the University, and in the broader community. They develop flyers and posters, and make use of targeted emails, email lists, and social media. The goal is to produce an event that is well-attended by people beyond the classroom and to mark the event *as* an event, a special occasion of communal importance. Students often express a degree of anxiety as the Public Knowledge open house approaches and they finalize their projects—an anxiety that can be understood as a keen awareness that rhetorical compositions will finally connect with an audience beyond the classroom. When asked in course evaluations whether the Public Knowledge open house is a worthwhile component of the course, students almost universally answered yes.

EVERYDAY ADS: CHANGING PERCEPTIONS OF MOUNTAINTOP REMOVAL

The work of one student will help illustrate the kinds of explorations and practices that this approach encourages. Mark Sleeman chose to explore the practice of mountaintop removal (MTR). In his CPA, Mark explored the multimodal rhetoric of TV ads produced by the West Virginia Coal Association to generate positive responses to MTR. Mark claimed that "coal companies influence the public's perception . . . by altering images of mountaintop removal to make it appear non-destructive. Because of their photo-realism, these images seem to provide 'proof' that MTR is harmless." He also examined efforts by activist groups to counteract the discourses circulated by coal companies. While he considered activist efforts valuable, his analysis revealed that these efforts are often framed in highly localized terms that limit their resonance with a broader American public.

Mark developed a Plan for a Rhetorical Intervention that builds on this analysis, ultimately proposing a campaign that he called "Search-MTR." Key to his approach was a set of "everyday ads" or "E.D.A.s": "shirts, rubber bracelets, pins and stickers" that "people themselves can spread around." Mark hoped that these "wearable, spreadable ads" would result in "connectedness" around the goal of opposing MTR. Components of this campaign would adopt a common visual style based on a "yellow background" ("Yellow can imply 'slow down'") coupled with hand-written words and simple hand-drawn illustrations. Mark suggested that the simplicity of this approach would contrast with the slickness of other national media campaigns: "it isn't too prestigious and encourages everyone to get involved." The E.D.A.s used in "phase one" of the campaign feature the short message "SearchM-TR" and the Web address for a website tied to the campaign, but they "never mention what MTR stands for." E.D.A.s, then, are designed to launch a visually distinctive, multifaceted campaign that relies on the rhetorical strategies of participation, display, solidarity, and awareness.

"Phase two" is the result of the Web traffic generated by the E.D.A.s. The SearchMTR website is designed to be a "source of information": "a place in which the public can come to learn about what MTR is." The website is designed to present information in a dynamic and compelling way, using the trope of "search" in animations. Visual images reinforce the environmental damage done by MTR. The emphasis of phase two is on convincing visitors that they should care about the issue even if they do not live in the localities directly affected by MTR.

For his Intervention Showcase, Mark developed a display that combined a banner, stickers, and two computers that presented working mock-ups of his website (figures 17 and 18). Stickers were presented on a mirror so that visitors could easily peel them off and wear them, which many did. The various components of the campaign were unified by their use of the same graphical components: a particular line drawing on a solid yellow background and the repetition of SearchMTR.

Figure 17. This photograph shows the Intervention Showcase that Mark developed for the Public Knowledge open house, including stickers positioned on the mirror, ready to be peeled off by visitors. The color scheme and the SearchMTR logo are applied consistently to the banner, the website, and the stickers, visually linking the disparate elements of the campaign. Photograph by David Sheridan.

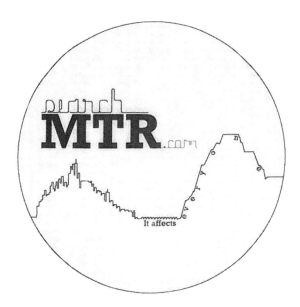

Figure 18. Mark's SearchMTR sticker.

Even in his relatively straightforward decision to produce the stickers, Mark negotiated a complex set of material considerations. The RCAH had made $10 available to each student in order to offset production costs. Mark's decision to proceed with the stickers was based in part on his knowledge that he could use the $10 to print his stickers on the large-format printer in the Language and Media Center (LMC) and that adhesive paper was one medium supplied by the LMC for $7/linear foot. Mark created the sticker using Adobe Illustrator, which he accessed on a workstation in the LMC. With the help of a peer consultant, Mark created a 42" x 12" image in Photoshop that was comprised of 120 iterations of his sticker. Many of those who stopped by Mark's Showcase at the open house were happy to take one of his stickers and wear it for the night.

Embodied in student projects like Mark's, we see several of the public rhetorical practices that we have been discussing in this book. Mark did not conceive of the rhetorical process as involving a single rhetor producing a single, word-based composition. Instead, Mark assessed kairotic opportunity as the function of multiple modes, media, genres, people, and other resources. Both Mark's Plan and his Showcase demonstrate a keen awareness of how multiple compositions, genres, and media can be coordinated. Not only did Mark produce an interconnected set of rhetorical compositions, but all of these compositions are unified by a flexible and effective visual style that Mark adopted because of his rhetorical goals. Mark seems to clearly illustrate the model of rhetor as point of articulation in a complex network of human and nonhuman agents.

We find the stickers placed on the mirror an interesting example of a student confronting the challenges of reproduction and distribution. Mark's process of rhetorical invention looked forward to a future moment at the open house when he would be able to distribute his stickers. He prepared for this moment through the coordination of people, technologies, and money. The separate stages of producing, reproducing, and distributing the stickers each required assessment, planning, effort, and imagination. Setting up the mirror as a mechanism for distributing the stickers was a final step in a long chain of human-nonhuman translations.

Traditional grading rubrics do not typically include the kinds of criteria necessary for valuing Mark's approach to reproduction and distribution. As a composition, the design for the sticker is modest, containing a simple line drawing against a solid yellow background. The only alphabetic text it includes is the SearchMTR.com logo (which functions simultaneously as a branding mechanism and as a pointer to online content) positioned above a three-word sentence: "It affects everyone." The full value of the sticker can only be seen when one takes into account its relationship to the entirety of Mark's approach. It is visually connected with other compositions, some of which contain more traditional arguments and presentations of information. As a carrier of the Web address, the sticker potentially helps people access this information; but it is also a simple form of display, like a political button, that signals the wearer's concern for the problem of MTR. It signifies membership in a larger group defined by this concern. All of these things are enabled by the fact that it is a sticker—something that can be affixed to people, backpacks, tote bags, walls, etc. It is specifically designed to travel, to circulate—which it visibly did the night of the open house. Many guests were happy to receive and wear one of Mark's stickers, and the bright yellow designs could be seen circulating throughout the corridors of the open house, a concatenation of texts whose bodily display made visible a relationship among strangers in the protopublic spaces of the RCAH. Even after the event, stickers

continued to travel, and in at least one verified case ended up in parts
several hundred miles from East Lansing.

Institutional Setting

We would like to close this chapter with a few words about the intu-
itional setting for the course David taught: Michigan State University's
Residential College in the Arts and Humanities. Our point of including this sketch of the broader curriculum is twofold. First, all courses
need to be adapted to the particular institutional contexts in which
they are embedded. So this sketch helps provide the context for the
course we just described. Second, we feel that the RCAH curriculum
provides one set of solutions to some of the pedagogical challenges we
have discussed in this book. First-year writing is certainly one place to
begin transforming rhetorical education, but to fully realize the potential of multimodal public rhetoric, broader institutional change is
necessary. The RCAH is characterized by a number of curricular and
infrastructural designs that are interesting in this context.

As a residential college, the RCAH—including classrooms, admin-
istrative offices, faculty offices, and other sites of learning and collaboration—is located within the Snyder-Phillips residence hall complex.
Students are expected to reside in Snyder-Phillips for at least their first
year of enrollment in the College. The residential component of the
program means that students have a chance to form a strong living-
learning community, laying the groundwork for collaboration, cocurricular learning, and self-sponsored learning.

The RCAH provides an integrated, interdisciplinary arts and humanities curriculum. One feature of the program is that first-year
writing is actually a two-course sequence for a total of six credits.
Spreading first-year writing across two courses provides additional opportunities to explore the ways writing is connected to other forms of
composing. Students routinely produce posters, brochures, websites,
videos, poems, and stories as well as compositions with a performative
dimension, such as music and spoken word compositions.

The connections between writing and other forms of communication are reinforced throughout the curriculum. All students are required to take four credits of "workshops," which focus on various
forms of creative expression: photography, poetry, screen-printing,
music, ceramics, and so on. The RCAH routinely offers a workshop

focused on "book arts"; students use traditional printing techniques and technologies to produce books and other printed artifacts.

Civic engagement is a major component of the curriculum. Students are required to take six credits of civic engagement courses, which involve substantial community-based work. Experience and interest in engaged learning is a major consideration in faculty hiring practices, and the College has a full-time professional staff member devoted to supporting engagement across the curriculum. Faculty routinely look for ways to connect their courses to public contexts. One visual arts workshop, for instance, traveled to public spaces surrounding Michigan's capitol building to stencil socially-minded visual compositions on the sidewalks. The students used a mixture of soil and water to create a nondestructive pigment that would not permanently deface public property. Instead of making art that remained locked away in a gallery, these students designed visual compositions appropriate for public venues.

The curriculum of the RCAH encourages students to respect the knowledge and skill sets of experts and professionals; faculty and artists in residence demonstrate the importance of long-term formal study within officially credentialed programs (such as MFA programs in studio art). At the same time, students are encouraged to experiment and to engage in self-sponsored learning. Students create films and photo essays even though they are not film or photography majors. This reinforces the possibilities associated with stepping outside culturally prescribed categories of expertise.

The infrastructural resources of the College are designed to support productive curricular and cocurricular experiences. For instance, the College's Language and Media Center provides a wide range of resources for language learning and media production: specialized workstations, media production software, cameras, camcorders, microphones, a large-format printer, a suite of spaces for collaboration, and more. The LMC is staffed by knowledgeable peer consultants who provide just-in-time support for students working in the Center on both curricular and self-sponsored projects.

Across the hall from the LMC is an Art Studio equipped with printing presses, paint, large worktables, and other resources for "old media" production. Students routinely move back and forth between these spaces as they work on projects that combine old and new media elements. The College includes lounges, conference rooms, and other informal spaces for discussion and collaboration. Students can exhibit and perform compositions in a variety of formal and informal spaces, including an art gallery, theater, glass display cases, and bulletin boards. All of these spaces of the College are in the same building where students live and are integrated into students' daily living and learning routines. Collaboration and cultural production are part of the fabric of daily life in the College. Walking through the corridors of the RCAH, even late at night, one is likely to encounter art exhibits, performances, readings, jam sessions, and students working on many different kinds of media projects, from posters to quilts.

We feel that a writing class focused on "the production of culture" has more traction as part of a broader curriculum and institutional setting of the sort provided by the RCAH. In this setting, a model of rhetorical practice that emphasizes the way multiple modes and media can be recruited to effect social change is reinforced and expanded by subsequent experiences as students navigate through the four-year curriculum. Moreover, a technology-rich, resource-rich, living-learning community supports an understanding of rhetoric as a social practice involving the orchestration of multiple modes, media, technologies, compositions, raw materials, and people.

Obviously the RCAH illustrates only one approach to preparing students to be makers of culture—one that would only be appropriate for certain contexts—but the key ingredients in this approach are worth thinking about: multimodal composing across the curriculum; a serious commitment to connecting rhetorical practices to community settings; ample infrastructural resources that support a wide variety of forms of cultural production; and a living-learning community that fosters peer-to-peer collaboration within a resource-rich environment. These ingredients are adaptable to many different contexts.

Conclusion: Habitual Publicity

We began this book by looking at the question of access. Drawing on the work of Don Slater and others, we suggested that rhetorical modes, media, and technologies are never simply *there*, never merely available to us. Instead, many different material and cultural dynamics enable certain opportunities and foreclose others. Is the camera a tool for engaging publics or is it a tool for capturing personal moments with friends and family? Is a 3D printer a newfangled gadget for geeks or an important tool for engaging in the production of culture? We suggested that sites of education in general, and the composition classroom in particular, have a role to play in quickening students to the public possibilities of rhetorical tools, broadly conceived. The rhetorics of digital video, 3D fabricated objects, immersive virtual reality environments, live musical performances, and more can all potentially serve a public sphere that embraces poesis.

More specifically, we suggested that sites of rhetorical education should open up four broad areas of critical reflection: should help students explore the *semiotic potentials, infrastructural accessibility, cultural position*, and practices of *de/specialization* associated with available rhetorical modes, media, and technologies. The pedagogy that we outline in this chapter is one attempt to open up these lines of inquiry. In the approach we outline above, no single mode, medium, or genre is privileged. Instead, students explore a wide range of rhetorical practices. Sophisticated academic critique (represented by journal articles) intermingles in the classroom with the rhetorics of the D Brand and *The Meatrix*. Students use their own imaginations to build on and expand available models, engaging in their own forms of cultural production. In the process of this critique and production, there are many opportunities to engage students in reflective discussions about what different rhetorical forms can do (*semiotic potentials*) and who values them (*cultural position*).

Readings like Gershenfeld's *Fab* help students think critically about the shifting dynamics of *infrastructural accessibility* and practices of *de/specialization*. Gershenfeld concretely and compellingly rehearses how contemporary culture has convinced itself that only industrial designers and engineers own the rhetoric of 3D fabricated objects, but this limited understanding of specialization is not inevitable. Developments like 3D printers allow all of us to design and manufacture toys, sculptures, tools, furniture, models, and many other forms of material culture. Gershenfeld helps us question our assumptions about what we can and can't do.

More importantly, asking students to plan and implement a multimodal-rhetorical campaign of their own involves them in the process of learning how to use new hardware and software, new interfaces and tools. They learn that they can learn. They discover that creative problem solving, perseverance, the help of knowledgeable peers, and the thorough assessment of resources enable them to push the boundaries of what forms of rhetorical production are *infrastructurally accessible* and what they are authorized to produce as *nonspecialists.* The Public Knowledge open house for first-year composition students contains many examples of multifaceted, multimodal campaigns like Mark's that demonstrate the results of students' inquiries into *semiotic potentials, infrastructural accessibility, cultural position,* and practices of *specialization.*

Obviously, in presenting our sketch of one class embedded within one institutional context, we are not attempting to impose a single approach on all teachers in all contexts. Every class needs to be designed with its own programmatic and institutional contexts in mind. A course developed for arts and humanities majors at MSU will need to be adapted. We hope that the broader principles that we have outlined in this book provide a foundation for that work.

Notes

1. In her footnote for the term, Fraser explains that she derives "subaltern counterpublic" by combining Gayatri Spivak's "subaltern" and Rita Felski's "counterpublic" (79).

2. For a summary of how nonverbal aurality functions in spoken performances, see McKee.

3. At this point, the literature on multimodality (and the related topics of visuality, aurality, multimediality, etc.) in composition-rhetoric and related fields is quite expansive, and we do not offer a comprehensive bibliography here. In the last sections of chapter 2, we offer a meta-analysis of scholarship that examines the way the field confronts new modalities, finding four topoi that, we argue, can serve a heuristic function. As evidenced by references throughout the book, our thinking has been particularly shaped by the work of Kevin Michael DeLuca, Dànielle Nicole DeVoss, Gunther Kress, Jody Shipka, and Anne Frances Wysocki. We have also found it useful to examine work on multimodal rhetorics in legal studies, visual anthropology, film studies, and media studies.

4. Paula Mathieu credits Stuart Brown for this phrase (23). Like work on multimodal rhetoric, the work on public rhetoric is too expansive to summarize here. Recent work on public rhetoric in composition studies includes Eberly; Edbauer Rice; Ervin; Flower; Long; Mathieu; Mathieu and George; Weisser; N. Welch; Wells.

5. "Lay actor" and related phrases like "ordinary" or "everyday" people, while somewhat awkward, are nevertheless important theoretical terms. In exploring the public sphere, it is useful to distinguish between lay actors and various specialists. One kind of specialist is comprised of those with an unusual amount of technical knowledge about a particular issue or topic (e.g., a climatologist who talks about global warming). Political systems in which experts hold power are sometimes referred to as "technocracies" (see Roberts-Miller 37). Official state actors are a different kind of specialist. The public sphere is often defined as the social space from which ordinary citizens (as distinct from state officials) exert pressure on the state (Warner 68). In this book, we are also interested in the distinction between lay actors and yet another kind of specialist—the creative professional. Creative professionals—such as graphic designers, illustrators, and filmmakers—are typically

(though not always) credentialed in formal and informal ways. They often have specialized degrees and training regimens. Graphic designers, for instance, often hold BFAs. At Michigan State University a student majoring in graphic design must take "foundational" courses (e.g., "Drawing I," "Color and Design") as well as "distribution" and "concentration" courses (e.g., "Typography I," "Three-Dimensional Design") ("Bachelor"). These distinctions are not, of course, absolute. Clearly there are professional graphic designers who don't hold BFAs. We are talking about broad trends. In chapter 2 we explore the need to critique discourses of specialization as an important precondition for multimodal public rhetoric.

6. See Sheridan, "Fabricating," for a fuller discussion of three-dimensional fabricated rhetoric.

7. Yates and Orlikowski credit for the record of this speech the account of Dorothy Height, chair of the National Council of Negro Women, who was interviewed on National Public Radio's *Morning Edition*, February 27, 1998.

8. A version of this heuristic appeared in Sheridan, "Fabricating Consent: Three-Dimensional Objects as Rhetorical Compositions."

9. Jim originally produced this video as a graduate student enrolled in Ellen Cushman's Multimedia Writing Class. Cushman and colleagues have written about the way student experiences in this course force us to rethink our understanding of "writing" (DeVoss, Cushman, and Grabill).

10. A number of writers allude to a similar decision making process, though usually only in passing (see, for instance, Hess 32–35; Kress "Gains" 19; Wysocki and Lynch). We discuss Jody Shipka's exploration of this decision making at some length in chapter 5.

11. For discussions of materiality, see Selzer and Crowley (especially contributions by Blair and by Faigley); Wysocki, "Opening."

12. Fleckenstein, et al. trace ecological approaches to writing back to Gregory Bateson, whose work influenced both Louise Rosenblatt's "transactional" model of reading and David Barton's *Literacy: An Introduction to the Ecology of Written Language.*

13. James Jasinski offers a useful summary of the literature on rhetoric and *contingency* in his *Sourcebook on Rhetoric: Key Concepts in Contemporary Rhetorical Studies.*

14. The very concept of Sendamessage.nl also raises serious questions about the role of the separation barrier and the Israeli-Palestinian conflict. There are also serious ethical questions involved in paying someone (potentially halfway around the world) to take dangerous physical and legal risks for personal amusement. We think scholars need to pay more explicit attention to distributed composing examples such as these.

15. At the time of writing this chapter we were unable to locate a trending topic on Twitter that had not been appropriated for discussions or advertising promotions of other topics and services.

16. Following the event, on April 5, 2005, the student groups involved in the protest were notified at an MSU Board of Trustee's meeting that the university intended to join the WRC (Davis).

17. For one attempt to examine pedagogy through a Warnerian lens, see Ronald Walter Greene.

18. Geisler summarizes conversations at the 2003 meeting of the Alliance of Rhetoric Societies that focused on the question, "How ought we to understand rhetorical agency?" *Philosophy and Rhetoric* devoted a special issue to the topic of agency (see Hauser). In addition to the works we cite in our own discussion, see Gaonkar; C. Miller, "What"; Sowards. See also Jasinski's discussion of "contingency."

19. Here Trimbur, arriving by a very different route, comes close to Warner's conception of the public sphere. Trimbur and Warner both locate the possibility of social transformation in our ability to operationalize new practices of textual production, circulation, and consumption.

20. We are grateful to one of the reviewers of our manuscript for encouraging us to clarify this distinction.

21. Take a look at the Write For Your Life (WFYL) program, in which students wrote grant proposals, submitted those proposals to program coordinators, and, when appropriate, received funding to implement their proposed projects (Swenson).

22. "I think we should call 'new media texts' those that have been made by composers who are aware of the range of materialities of texts and who then highlight the materiality: such composers design texts that help readers/consumers/viewers stay alert to how any text—like its composers and readers—doesn't function independently of how it is made and in what contexts. Such composers design texts that make as overtly visible as possible the values they embody" (Wysocki, "Opening" 15).

23. For general discussions of remix, see Lessig; P. D. Miller. Remix has been a popular topic in composition studies in recent years (see, for instance, DeVoss and Webb; digirhet; Johnson-Eilola and Selber; J. Rice). Dubisar and Palmeri offer a useful discussion of remix in the composition classroom and include a thorough bibliography of works that address the issue.

24. 2 Live Crew's "Pretty Woman" has been discussed by Woodmansee and Jaszi, among others.

25. For discussions of how the city of Detroit is constructed by dominant discourses, see Herron; Marback; Sheridan, "Narrative."

26. Gwendolyn D. Pough draws on the expanded model of the public sphere outlined in *The Black Public Sphere* in order to develop a foundation for her discussion of how examining the Black Panther Party in a writing-

intensive classroom can help students create "their own empowering rhetorics" (466).

27. For other explorations of the public sphere that draw on poesis, see Ivie, "Rhetorical"; Young, "Activist." In his excellent review essay, "Reason and Passion in the Public Sphere," John L. Brook reviews multiple historical studies of public-sphere practices that would fall under the category of poesis, as we define it here.

28. We are grateful to Michael Leff and Andrew Sachs's "Words the Most Like Things: Iconicity and the Rhetorical Text" for introducing us to the work of Fisher, Ivie, and Osborn.

Works Cited

"About." *360degrees: Perspectives on the U.S. Criminal Justice System.* Web. 1 February 2006.

Acuff-Rose Music, Inc. v. Campbell. No. 91–6225. United States Court of Appeals, Sixth Circuit. 1992. Open Jurist. Web. 20 June 2011.

Adbusters. "First Things First Manifesto 2000." *Emigre.* Web. 23 December 2009.

Adler-Kassner, Linda, and Heidi Estrem. "Reaching Out from the Writing Classroom: Research Writing as a Situated, Public Act." *Writing in Context(s): Textual Practices and Learning Processes in Sociocultural Settings.* Ed. Triantafillia Kostouli. Studies in Writing 15. New York: Springer, 2005. 229–46.

Allen, Nancy. "Ethics and Visual Rhetorics: Seeing Is Not Believing Anymore." *Technical Communication Quarterly* 5.1 (1996): 87–105. Print.

Alsultany, Evelyn. "Selling American Diversity and Muslim American Identity through Nonprofit Advertising Post-9/11." *American Quarterly* 59.3 (2007): 593–622. Print.

Anderson, Daniel. "Prosumer Approaches to New Media Composition: Consumption and Production in Continuum." *Kairos: A Journal of Rhetoric, Technology, and Pedagogy* 8.1 (2003): n. pag. Web. 20 June 2011.

Armstrong, Mark Robertson. *Emotional Eloquence: The Argument from Pathos in Deliberation.* Diss. U of North Carolina at Greensboro, 1996. Print.

Asen, Robert, and Daniel C. Brouwer. *Counterpublics and the State.* New York: SUNY P, 2001. Print.

"Bachelor of Fine Arts Studio Art Program." Department of Art and Art History. Michigan State University. 2010. Web. 15 January 2011.

Bagdikian, Ben H. *The Media Monopoly.* Boston, MA: Beacon P, 1983. Print.

Baker, Houston A., Jr. "Critical Memory and the Black Public Sphere." *The Black Public Sphere: A Public Culture Book.* Ed. Black Public Sphere Collective. Chicago: U of Chicago P, 1995. 7–37. Print.

Barton, David. *Literacy: An Introduction to the Ecology of Written Language.* Oxford: Blackwell, 1994. Print.

Barthes, Roland. "Rhetoric of the Image." *Image—Music—Text.* Trans. Stephen Heath. New York: Hill and Wang, 1988. 32–51. Print.

Bazerman, Charles. *Constructing Experience.* Carbondale and Edwardsville: Southern Illinois UP, 1994. Print.

Benhabib, Seyla. "The Utopian Dimension in Communicative Ethics." *New German Critique* 35 (1985): 83–96. Print.

Berger, Arthur Asa. *Seeing Is Believing: An Introduction to Visual Communication.* 2nd ed. Mountain View, CA: Mayfield, 1989. Print.

Berlin, James A. *Rhetorics, Poetics, and Cultures: Refiguring College English Studies.* West Lafayette, IN: Parlor, 2003. Print.

Bettini, Maurizio. "Preface." *Poet, Public, and Performance in Ancient Greece.* Ed. Lowell Edmunds and Robert W. Wallace. Baltimore: Johns Hopkins UP, 1997. vii-xiii. Print.

Bianculli, David. "Down on the 'Boardwalk' with Terence Winter." *Fresh Air.* 28 Sept. 2010. Web. 18 January 2012.

Bitzer, Lloyd. "The Rhetorical Situation." *Philosophy and Rhetoric* 1.1 (1968): 1–14. Print.

Black, Max. "Metaphor." *Philosophical Perspectives on Metaphor.* Ed. Mark Johnson. Minneapolis: U of Minnesota P, 1981. 63–82. Print.

Blair, Carole. "Contemporary U.S. Memorial Sites as Exemplars of Rhetoric's Materiality." *Rhetorical Bodies.* Ed. Jack Selzer and Sharon Crowley. Madison: U of Wisconsin P, 1999. 16–57. Print.

Blakesley, David. "Defining Film Rhetoric: The Case of Hitchcock's *Vertigo.*" *Defining Visual Rhetorics.* Ed. Charles A. Hill and Marguerite Helmers. Mahawah, NJ: Erlbaum, 2004: 111–134. Print.

Blaustein, Jessica. "How Publics Matter: A Handbook for Alternative World-Making." Rev. of *Publics and Counterpublics,* Michael Warner. *American Quarterly* 56.1 (2004): 171–181. Print.

"Blind Date." Detroit Metro Convention & Visitors Bureau. visitdetroit. com. 2012. Web. 18 January 2012.

Blumrich, Eric. "Grand Theft America." 2003. Web.

Booth, Wayne C., and Marshall W. Gregory. *The Harper & Row Rhetoric: Writing as Thinking, Thinking as Writing.* New York: Harper and Row, 1988. Print.

Bourdieu, Pierre, and Randal Johnson. *The Field of Cultural Production: Essays on Art and Literature.* New York: Columbia UP, 1993. Print.

Brecht, Bertolt. "The Radio as an Apparatus of Communication." *Communication for Social Change Anthology: Historical and Contemporary Readings.* Ed. Alfonso Gumucio Dagron and Thomas Tufte. South Orange, NJ: Communication for Social Change Consortium, 2006. Print.

Brooke, John L. "Reason and Passion in the Public Sphere: Habermas and the Cultural Historians." *Journal of Interdisciplinary History* 29.1 (1998): 43–67. Print.

Brouwer, Daniel C., and Robert Asen. *Public Modalities: Rhetoric, Culture, Media, and the Shape of Public Life.* Tuscaloosa: U Alabama P, 2010. Print.

Buchanan, Richard. "Declaration by Design: Rhetoric, Argument, and Demonstration in Design Practices." *Design Discourse: History, Theory, Criticism.* Ed. Victor Margolin. Chicago: U Chicago P, 1989. 91–109. Print.

Burgin, Victor. "Looking at Photographs." *Thinking Photography.* London: Macmillan, 1982. 142–53. Print.

Burke, Kenneth. *A Rhetoric of Motives.* Berkeley: U of California P, 1969. Print.

Caldwell, Lt. Gen. William B., IV. "A Soldier Interacting, Without Mediation." Interview by Mike Edwards and D. Alexis Hart. *Kairos: A Journal of Rhetoric, Technology, and Pedagogy* 14.3 (2010): n. pag. Web. 20 June 2011.

Calhoun, Craig J. "Introduction: Habermas and the Public Sphere." *Habermas and the Public Sphere.* Ed. Craig J. Calhoun. Cambridge: MIT P, 1992. 1–48. Print.

—. "Rethinking the Public Sphere." *Presentation to the Ford Foundation.* 7 Feb. 2005. Web. 20 June 2011.

Carney, Brian, and Neal Feigenson. "Visual Persuasion in the Michael Skakel Trial: Enhancing Advocacy through Interactive Media Presentations." *Criminal Justice Magazine* 19.1 (2004): n. pag. Web. 20 June 2011.

CCCC. "Students' Right to Their Own Language." *College Composition and Communication* 25.3 (1974): 2–3. Print.

Chaudhuri, Arjun, and Ross Buck. "Media Differences in Rational and Emotional Responses to Advertising." *Journal of Broadcasting and Electronic Media* 39 (1995): 109–25. Print.

Chion, Michel. *Audio-Vision: Sound on Screen.* New York: Columbia UP, 1994. Print.

Christoph, Julie Nelson. "Reconceiving Ethos in Relation to the Personal: Strategies of Placement in Pioneer Women's Writing." *College English* 64.6 (2002): 660–679. Print.

"Com-." *Oxford English Dictionary.* 2nd ed. Oxford: Oxford UP, 1989. Web. 15 Jan. 2011.

Connecticut v. Skakel. "Brief of the State of Connecticut/Appellee." Supreme Court of the State of Connecticut. S.C. 16844. State of Connecticut Division of Criminal Justice. Web. 20 January 2009.

Consigny, Scott. "Rhetoric and Its Situations." *Philosophy and Rhetoric* 7 (1974): 175–86. Print.

"Contingency." The *Oxford English Dictionary.* 2nd ed. Oxford: Oxford UP, 1989. Web. 15 Jan. 2011.

"Contingent." The *Oxford English Dictionary.* 2nd ed. Oxford: Oxford UP, 1989. Web. 15 Jan. 2011.

Cooper, Marilyn M. "The Ecology of Writing." *College English* 48.4 (1986): 364–75. Print.

Corbett, Edward P. J. "The Rhetoric of the Open Hand and the Rhetoric of the Closed Fist." *College Composition and Communication* 20.5 (1969): 288–96. Print.

Craddock, Linda. "One on One with Chris Caldovino." *HoboTrashcan*. 31 May 2007. Web. 23 January 2012.

Cramer, Janet M. "Discourses of Sexual Morality in *Sex and the City* and *Queer as Folk*." *Journal of Popular Culture* 40.3 (2007): 409–432. Print.

Crowley, Sharon. Rev. Phillip Sipiora and James S. Baumlin, eds. *Rhetoric and Kairos: Essays in History, Theory, and Praxis. Rhetoric Review* 22.1 (2003): 82–85. Print.

Cussins, Charis. "Ontological Choreography: Agency through Objectification in
Infertility Clinics." *Social Studies of Science* 26 (1996): 575–610. Print.

Davey, Andy. "Model Behavior." *Design Week.* (27 February 2003): 16–17. Web. 15 June 2009.

Davis, Amy. "MSU joins group for workers' rights." *The State News.* 5 April 2005. 3 March 2006. Web.

Dean, Jodi. "Why the Net Is Not a Public Sphere." *Constellations* 10.1 (2003): 95–112. Print.

DeLuca, Kevin Michael. *Image Politics: The New Rhetoric of Environmental Activism.* New York: Guilford P, 1999. Print.

Detroit Metro Convention & Visitors Bureau. visitdetroit.com. 2012. Web. 23 January 2012.

DeVoss, Dànielle Nicole, and Suzanne Webb. "Media Convergence: Grand Theft Audio: Negotiating Copyright as Composers." *Computers and Composition* 25.1 (2008): 79–103. Print.

DeVoss, Dànielle Nicole, and Cynthia L. Selfe. "'This Page Is under Construction': Reading Women Shaping Online Identities." *Pedagogy: Critical Approaches to Teaching Literature, Language, Composition, and Culture* 2.1 (2002): 31–49. Print.

DeVoss, Dànielle Nicole, Ellen Cushman, and Jeffrey T. Grabill. "Infrastructure and Composing: The *When* of New-Media Writing." *College Composition and Communication* 57.1 (2005): 14–44. Print.

Dias, Patrick, et al. *Worlds Apart: Acting and Writing in Academic and Workplace Contexts.* Mahwah, NJ: Erlbaum, 1999. Print.

digirhet. "Old + Old + Old = New." *Kairos: A Journal of Rhetoric, Technology, and Pedagogy* 12.3 (2008): n. pag. Web. 20 June 2011.

Dobrin, Sidney I., and Christian R. Weisser. *Natural Discourse: Toward Ecocomposition.* Albany: SUNY P, 2002. Print.

Dragga, Sam. "The Ethics of Delivery." *Rhetorical Memory and Delivery: Classical Concepts for Contemporary Composition and Communication.* Ed. John Frederick Reynolds. Hillsdale, NJ: Erlbaum, 1993. 79–95. Print.

Dubisar, Abby M., and Jason Palmeri. "Palin/Pathos/Peter Griffin: Political Video Remix and Composition Pedagogy." *Computers and Composition* 27.2 (2010): 77–93. Print.

Eberly, Rosa A. "'Everywhere You Go It's There': Forgetting and Remembering the University of Texas Tower Shootings." *Framing Public Memory.* Ed. Kendall R. Phillips. Tuscaloosa: U Alabama P, 2004. 65–88. Print.

—. "From *Writers, Audiences,* and *Communities* to *Publics*: Writing Classrooms as Protopublic Spaces." *Rhetoric Review* 18.1 (1999): 165–78. Print.

—. "Rhetoric and the Anti-Logos Doughball: Teaching Deliberating Bodies the Practices of Participatory Democracy." *Rhetoric & Public Affairs* 5.2 (2002): 287–300. Print.

Eco, Umberto. "Critique of the Image." *Thinking Photography.* Ed. Victor Burgin. London: Macmillan, 1982. 32–38. Print.

Edbauer, Jenny. (See Rice, Jenny Edbauer.)

"Edgy Ads Promote Detroit." *Crain's Detroit Business,* 10 February 2008. Web. 20 June 2011.

Enzensberger, Hans Magnus, and Michael Roloff. *The Consciousness Industry: On Literature, Politics and the Media.* New York: Seabury P, 1974. Print.

Ervin, Elizabeth. "Encouraging Civic Participation among First-Year Writing Students; or, Why Composition Class Should Be More like a Bowling Team." *Rhetoric Review* 15.2 (1997): 382–399. Print.

Eyman, Douglas Andrew. "Digital Rhetoric: Ecologies and Economics of Digital Circulation." Diss. Michigan State University, 2007. Print.

Feigenson, Neal, and Meghan A. Dunn. "New Visual Technologies in Court: Directions for Research." *Law and Human Behavior* 27.1 (2003): 109–26. Print.

Feigenson, Neal, and Richard K. Sherwin. "Thinking Beyond the Shown: Implicit Inferences in Evidence and Argument." *Law, Probability and Risk* 6 (2007): 295–310. Print.

Felski, Rita. *Beyond Feminist Aesthetics.* Cambridge, MA: Harvard UP, 1989. Print.

Fisher, Walter R. "Narration as a Human Communication Paradigm: The Case of Public Moral Argument." *Communication Monographs* 51 (1984): 1–22. Print.

Fleckenstein, Kristie S., Clay Spinuzzi, Rebecca J. Rickly, and Carole Clark Papper. "The Importance of Harmony: An Ecological Metaphor for Writing Research." *College Composition and Communication* 60.2 (2008): 388–419. Print.

Flower, Linda. *Community Literacy and the Rhetoric of Public Engagement.* Carbondale: Southern Illinois UP, 2008. Print.

Fraser, Nancy. "Rethinking the Public Sphere: A Contribution to the Critique of Actually Existing Democracy." *Social Text* 25/26 (1990): 56–80. Print.

Freedman, Aviva, Christine Adam, and Graham Smart. "Wearing Suits to Class: Simulating Genres and Simulations as Genre." *Written Communication* 11 (1994): 193–226. Print.

Fulkerson, Richard. *Teaching the Argument in Writing*. Urbana, IL: NCTE, 1996. Print.

Gaonkar, Dilip Parameshwar. "The Idea of Rhetoric in the Rhetoric of Science." *The Southern Communication Journal* 58.4 (1993): 258–95. Print.

Garland, Ken. "First Things First." *Looking Closer 3: Classic Writings on Graphic Design*. Ed. Michael Bierut, et al. New York: Allworth P, 1999. 283. Print.

Garnham, Nicholas. "The Media and the Public Sphere." *Habermas and the Public Sphere*. Ed. Craig J. Calhoun. Cambridge: MIT P, 1992. 359–376. Print.

Gayford, Martin. "The Mind's Eye." *Technology Review*. September/October 2011. Web. 24 September 2011.

Geary, James. *The World in a Phrase: A Brief History of the Aphorism*. New York: Bloomsbury, 2005. Print.

Geisler, Cheryl. "How Ought We to Understand the Concept of Rhetorical Agency? Report from the ARS." *Rhetoric Society Quarterly* 34.3 (2004): 9–17. Print.

Gentili, Bruno. *Poetry and Its Public in Ancient Greece: From Homer to the Fifth Century*. Baltimore, MD: Johns Hopkins UP, 1988. Print.

George, Diana. "From Analysis to Design: Visual Communication in the Teaching of Writing." *College Composition and Communication* 54 (2002): 11–38. Print.

—. "Wonder of It All: Computers, Writing Centers, and the New World." *Computers and Composition* 12 (1995): 331–34. Print.

Gershenfeld, Neil A. *Fab: The Coming Revolution on Your Desktop—from Personal Computers to Personal Fabrication*. New York: Basic Books, 2005. Print.

Glaser, Milton, and Mirko Ilic. *The Design of Dissent*. Gloucester, MA: Rockport, 2005. Print.

González, Jennifer A. "Rhetoric of the Object: Material Memory and the Artwork of Amalia Mesa-Bains." *Visual Anthropology Review* 9.1 (1993): 82–91. Print.

—. "Morphologies: Race as a Visual Technology." *Only Skin Deep: Changing Visions of the American Self*. Ed. Coco Fusco and Brian Wallis. New York: International Center of Photography in association with H N Abrams, 2003. 379–393. Print.

Goodnight, G. Thomas. "A 'New Rhetoric' For A "New Dialectic": Prolegomena to a Responsible Public Argument." *Argumentation* 7 (1993): 329-42.

Graas, David. *Not a Box.* 2007. Web. 27 December 2010.

GRACE and Free Range Studios. "The Meatrix." 2003. Web. 20 June 2011.

Graham, Ted, Sam Boardman, and David Pearson, eds. *Advancing Maths for AQA: Mechanics 1 (M1).* 2nd ed. Oxford: Pearson Education, 2004. Print.

Grandmont Rosedale Development Corporation. (2003). Web. 26 December 2003.

Greene, Ronald Walter. "Rhetorical Pedagogy as a Postal System: Circulating Subjects through Michael Warner's 'Publics and Counterpublics.'" *Quarterly Journal of Speech.* 88.4: 434–443. Print.

Grier, Katherine C. "Material Culture as Rhetoric: 'Animal Artifacts' as a Case Study." *American Material Culture: The Shape of the Field.* Ed. Ann Smart Martin and J. Ritchie Garrison. Knoxville: Henry Francis du Pont Winterthur Museum; Distributed by U Tennessee P, 1997. 65–104. Print.

Griffioen, James D. "But Where Do You Shop (for Thanksgiving)?" *Sweet Juniper.* 25 November 2010. Web. 20 June 2011.

—. "Honey Bee Market La Colmena, Est. 1956." *Sweet Juniper.* 27 May 2010. Web. 20 June 2011.

—. "Yes There Are Grocery Stores in Detroit." *Urbanophile.* 25 January 25 2011. Web. 20 June 2011.

Gross, Alan G. "Presence as Argument in the Public Sphere." *Rhetoric Society Quarterly* 35.2 (2005): 5–21. Print.

Grossman, Bathsheba. Bathsheba Sculpture LLC. Web. 23 January 2012.

Gvion, Liora, and Naomi Trostler. "From Spaghetti and Meatballs through Hawaiian Pizza to Sushi: The Changing Nature of Ethnicity in American Restaurants." *The Journal of Popular Culture* 41.6 (2008): 950–974. Print.

Haas, Angela M. "Wampum as Hypertext: An American Indian Intellectual Tradition of Multimedia Theory and Practice." *Studies in American Indian Literatures* 19.4 (2007): 77–100. Print.

Haas, Christina, and Christine M. Neuwirth. "Writing the Technology That Writes Us: Research on Literacy and the Shape of Technology." Ed. Cynthia L. Selfe and Susan Hilligoss. *Literacy and Computers: The Complications of Teaching and Learning with Technology.* New York: MLA, 1994. 319–335. Print.

Habermas, Jürgen. *Moral Consciousness and Communicative Action.* Studies in Contemporary German Social Thought. Cambridge: MIT P, 1990. Print.

—. *The Structural Transformation of the Public Sphere: An Inquiry into a Category of Bourgeois Society.* Cambridge: MIT P. Print.

Hacker, Kenneth L., and Jan van Dijk. *Digital Democracy: Issues of Theory and Practice.* London, Thousand Oaks, CA: SAGE, 2000. Print.

Hague, Barry N., and Brian Loader. *Digital Democracy: Discourse and Decision Making in the Information Age.* London: Routledge, 1999. Print.

Halbritter, Bump, and Todd Taylor. "Remembering Composition (The Book): A DVD Production." *JAC* 26.3–4 (2006): 389–396. Print.

Hariman, Robert, and John Louis Lucaites. *No Caption Needed: Iconic Photographs, Public Culture, and Liberal Democracy.* Chicago: U of Chicago P, 2007. Print.

Harris, Michael D. *Colored Pictures: Race and Visual Representation.* Chapel Hill: U of North Carolina P, 2003. Print.

Hauser, Gerard A. "Editor's Introduction." *Philosophy and Rhetoric* 37.3 (2004): 181–87. Print.

—. *Vernacular Voices: The Rhetoric of Publics and Public Spheres.* Columbia: U of South Carolina P, 1999. Print.

Hawisher, Gail E., and Patricia A. Sullivan. "Fleeting Images: Women Visually Writing the Web." *Passions, Pedagogies, and 21st Century Technologies.* Ed. Gail E. Hawisher and Cynthia L. Selfe. Urbana, IL: National Council of Teachers of English, 1997. 268–91. Print.

Hawk, Byron. "The Shape of Rhetoric to Come: Musical *Worlding* as Public Rhetoric." *Pre/Text* 20.1–4 (2010): 7–42. Print.

Hebdige, Dick. *Subculture, the Meaning of Style.* London: Methuen, 1979. Print.

Henderson, Tom. "Bureau Webinar to Show How to Use 'D' Branding to Help with Marketing." *Crain's Detroit Business* (9 July 2007): 17. LexisNexis. Web. 20 June 2011.

Herman, Edward S., and Noam Chomsky. *Manufacturing Consent: The Political Economy of the Mass Media.* New York: Pantheon Books, 2002. Print.

Herndl, Carl G., and Adela C. Licona. "Shifting Agency: Agency, *Kairos*, and the Possibilities of Social Action." *Communicative Practices in Workplaces and the Professions: Cultural Perspectives on the Regulation of Discourse and Organizations.* Ed. Mark Zachry and Charlotte Thralls. Amityville, NY: Baywood Publishing Company, 2007. Print.

Herron, Jerry. *Afterculture: Detroit and the Humiliation of History.* Detroit, MI: Wayne State UP, 1993. Print.

Hesse, Douglas D. "2005 CCCC Chair's Address: Who Owns Writing?" *College Composition and Communication* 57.2 (2005): 335–57. Print.

Hill, Charles A. "The Psychology of Rhetorical Images." *Defining Visual Rhetorics.* Ed. Charles A. Hill and Marguerite Helmers. Mahwah, NJ: Erlbaum, 2004: 25–40. Print.

Hine, Lewis. "Social Photography." *Classic Essays on Photography.* Ed. Alan Trachtenberg. New Haven, CT: Leetes Island Books, 1981. 109–13. Print.

Howley, Kevin. *Community Media: People, Places, and Communication Technologies.* Cambridge: Cambridge UP, 2005. Print.

Hughes, Joseph J. "Kairos and Decorum: Crassus Orator's Speech De Lege Servilia." *Rhetoric and Kairos: Essays in History, Theory, and Praxis.* Ed. Phillip Sipiora and James S. Baumlin. Albany: SUNY P, 2002. 129–137. Print.

Iedema, Rick. "Multimodality, Resemiotization: Extending the Analysis of Discourse as Multi-Semiotic Practice." *Visual Communication* 2.1 (2003): 29–57. Print.

"Inspiring Possibilities: The Power of the D Brand." October 2007. Detroit Metro Convention & Visitors Bureau. visitdetroit.com. Web. 20 June 2011.

Ivie, Robert L. "Metaphor and the Rhetorical Invention of Cold War 'Idealists.'" *Communication Monographs* 54 (1987): 165–82. Print.

—. "Rhetorical Deliberation and Democratic Politics in the Here and Now." *Rhetoric and Public Affairs* 5.2 (2002): 277–85. Print.

Jarman, Josh. "Taking a Stand: Students Push MSU to Support Workers' Rights." *The State News.* 25 February 2005. Web. 2 April 2009.

Jasinski, James. *Sourcebook on Rhetoric: Key Concepts in Contemporary Rhetorical Studies.* Thousand Oaks, CA: Sage, 2001. Print.

Jenkins, Henry. *Convergence Culture: Where Old and New Media Collide.* New York: New York UP, 2006. Print.

Johns, Adrian. *The Nature of the Book Print and Knowledge in the Making.* Chicago, IL: U of Chicago P, 2005. Print.

Johnson-Eilola, Johndan, and Stuart A. Selber. "Plagiarism, Originality, Assemblage." *Computers and Composition* 24.4 (2007): 375–403. Print.

Johnson, Randal. "Editor's Introduction: Pierre Bourdieu on Art, Literature and Culture." Pierre Bourdieu. *The Field of Cultural Production: Essays on Art and Literature.* New York: Columbia UP, 1993. 1–25. Print.

Jonsen, Albert R., and Stephen Toulmin. *The Abuse of Casuistry: A History of Moral Reasoning.* Berkeley: U California, 1988. Print.

Jowett, Garth, and Victoria O'Donnell. *Propaganda and Persuasion.* Thousand Oaks, CA: Sage Publications, 1999. Print.

Keane, John. "Democracy and the Media—Without Foundations." *Political Studies* 40 (1992): 116–29. Print.

Kellner, Douglas. "New Media and New Literacies: Reconstructing Education for the New Millennium." *Handbook of New Media: Social Shaping and Consequences of ICTs.* Ed. Leah A. Lievrouw and Sonia Livingstone. London: SAGE, 2002. Print. 90-104.

Kennerly, David H. "Essay: Chop and Crop." *Lens: Photography, Video and Visual Journalism.* 17 Sept. 2009. Web. 23 Sept. 2009.

Kenney, Keith. "Building Visual Communication Theory by Borrowing from Rhetoric." *Visual Rhetoric in a Digital World.* Ed. Carolyn Handa. New York: Bedford/St. Martin's, 2004. 321–343. Print.

Kienzler, Donna S. "Visual Ethics." *Journal of Business Communication* 34.2 (1997): 171–187. Print.

Kinneavy, James L. "Kairos: A Neglected Concept in Classical Rhetoric." *Rhetoric and Praxis: The Contribution of Classical Rhetoric to Practical Reasoning.* Ed. Jean Dietz Moss. Washington, DC: Catholic U of America P, 1986. 79–105. Print.

—. "Kairos Revisited: An Interview with James Kinneavy." Roger Thompson. *Rhetoric Review* 19.1/2 (2000): 73–88. Print.

Klein, Julie Thompson. *Interdisciplinarity: History, Theory, and Practice.* Detroit, MI: Wayne State UP, 1990. Print.

Kress, Gunther. "'English' at the Crossroads: Rethinking Curricula of Communication in the Context of the Turn to the Visual." *Passions, Pedagogies, and 21ˢᵗ Century Technologies.* Ed. Gail E. Hawisher and Cynthia Selfe. Logan: Utah State UP, 1999. 66–88. Print.

—. "Gains and Losses: New Forms of Texts, Knowledge, and Learning." *Computers and Composition* 22 (2005): 5–22. Print.

Kress, Gunther R., and Theo Van Leeuwen. *Multimodal Discourse: The Modes and Media of Contemporary Communication.* London: Oxford UP, 2001. Print.

La Brecque, Eric. "Creating Destination Detroit." *Detroiter Online.* 7 July 2008. Web. 20 June 2011.

—. "Metro Detroit Tourism Brand: Preliminary Findings 0.1b." Detroit Metro Convention & Visitors Bureau. visitdetroit.com. 5 Oct. 2006. Web. 20 June 2011.

Lanham, Richard A. *The Electronic Word: Democracy, Technology, and the Arts.* Chicago, IL: U of Chicago P, 1993. Print.

—. *A Handlist of Rhetorical Terms.* 2ⁿᵈ ed. Berkeley: U of California P, 1991. Print.

Lansing State Journal. "Demonstrators Shout, Dance, Urge MSU to Code: Students Protest for Human Rights." *Lansing State Journal.* 25 Feb. 2005. Web. 25 Feb. 2005.

Lasn, Kalle. *Design Anarchy.* Vancouver, BC: Adbusters, 2006. Print.

Latour, Bruno. "On Recalling ANT." *Actor Network Theory and After.* Ed. John Law and John Hassard. Oxford: Blackwell/Sociological Review, 1999. 15–25. Print.

—. "Where Are the Missing Masses? The Sociology of a Few Mundane Artifacts." *Technology and Society: Building Our Sociotechnical Future.* Ed. Debroah G. Johnson and Jameson M. Wetmore. Cambridge: MIT P, 2009. 151–79. Print.

Lauer, Janice M. "Persuasive Writing on Public Issues." *Composition in Context: Essays in Honor of Donald C. Stewart.* Ed. W. Ross Winterowd and Vincent Gillespie. Carbondale: Southern Illinois UP, 1994. 62–72. Print.

Law, John. "Notes on the Theory of the Actor Network: Ordering, Strategy and Heterogeneity." *Centre for Science Studies.* Lacaster, UK: Lancaster University, 1992. Web. 20 June 2011.

—. "On the Methods of Long-Distance Control: Vessels, Navigation and the Portuguese Route to India" *Power, Action, and Belief: A New Sociology of Knowledge?* Ed. John Law. London: Routledge & Kegan Paul, 1986. 234–63. Print.

Leff, Michael, and Andrew Sachs. "Words the Most Like Things: Iconicity and the Rhetorical Text." *Western Journal of Speech Communication* 54 (1990): 252–73. Print.

Lessig, Lawrence. *Remix: Making Art and Commerce Thrive in the Hybrid Economy.* New York: Penguin, 2008. Print.

Lippi-Green, Rosina. *English with an Accent: Language, Ideology, and Discrimination in the United States.* New York: Routledge, 1997. Print.

Long, Elenore. *Community Literacy and the Rhetoric of Local Publics.* West Lafayette, IN: Parlor, 2008. Print.

Louw, Eric. *The Media and Cultural Production.* London: Sage, 2001. Print.

Lowe, Charles. "Considerations for Creative Commons Licensing of Open Educational Resources: The Value of Copyleft." *Computers and Composition Online.* Fall (2010): n. pag. Web. 20 June 2011.

Lynch, Dennis A., Diana George, and Marilyn M. Cooper. "Moments of Argument: Agonistic Inquiry and Confrontational Cooperation." *College Composition and Communication* 48.1 (1997): 61–85. Print.

"Mac Expo 2005." Web. 3 February 2006.

MacAvoy, Leslie. "Rev. Habermas, Kristeva, and Citizenship." *The Journal of Speculative Philosophy* 17.2 (2003): 144–47. Print.

Mah, Harold. "Phantasies of the Public Sphere: Rethinking the Habermas of Historians." *The Journal of Modern History* 72.1 (2000): 153–82. Print.

Maira, Sunaina. "Belly Dancing: Arab-Face, Orientalist Feminism, and U.S. Empire." *American Quarterly* 60.2 (2008): 317–345. Print.

"Making Movies Roadshow." *George Negus Tonight.* 14 September 2004. Episode 126. Web. 20 June 2011.

Marback, Richard. "Detroit and the Closed Fist: Toward a Theory of Material Rhetoric." *Rhetoric Review* 17.1 (1998): 74–91. Print.

Mathieu, Paula. *Tactics of Hope: The Public Turn in English Composition.* Portsmouth, NH: Boynton/Cook, 2005. Print.

Mathieu, Paula, and Diana George. "*Not* Going It Alone: Public Writing, Independent Media, and the Circulation of Homeless Advocacy." *College Composition and Communication* 61.1 (2009): 130–49. Print.

McAfee, Noëlle. *Habermas, Kristeva, and Citizenship.* Ithaca, NY: Cornell UP, 2000. Print.

McCarthy, Thomas. "Introduction." Jürgen Habermas. *Moral Consciousness and Communicative Action.* Cambridge: MIT P, 1990. vii-xiii. Print.

McChesney, Robert W. *The Problem of Media: U.S. Communication Politics in the Twenty-First Century.* New York: Monthly Review P, 2004. Print.

McComiskey, Bruce. "Disassembling Plato's Critique of Rhetoric in the *Gorgias* (447a-466a)." *Rhetoric Review* 10.2 (1992): 205–16. Print.

—. "Visual Rhetoric and the New Public Discourse." *JAC* 24.1 (2004): 187–206. Print.

—. Rev. of *Rhetorical Bodies* Ed. Jack Selzer and Sharon Crowley. *JAC* 20.3 (2000): 699–703. Print.

—. *Teaching Composition as a Social Process.* Logan: Utah State UP, 2000. Print.

McCracken, Grant David. *Culture and Consumption: New Approaches to the Symbolic Character of Consumer Goods and Activities.* Bloomington: Indiana UP, 1988. Print.

McKee, Heidi. "Sound Matters: Notes Toward the Analysis and Design of Sound in Multimodal Webtexts." *Computers and Composition* 23 (2006): 335–354.

McQuiston, Liz. *Graphic Agitation 2: Social and Political Graphics in the Digital Age.* London: Phaidon, 2004. Print.

—. *Graphic Agitation: Social and Political Graphics Since the Sixties.* London: Phaidon, 1993. Print.

"Meet the Parents." Detroit Metro Convention & Visitors Bureau. visitdetroit.com. Web. 20 June 2011.

Messaris, Paul. *Visual Persuasion: The Role of Images in Advertising.* Thousand Oaks, CA: Sage, 1997. Print.

Micciche, Laura R. *Doing Emotion: Rhetoric, Writing, Teaching.* Portsmouth, NH: Boynton/Cook, 2007. Print.

Miller, Carolyn R. "Kairos in the Rhetoric of Science." *A Rhetoric of Doing: Essays on Written Discourse in Honor of James L. Kinneavy.* Ed. Neil Nakadate, Stephen P. Witte, and Roger D. Cherry. Carbondale: Southern Illinois UP, 1992. 310–27. Print.

—. "What Can Automation Tell Us About Agency?" *Rhetoric Society Quarterly* 37 (2007): 137–57. Print.

Miller, Paul D. (aka DJ Spooky that Subliminal Kid). *Rhythm Science.* Cambridge: Mediawork/MIT P, 2004. Print.

Miller, Susan. *Textual Carnivals: The Politics of Composition.* Carbondale: Southern Illinois UP, 1993. Print.

—. *Trust in Texts: A Different History of Rhetoric.* Carbondale: Southern Illinois UP, 2008. Print.

Mitchell, W. J. T. *Picture Theory: Essays on Verbal and Visual Representation.* Chicago, IL: U of Chicago P, 1994. Print.

Monroe, Barbara Jean. *Crossing the Digital Divide: Race, Writing, and Technology in the Classroom.* New York: Teachers College P, 2004. Print.

Morris, Glen E. "Desktop Manufacturing Hits the Home Market." *Advertising and Marketing Review.* 22 October 2008. Web. 21 May 2009.

The Moth: True Stories Told Live. Web. 24 September 2011.

Murphy, Joel. "One on One with Terence Winter." *HoboTrashcan.* 7 June 2007. Web. 20 June 2011.

National Council of Teachers of English. "The NCTE Definition of 21st-Century Literacies." 15 February 2008. Web. 18 August 2008.

National Institute on Media and the Family. *Who's in Charge?* Minneapolis, MN: Mediawise, 2007. Web. 18 August 2008.

New London Group. "A Pedagogy of Multiliteracies: Designing Social Futures." *Multiliteracies: Literacy Learning and the Design of Social Futures.* Ed. Bill Cope and Mary Kalantzis. New York: Routledge, 2000. 9–37. Print.

Norris, Pippa, ed. *Public Sentinel: News Media & Governance Reform.* Washington, DC: World Bank, 2009. Web. 20 June 2011.

Okrent, Daniel. "Notown." *Time* 174.13 (2009): 26. Print.

Onians, Richard Broxton. *The Origins of European Thought About the Body, the Mind, the Soul, the World, Time and Fate.* Cambridge: Cambridge UP, 1951. Print.

Orson, Diane. "Multimedia Display at Issue in Skakel Appeal." NPR. 4 Feb 2005. Web. 30 July 2008.

—. "Multimedia in the Courtroom." NPR. 20 November 2002. Web. 30 July 2008.

Osborn, Michael. "Rhetorical Depiction." *Form, Genre, and the Study of Political Discourse.* Ed. Herbert W. Simons and Aram A. Aghazarian. Columbia: U of South Carolina P, 1986. 79–107. Print.

Parr, Ben. "HOW TO: Retweet on Twitter." Social Media News and Web Tips—*Mashable—The Social Media Guide.* 16 April 2009. Web. 03 Sept. 2009.

Plato. *The Dialogues of Plato.* Trans. Benjamin Jowett. New York: Random House, 1920. Print.

Porter, James E. "Recovering Delivery for Digital Rhetoric." *Computers and Composition* 26.4 (2009): 207–24. Print.

—. *Rhetorical Ethics and Internetworked Writing.* Greenwich, CT: Ablex, 1998. Print.

Poster, Mark. "Cyberdemocracy: Internet and the public sphere." Ed. David Porter. *Internet Culture.* New York: Routledge, 1997. 202–217. Print.

Pough, Gwendolyn D. "Empowering Rhetoric: Black Students Writing Black Panthers." *College Composition and Communication* 53.3 (2002): 466–86. Print.

Prior, Paul. "Moving Multimodality Beyond the Binaries: A Response to Gunther Kress' 'Gains and Losses.'" *Computers and Composition* 22 (2005): 23–30. Print.

Pritzlaff, Mark. "Detroit Doesn't Measure up Economically, Socially." *The State News*. 13 January 1999. Web. 13 May 2000.

Ramsey, Clare Pfeiffer. "The D Brand and You." *Model D*. 15 January 2008. Web. 20 June 2011.

Rice, Jeff. "The Making of Ka-Knowledge: Digital Aurality." *Computers and Composition* 23.3 (2006): 266–79. Print.

Rice, Jeff, and Marcel O'Gorman. "Getting Schooled: Introduction to the Florida School." *New Media/New Methods: The Academic Turn from Literacy to Electracy*. Ed. Jeff Rice and Marcel O'Gorman. West Lafayette, IN: Parlor Press, 2008. Print.

Rice, Jenny Edbauer. "Rhetoric's Mechanics: Retooling the Equipment of Writing Production." *College Composition and Communication* 60.2 (2008): 366–387. Print.

—. "Unframing Models of Public Distribution: From Rhetorical Situation to Rhetorical Ecologies." *Rhetoric Society Quarterly* 35.4 (2005): 5–24. Print.

Richards, I. A. *The Philosophy of Rhetoric*. New York, London: Oxford UP, 1965. Print.

Ridolfo, Jim, and Dànielle Nicole DeVoss. "Composing for Recomposition: Rhetorical Velocity and Delivery." *Kairos: A Journal of Rhetoric, Technology, and Pedagogy* 13.2 (2009): n. pag. Web. 20 June 2011.

Ridolfo, Jim, and Martine Courant Rife. "Rhetorical Velocity and Copyright: A Case Study on the Strategies of Rhetorical Delivery." *Copy(write): Intellectual Property in the Writing Classroom*. Ed. Martine Rife, Shaun Slattery, and Dànielle Nicole DeVoss. WAC Clearinghouse and Parlor Press, 2011. 223-243. Print.

Roberts-Miller, Patricia. *Deliberate Conflict: Argument, Political Theory, and Composition Classes*. Carbondale: Southern Illinois UP, 2004. Print.

Rose, Mike. "Rigid Rules, Inflexible Plans, and the Stifling of Language: A Cognitivist Analysis of Writer's Block." *College Composition and Communication* 31.4 (1980): 389–401. Print.

Ruby, Jay. *Picturing Culture: Explorations of Film and Anthropology*. Chicago, IL: U of Chicago P, 2000. Print.

Rude, Carolyn D. "Toward an Expanded Concept of Rhetorical Delivery: The Uses of Reports in Public Policy Debates." *Technical Communication Quarterly* 13.3 (2004): 271–88. Print.

Sanders, Lynn M. "Against Deliberation." *Political Theory* 25.3 (1997): 347-76. Print.

Santos, Hubert J., Hope C. Seeley, Patrick S. Bristol, and Sandra L. Snaden. "Brief of the Defendant-Appellant." State of Connecticut v. Michael Skakel. S.C. 16844. *CourtTV.* Web. 20 Jan 2008.

Scholes, Robert E. *Textual Power: Literary Theory and the Teaching of English.* New Haven, CT: Yale UP, 1985. Print.

Selber, Stuart A. "Reimagining the Functional Side of Computer Literacy." *College Composition and Communication* 55 (2004): 470–503. Print.

—. "Technological Dramas: A Meta-Discourse Heuristic for Critical Literacy." *Computers and Composition* 21 (2004): 171-95.

Selfe, Cynthia. "Students Who Teach Us: A Case Study in a New Media Text Designer." *Writing New Media: Theory and Applications for Expanding the Teaching of Composition.* Ed. Anne Wysocki, Johndan Johnson-Eilola, Cynthia Selfe, and Geoffrey Sirc. Logan: Utah State UP, 2004. 43–66. Print.

Selfe, Richard J. *Sustainable Computer Environments: Cultures of Support in English Studies and Language Arts.* Cresskill, NJ: Hampton, 2005. Print.

Selzer, Jack, and Sharon Crowley. *Rhetorical Bodies.* Madison: U of Wisconsin P, 1999.

"Send.a.message." The Longest Letter (It's on the Wall!). Web. 03 Sept. 2009.

Shapiro, Michael J. *The Politics of Representation: Writing Practices in Biography, Photography, and Policy Analysis.* Madison: U of Wisconsin P, 1988. Print.

Shapiro, Nat. *An Encyclopedia of Quotations About Music.* New York: Da Capo P, 1981. Print.

Sheard, Cynthia Miecznikowski. "Kairos and Kenneth Burke's Psychology of Political and Social Communication." *College English* 55.3 (1993): 291–310. Print.

Sheridan, David. "Fabricating Consent: Three-Dimensional Objects as Rhetorical Compositions." *Computers and Composition* 27 (2010): 249–265. Print.

—. "Narrative and Counter-Narrative in Detroit." Diss. Michigan State U, 2001. Print.

Shipka, Jody. "A Multimodal Task-Based Framework for Composing." *College Composition and Communication* 57.2 (2005): 277–306. Print.

Shirky, Clay. "Weblogs and the Mass Amateurization of Publishing." 3 October 2002. Web. 15 October 2009.

Sipiora, Phillip, and James S. Baumlin. *Rhetoric and Kairos: Essays in History, Theory, and Praxis.* Albany: SUNY P, 2002. Print.

Slater, Don. "Marketing Mass Photography." *Visual Culture: The Reader.* Ed. Jessica Evans and Stuart Hall. London: Sage, 1999. 289–306. Print.

Smith, Paul. *Discerning the Subject.* Minneapolis: U Minnesota P, 1988. Print.

Sontag, Susan. *On Photography.* New York: Doubleday, 1990. Print.

Sowards, Stacey. "Rhetorical Agency as Haciendo Caras and Differential Consciousness through Lens of Gender, Race, Ethnicity, and Class: An Examination of Dolores Huerta's Rhetoric." *Communication Theory* 20.2 (2010): 223–47. Print.

Spellmeyer, Kurt. *Arts of Living: Reinventing the Humanities for the Twenty-First Century.* Albany: SUNY P, 2003. Print.

Spinuzzi, Clay, and Mark Zachry. "Genre Ecologies: An Open System Approach to Understanding and Constructing Documentation." *ACM Journal of Computer Documentation* 24.3 (2000): 169–81. Print.

Spivak, Gayatri. "Can the Subaltern Speak?" *Marxisma and the Interpretation of Culture.* Ed. Cary Nelson and Larry Grossberg. Chicago: U Illinois P, 1988. 271–313. Print.

Sproule, J. Michael. *Channels of Propaganda.* Bloomington, IN: ERIC: Edinfo P, 1994. Print.

Stegmair, John. "Student Groups Bring Sweat Straight to MSU Administration." *The Lansing City Pulse.* 2 March 2005. Web. 2 April 2009.

Stolley, Karl. "The Lo-Fi Manifesto." *Kairos: A Journal of Rhetoric, Technology, and Pedagogy* 12.3 (2008): n. pag. Web. 14 Sept. 2010.

Stott, William. *Documentary Expression and Thirties America.* New York: Oxford UP, 1973. Print.

Streeter, Thomas, Nicole Hintlian, Samantha Chipetz, and Susanna Callender. "This Is Not Sex: A Web Essay on the Male Gaze, Fashion Advertising, and the Pose." *Semiotics and the Media.* Web. 18 December 2009.

Stroupe, Craig. "Visualizing English: Recognizing the Hybrid Literacy of Visual and Verbal Authorship on the Web." *College English* 62.5 (2000): 607–32. Print.

Sutton, Jane. "Kairos." *Encyclopedia of Rhetoric.* Ed. Thomas O. Sloane. Oxford: Oxford UP, 2001. 413–417. Print.

Swenson, Janet. "Transformative Teacher Networks, On-Line Professional Development, and the Write for Your Life Project." *English Education* 35.4 (2003): 262–321. Print.

Swistock, Janet. "It Takes More Than a Computer to Make a Graphic Designer." American Institute of Graphic Arts, Baltimore Chapter. Web. 30 July 2008.

Syverson, Margaret A. *The Wealth of Reality: An Ecology of Composition.* Carbondale: Southern Illinois UP, 2009. Print.

Tagg, John. *The Burden of Representation: Essays on Photographies and Histories.* Amherst: U of Massachusetts P, 1988. Print.

Taylor, Timothy D. "A Riddle Wrapped in a Mystery: Transnational Music Sampling and Enigma's 'Return to Innocence.'" *Music and Technoculture.*

Ed. René T. A. Lysloff and Leslie C. Gay. Middletown, CT: Wesleyan UP, 2003. 64–92. Print.

"*Tangere*." *Oxford English Dictionary*. 2nd ed. Oxford: Oxford UP, 1989. Web. 20 June 2011.

Townsend, Jim. "Guest Blogger: Jim Townsend." *Metromode*. 22 March 2007. Web. 20 June 2011.

Trimbur, John. "Composition and the Circulation of Writing." *College Composition and Communication* 52.2 (2000): 188–219. Print.

—. "Delivering the Message: Typography and the Materiality of Writing." *Visual Rhetoric in a Digital World: A Critical Sourcebook*. Ed. Carolyn Handa. Boston, MA: Bedford, 2004. Print.

—. "Multiliteracies, Social Futures, and Writing Centers." *The Writing Center Journal* 20.2 (2000): 29–32. Print.

Vatz, Richard E. "The Myth of the Rhetorical Situation." *Philosophy and Rhetoric* 6 (1973): 154–61. Print.

Voltmer, Katrin. "The Media, Government Accountability, and Citizen Engagement." *Public Sentinel: News Media and Governance Reform*. Ed. Pippa Norris. Washington, DC: The International Bank for Reconstruction and Development / The World Bank, 2010. 137–59. Web. 15 January 2011.

Wade, Lisa. "Doctoring Diversity: Race and Photoshop." *The Society Pages*. 2 September 2009. Web. 15 January 2012.

Walker, Jeffrey. "The Body of Persuasion: A Theory of the Enthymeme." *College English* 56.1 (1994): 46–65. Print.

—. *Rhetoric and Poetics in Antiquity*. Oxford: Oxford UP, 2000. Print.

Ward, Brad J. "The Anatomy of #WatchItSpread." *SquaredPeg*. 8 June 2009. Web. 03 September 2009.

Warner, Michael. *Publics and Counterpublics*. New York: Zone Books, 2002. Print.

Warnick, Barbara. *Rhetoric Online: Persuasion and Politics on the World Wide Web*. Frontiers in Political Communication. New York: Peter Lang, 2007. Print.

Weisser, Christian R. *Moving Beyond Academic Discourse: Composition Studies and the Public Sphere*. Carbondale: Southern Illinois UP, 2002. Print.

Welch, Kathleen E. *Electric Rhetoric: Classical Rhetoric, Oralism, and a New Literacy*. Digital Communication. Cambridge: MIT P, 1999. Print.

Welch, Nancy. *Living Room: Teaching Public Writing in a Privatized World*. Portsmouth, NH: Boynton/Cook, 2008. Print.

Wells, Susan. "Rogue Cops and Health Care: What Do We Want from Public Writing?" *College Composition and Communication* 47.3 (1996): 325–341. Print.

Welsh, Scott. "Deliberative Democracy and the Rhetorical Production of Political Culture." *Rhetoric and Public Affairs* 5.4 (2002): 679–708. Print.

Westside Neighborhood Association, *Westsider.* Summer 2011. Print & Web.

Westbrook, Steve. "Visual Rhetoric in a Culture of Fear: Impediments to Multimedia Production." *College English* 68.5 (2006): 457–80. Print.

White, Ann Folino. "Page 48: Vaudeville of a Historian." *Performing Arts Resources* 28 (2011). Print.

White, Eric Charles. *Kaironomia: On the Will-to-Invent.* Ithaca, NY: Cornell UP, 1987. Print.

Whitesall, Amy E. "Firms Pitch D Brand to Would-Be Hires, Out-of-Town Visitors." *Crain's Detroit Business.* 10 February 2008. Web. 20 June 2011.

—. *Problems in Materialism and Culture: Selected Essays.* London: Verso, 1980. Print.

Williams, Sean D. "Part 1: Thinking Out of the Pro-Verbal Box." *Computers and Composition* 18 (2001): 21–32. Print.

Williams-Jones, Bryn, and Janice E. Graham. "Actor-Network Theory: A Tool to Support Ethical Analysis of Commercial Genetic Testing." *New Genetics and Society* 22.3 (2003): 271–296. Print.

Winston, Brian. *Technologies of Seeing: Photography, Cinematography and Television.* London: British Film Institute, 1996. Print.

Wong, Shawn. *Homebase.* Baltimore, MD: U of Washington P, 2008.

Woodmansee, Martha, and Peter Jaszi. "The Law of Texts: Copyright in the Academy." *College English* 57.7 (1995): 769–787. Print.

Wysocki, Anne Frances. "Awaywithwords: On the Possibilities in Unavailable Designs." *Computers and Composition* 22 (2005): 55–62. Print.

—. "Opening New Media to Writing: Openings and Justifications." *Writing New Media: Theory and Applications for Expanding the Teaching of Composition.* Ed. Anne Frances Wysocki, et al. Logan: Utah State UP, 2004. 1–41. Print.

Yates, JoAnne, and Wanda Orlikowski. "Genre Systems: Chronos and Kairos in Communicative Interaction." *The Rhetoric and Ideology of Genre: Strategies for Stability and Change.* Ed. Richard M. Coe, Lorelei Lingard, and Tatiana Teslenko. Cresskill, NJ: Hampton, 2002. 103–21. Print.

The Yes Men. "reBurger." 2 November 2006. Web. 20 June 2011.

Young, Iris Marion. "Activist Challenges to Deliberative Democracy." *Debating Deliberative Democracy.* Ed. James S. Fishkin and Peter Laslett. Malden, MA: Blackwell, 2003. 102–20. Print.

—. "Communication and the Other: Beyond Deliberative Democracy." *Democracy and difference: Contesting the Boundaries of the Political.* Ed. Seyla Benhabib. Princeton, NJ: Princeton UP, 1996. Print.

Zimmermann, Patricia Rodden. *Reel Families: A Social History of Amateur Film.* Arts and Politics of the Everyday. Bloomington: Indiana UP, 1995. Print.

Appendix

Design for a Cultural Intervention

Assignment Sequence • RCAH 112 Writing, Research, and Technologies[*]

As you know, this course focuses on a set of assignments that collectively make up a "Design for a Cultural Intervention." The basic template for this set of assignments calls for us to identify a "cultural problem," analyze that problem in the context of existing research and your own novel insights, develop a plan for addressing the problem through some form of cultural production, and then produce a showcase of the kinds of cultural production that your plan calls for.

Mini Proposal

due week 3 • approximately half a page

The mini proposal is a one-paragraph statement of your idea for you're your Cultural Intervention. It should include a description of the cultural problem you hope to focus on, examples of cultural artifacts that illustrate the problem, and a brief suggestions of the kinds of rhetorical actions that might be taken to help address the problem. This is an informal, ungraded assignment. The primary purpose of the mini proposal is to facilitate a short conversation between you and me about possible directions for you to take for this assignment sequence.

Research Proposal

due week 5 • approximately 5 pp

Humanities scholars are frequently asked to submit proposals for research projects. Scholars need to convince funders and reviewers that planned research will be fruitful and compelling.

You can think of this research proposal as a micro version of your Cultural Problem Analysis (CPA), so you should read through the description of that assignment before embarking on your proposal.

---

[*] This assignment sequence appears here in slightly modified form.

As a micro version of your CPA, your proposal should include the following components:

- An introduction of the cultural problem that you plan to address.
- A clear thesis statement that summarizes your primary insight into your cultural problem.
- A presentation of at least one academic source that attempts to explore this problem.
- Your own original analysis of at least one cultural artifact (i.e., a "primary source") that helps to illustrate the nature of the cultural problem you're exploring.

Your proposal should be informed by a clear understanding of the three assignments that follow below.

Cultural Problem Analysis

first draft due week 9 • revised draft due week 11 • approximately 10 pp

For the purposes of this class, a "cultural problem" is a set of attitudes, perceptions, beliefs, and/or practices that undermine the goals of social justice. Examples include racial stereotypes, unfair perceptions of labor unions, negative attitudes toward immigrants, etc. In the humanities, cultural problems are often explored through analysis of primary sources like films, TV shows, advertisements, websites, novels, poems, paintings, photographs, magazines and other cultural forms.

The example of a cultural problem that we're using as a "textbook case" is the set negative perceptions that many people have of the city of Detroit. Many people share the sentiments and attitudes of Mark Pritzlaff, who claims that "Detroit truly has nothing of any real value to offer." Like Pritzlaff, many people associate Detroit with crime, drugs, violence, abandoned buildings, and emptiness. These associations often render invisible the many assets the city has to offer: world-class architecture and museums; historic restaurants and music venues; beautiful parks, public spaces, and vistas on the Detroit River (e.g., Belle Isle, Hart Plaza), etc. Even more importantly, negative perceptions tend to erase the 713,777 people who live in the city, whose daily existence is defined by homes, streets, schools, places of worship, parks, stores, and restaurants located in the city. Before we dismiss

Detroit as "pathetic" (as Pritzlaff does), we need to acknowledge the people who live there and the meaning and value the city has for them.

Detroit's image problem is an example of the kind of problem you might explore in your CPA. A paper focused on this cultural problem could draw on scholarly research that explores how cities are depicted in novels, poems, movies, news broadcasts, and other cultural forms. The paper would include original analysis of cultural artifacts related to the problem. For instance, it might explore the images presented in *8 Mile* and/or might examine a network news story on Detroit. It might even take a look at the language and metaphors used by writers like Pritzlaff.

As a class, we will develop a detailed set of criteria that will be used to assess CPAs, but in general CPAs should include the following components:

1. A clear thesis statement that summarizes your primary insights into your cultural problem.
2. Analysis of at least three primary sources that help to establish the nature of your cultural problem.
3. Substantial use of at least three academic sources that help to illustrate existing insights into the cultural problem you're exploring.

Plan for Rhetorical Intervention

first draft due week 9 • revised draft due week 11 • approximately 8 pp

Let's imagine that, based on the extensive research produced for the CPA, you have been hired by a non-profit organization to address the problem in question through strategically chosen forms of cultural production. You have been tasked with designing a **campaign** that makes best use of existing resources. The Plan for Rhetorical Intervention is your proposal for the campaign.

Your Plan should include the following components:

1. A detailed description of the purpose of the campaign/intervention: What attitudes, beliefs, perceptions, behaviors would you like to change or encourage?
2. A detailed description of your audience: Who do you hope to reach? Why is this audience key to addressing your problem?

3. A detailed description of what forms of cultural production: What kinds of media will you deploy? What pieces of writing will you develop? (Note: I'm using the term "campaign" to suggest an approach in which multiple media and compositions work together to address a problem.)
4. A detailed plan for circulating the writing and media that constitutes your campaign: How will your videos, press releases, brochures, etc. get to the target audience?
5. A rationale for the choices that you are making: Why did you choose this kind of writing and media? Why do you hypothesize that your audience will respond to video better than a poster? Why do you believe the strategies for circulating your writing are effective?

As a class, we will develop more detailed criteria for how these Plans are assessed.

Before you begin work on your Plan, you should produce a brief description of the kind of context that you would like to work within. This description should include a sketch of the organizations you are working with, the goals of these organizations, the budget that you expect to have for the project, and other contextual factors.

Intervention Showcase

due week 15

You will not have time to fully implement the Plan for a Rhetorical Intervention that you develop for this class. Instead, you are asked to develop an Intervention Showcase—a scaled-down version of your Plan that provides a sense of what you have in mind. For instance, if your Plan calls for a twenty-minute film, your Showcase might include the thirty-second trailer for the film. If your plan calls for a series of three brochures with matching posters, your Showcase might include one brochure and one poster. I will meet with each student individually to develop an outline of what his/her Showcase should entail. Showcases will be presented at the Public Knowledge open house (date TBA).

Index

2 Live Crew, 139, 191
360degrees, 137–138
3D: 3D compositions; 3D printers, xviii, xix, xxiv, xxv, 25–27, 47–48, 50, 99, 119, 186–187

Access, xii, xiv, xxiv, 15–17, 25–26, 28–33, 36–38, 41, 43, 47–48, 51, 56, 58–59, 62–64, 66, 68, 70, 78, 81, 132, 162, 166, 183, 186
Actor-network theory, 102–103, 106; Actor-network theorists, xxvii, 20, 72, 102, 107
Actors, xxiii, xxvii, 11, 20, 72, 102–103, 106–107, 189; Human actors, xxii-xxiii, xxvi-xxvii, 11, 13, 97, 102, 104–108, 124–125, 140–141, 165, 168, 175, 189
Acuff-Rose Music, Inc. v. Campbell, 140
Adbusters, xi-xii
Affordances, xviii, 33, 39–41, 67, 74, 96, 146, 153
Agency, xxvii, 7, 11, 19–20, 69, 72, 99–100, 102–104, 106–109, 112, 141, 171, 191; rhetorical, xvii, xxiii, xxvii, 7–8, 98–100, 102, 191
Allen, Nancy, 139
Alsultany, Evelyn, 177
Amateur: Amateur film, 36, 64
Anderson, Daniel, 31, 43, 45

Appropriation, 47, 79, 82, 84, 86, 90, 91, 95–96, 125, 139–140, 142
Argument: Argumentation, xvii, xxv, xxviii, 13, 15, 19–20, 39–45, 47–51, 102, 123–128, 133, 135–137, 143, 147, 150–152, 155, 164, 169, 172, 175, 183
Armstrong, Mark Robertson, 151
Asen, Robert, 14, 17, 21
Audience, xiv, xxiii, xxvi-xxvii, 7–8, 12, 15, 30–32, 34, 51, 53, 55, 57, 61–62, 64, 68, 70, 73–74, 78, 85, 99–100, 107–117, 131, 133–134, 136, 140, 143, 147, 157, 165, 167, 171, 175, 178–179
Aurality, xv, xviii, xxvii, 31, 53, 78, 124, 126, 134, 154, 165, 189

Baker, Houston A., Jr., xiii, 146, 148–149
Barthes, Roland, 129–130
Barton, David, 190
Baumlin, James S., 6
Bazerman, Charles, 6, 167–168
Benhabib, Seyla, 16
Berger, Arthur Asa, 126
Berlin, James A., xxx, 149, 150, 156, 162, 173–174, 176
Bitzer, Lloyd, 6, 108, 170
Black, Max, xiii, 139, 148, 151, 191
Blakesley, David, xiv

Blaustein, Jessica, 101
Blogs, 145
Blumrich, Eric, 142, 176
Booth, Wayne C., 153
Bourdieu, Pierre, 59
Brecht, Bertolt, 31–32
Brooke, John L., 19
Brouwer, Daniel C., 14, 17, 21
Buck, Ross, 135
Burgin, Victor, 129
Burke, Kenneth: Pentad, 6, 69, 70, 103, 135, 151

Caldwell, Lt. Gen. William B., IV, 80
Calhoun, Craig J., 14, 16
Camera, xxiv, 25, 27, 30, 33–37, 39, 44–46, 50, 52, 55, 58, 64, 73–74, 118, 124–126, 131, 138, 163, 185–186
Carney, Brian, 123, 134–136
Case analysis, xviii
Chaudhuri, Arjun, 135
Chion, Michel, 132
Chomsky, Noam, 28
Christoph, Julie Nelson, 51
Circulation, xii, xvii, xxi, xxvi, 15, 29–30, 56, 58, 61–64, 66–68, 71, 73, 78, 80, 83, 92, 97, 101, 107–108, 111–115, 117, 163, 165, 169, 172, 175, 191
Civic, 109, 127, 163, 166, 171, 173, 175, 185
Class (socioeconomic), 28, 33–34, 43, 47, 86, 116, 144, 153–155, 171–172, 186, 188
Closed fist, 129
Composition, xvii-xviii, xxi, xxvi-xxviii, 7, 15, 20, 30–33, 51, 53, 55, 57- 62, 64, 66, 68, 71, 73, 74, 77–80, 82–83, 86, 91–92, 96–97, 99, 107–112, 114–115, 117–118, 124–125, 132–134,

139, 142–144, 161, 164–165, 169, 175, 177–179, 182–185; field of, xii-xiii, xv, xvii-xxv, 11, 19, 26, 40, 42, 57, 61, 74, 78, 84, 102, 108, 110, 115, 118, 146, 149, 155–156, 168–175, 186–189, 191
Considerations, xvii-xviii, xxi, xxiii, xxvi-xxviii, 15, 50, 55, 60, 62–64, 73, 79, 81, 100, 115, 125–126, 139–141, 143, 172, 179, 182
Consigny, Scott, 6, 9
Constructions of race, 28, 153–154, 168
Contingency, 8, 11, 48, 72–73, 101–102, 107, 127, 131, 190–191
Cooper, Marilyn M., 70–71, 129
Cooperative-rational model, 143; Cooperative-rational approach, 127–129, 136–137
Corbett, Edward P. J., 127, 129, 143
Counterpublic, 16, 18, 101, 189
Crowley, Sharon, 9, 190
Culture, xi-xiii, xvi- xix, xxiv, xxviii, 18, 28, 38–39, 41–43, 46, 48, 64, 78, 101, 104, 112, 119, 124, 137, 139–140, 145–149, 151, 153, 155–157, 161, 163–164, 169, 173–174, 176–177, 186–187
Cushman, Ellen, 43, 73, 78, 116, 190
Cussins, Charis, xxvii, 107
Dean, Jodi, 14
Deliberation, 12, 18–20, 127, 130, 137, 144, 149, 151–152, 171–172
Delivery, 7, 53, 59, 66, 68, 70, 73, 78, 80, 83–85, 97, 99, 109, 114

DeLuca, Kevin Michael, xxviii, 13, 21, 148–149, 189
Demassification, 32
Depiction, 150–152
Desktop manufacturing, xviii
Desktop publishing, xviii, 43, 45
Detroit, Michigan: D Brand, xxviii, 62–63, 67, 145–147, 153, 161–164, 166–168, 191
DeVoss, Dànielle Nicole, 43, 73, 78, 81, 90, 97, 116, 156, 189–191
Dialectic, 39, 42, 112, 149–150, 152
Digital technologies, xiv-xv, 30, 32, 36
Distribution, xvi, xxi, xxvi-xxviii, 11, 18, 30, 32, 58–60, 63–64, 66–68, 70, 73, 80–82, 96–98, 108–116, 125, 166, 169, 171–172, 175, 177–178, 183, 190
Dragga, Sam, 139, 142
Dubisar, Abby M., 191

Eberly, Rose A., xii, xxx, 28–29, 171–174, 189
Eco, Umberto, 130
Ecology, xvii, xxiii, xxvi-xxviii, 14, 21, 32, 37, 70–71, 73, 109, 142
Edwards, Mike, 80
Emergent technologies, 27, 30–31, 33, 46, 176
Emotion, 18, 42, 74, 97, 124, 127, 129, 135–136, 148–149, 151–152, 157
Enzensberger, Hans Magnus, 31–32, 154, 176
Ervin, Elizabeth, 171, 173, 189
Ethics, xvii-xviii, xxiii-xxvii, 5, 12, 83, 109, 125–126, 128, 135–137, 139, 140–143, 190; Rhetorical ethics, xxiii, xxvii-xx-

viii, 12, 125–126, 136, 139–143, 168
Exigency, xxvi-xxvii, 50, 53–54, 70, 73, 77, 108–109, 114–118, 161, 165, 168, 171, 173–176, 178

Feigenson, Neal, 39, 123, 133–137
Felski, Rita: counterpublic, 16, 101, 189
Films, xi, 18, 25, 28, 30–32, 34–35, 45, 52–53, 55, 58, 64, 67, 70, 74, 83, 118, 125, 130–132, 134, 138, 146, 154–156, 158, 177, 185, 189
First Things First Manifesto, xi-xii, xvi
Fisher, Walter R., 150, 192
Fraser, Nancy: subaltern counter-public, xii-xxiv, 13, 16–18, 21, 29, 148, 189
Free Trade Area of the Americas (FTAA), 52
Fulkerson, Richard, 127–128

Gaonkar, Dilip Parameshwar: point of articulation, xxvi, 72, 99–100, 191
Garnham, Nicholas, 16
Geary, James, 61
Geisler, Cheryl, 102, 191
Gender, 17–18, 153–155
Genre, xxi, 38, 61, 73, 83, 85–86, 109, 111–113, 134, 187
Gentili, Bruno, 150, 157
George, Diana, 27, 39, 42–43, 48, 61, 71, 129, 189
Gershenfeld, Neil A., xviii, 31, 176, 187 ·
González, Jennifer A., 49, 154
Gorgias, 9–10, 149
Graas, David: *Not a Box*, xix-xxi, 67

Grabill, Jeffrey T., 43, 73, 78, 116, 190
GRACE and Free Range Studios, 176
Graham, Janice E., 79, 107
Gregory, Marshall W., 153, 190
Griffioen, James D., 145–146, 161
Gross, Alan G., 151–152
Grossman, Bathsheba, xv
Gunther, Kress, 39–40, 189

Haas, Angela M., xiv, 115
Haas, Christina, xiv, 115
Habermas, Jürgen, xiii, xxiv, xxviii, 13, 15–21, 28, 70, 102, 127–128, 146, 152
Hague, Barry N., xv
Halbritter, Bump, 50
Hariman, Robert, xvi, 14
Harris, Michael D., 154
Hart, Alexis, 80, 163
Hawisher, Gail E., 156
Hawk, Byron, 20
Hebdige, Dick, 176
Herman, Edward S., 28
Herndl, Carl G., xxvii, 6, 11, 70, 72, 102–103, 106, 141
Hesse, Douglas D., 171
Heuristic, xviii, xxv, 27, 38, 40–41, 43, 45–46, 48, 50, 70, 74, 97, 112, 142, 189–190
Hill, Charles A., 135, 162
Hine, Lewis, 34, 38–39
Hockney, David, xiv
Hughes, Joseph J., xiv, 6, 50

Icon, 130, 142
Iedema, Rick, xiv, 154
Image, xiv, xvii, xxvi, 19, 32, 34–36, 43, 47, 54, 63, 66, 79, 83, 87, 95, 124, 126, 130–131, 135–136, 138, 142, 144–148, 151, 153, 155–156, 161, 163–165, 169, 179–180, 182
Infrastructure: Infrastructural accessibility, 43–44, 80, 81
Internet, xi, xiv, xvi, 21, 29, 32–33, 37, 43, 52, 63, 66, 68, 70
Intervention, 26, 36, 63, 171
Ivie, Robert L., 13, 149, 151, 157, 192

Jasinski, James, 72, 190–191
Jaszi, Peter, 191
Johns, Adrian, 78
Johnson, Randal, 60, 112, 191
Johnson-Eilola, Johndan, 191
Jonsen, Albert R., xviii

Kairos, xxiv-xxv, xxvii-xxviii, 5–14, 20–21, 26–27, 37, 48, 50–51, 53–55, 69, 73–74, 77, 80, 99–101, 103, 115, 119, 126, 167, 169, 175
Kairotic, xxviii, 7, 9, 10, 12, 17, 39, 53–55, 57, 68–69, 73, 99, 110, 113, 116–117, 143, 167, 168, 172; approach, 10, 20–21, 25–27, 128–129; inventiveness, xxv, 10–11, 21, 48, 50, 53, 60, 69, 79, 97, 99, 110; moments, 9, 57; opportunities, xxiv-xxv, 50–51, 59, 72, 100, 168, 178, 182; struggle, 50–51, 53, 57, 60, 64, 68, 70, 73, 99, 104, 109–110
Kennerly, David Hume, 91, 94–96, 141–142
Kienzler, Donna S., 139
Kinneavy, James L., 5–10, 12

La Brecque, Eric, 162–163, 165
Lanham, Richard A., 30–31, 44, 47–48, 53

Lansing, Michigan; Westside Neighborhood Association, 64–65, 87, 89, 178, 184
Lansing State Journal, 87, 90
Latour, Bruno, xxiii, 11, 21, 103–106, 141
Lauer, Janice M., 171–172
Law, John, xxiii, 11, 105–106, 141
Lay actor, xvi, 31, 189
Leff, Michael, 151, 192
Lessig, Lawrence, 191
Licona, Adela C., xxvii, 6, 11, 70, 72, 102–103, 106, 141
Lippi-Green, Rosina, 154
Loader, Brian, xv
Logic, 33, 38, 41, 43, 49, 59, 128, 133, 135–136, 149–150, 152–153, 169
Louw, Eric, 28, 30
Lowe, Charles, 80
Lucaites, John Louis, xvi, 14
Lynch, Dennis A., 129, 190

Maira, Sunaina, 177
Manifesto: First Things First, xi-xii, xvi
Marback, Richard, 191
Mathieu, Paula, xv, 61, 71, 189
McAfee, Noëlle, 20
McCarthy, Thomas, 128
McChesney, Robert W., 28–29
McComiskey, Bruce, xviii, xxx, 6, 10, 32, 42, 46–47, 50, 110, 112–113, 118, 126, 156, 162, 173–174, 176
McCracken, Grant David, 48
McKee, Heidi, 189
Media, xiv-xvii, xxiv, xxvi, xxviii, 11, 26, 28–29, 31–33, 38–40, 43–44, 47–48, 53–55, 63, 67–68, 70–71, 73–74, 80–81, 83–85, 87, 90, 93–94, 96–97, 109, 111–112, 114–117, 123–126,

130–131, 134, 139–140, 142–143, 162, 164–166, 169–172, 175–180, 182–183, 185–187, 189; Commercial media, xvi, 25, 32, 155; For-profit media, xii, xvi, 28, 33; Mainstream media, 52, 64, 145, 147, 153, 163; Mass media, 28–31, 154, 163; Mixed media, 20, 178–179; New media, xvi, xviii, xxiii, 32–33, 78, 109, 131, 156, 185, 191
Messaris, Paul, 130
Metaphor, 6, 14–15, 32, 43, 79, 103, 138, 146, 150–152, 161, 163
Micciche, Laura R., 151
Michigan State University: MSU, 86, 175, 184, 190
Miller, Carolyn R., 8–9, 191
Miller, Paul D., 191
Miller, Susan, 118, 171
Mitchell, W. J. T., xvi, 45
Modes, xvii, xix, xxiv, xxvi, xxviii, 26, 36, 38–41, 43–44, 47–48, 51, 53, 55, 64, 70, 72–74, 90, 92, 97, 99, 108–116, 126, 130, 141, 143, 148, 150, 154, 169–170, 172, 175, 177–178, 182, 186–187
Moment of crisis, xxv, 26–27, 37, 99
Monroe, Barbara Jean, 28, 33
Morano, Christopher, 41, 123–124, 134
Movies, xxiv, 27, 35–37, 124, 153
Multimodal, xii-xix, xxiii, xxvi-xxviii, 12, 20, 30–32, 38, 41, 51–53, 55, 63, 79, 84, 86, 90, 92, 96, 107–108, 113, 115- 118, 123, 125–126, 129, 131, 133-137, 139, 141- 143, 146–147, 152–158, 161, 168, 170, 173- 175, 179, 184, 186–187,

189–190; composition, xiv, xvii,
xxvii, 12, 31, 51, 68, 79, 96,
126, 134–135, 142, 152, 154,
158; public rhetoric, xvii–xix, xxi,
xxiii, xxiv-xxv, xxviii, 5, 12–13,
19, 21 25, 50–51, 53, 55, 63, 73,
86, 125–126, 139, 141, 146–
147, 161, 170, 174, 184, 190
Multimodality, xii- xvii, xxiii,
xxvii-xxviii, 7, 10, 12, 15, 19, 41,
63, 84, 97, 125–126, 133, 137,
142–143, 146, 152, 170, 175,
189
Music, xiii-xiv, xxvi, 30–31, 36,
87, 92, 118–119, 139, 142–143,
154–156, 163, 184

Narrative, 53, 64, 146–147,
149–150, 152, 155, 158, 164
Neuwirth, Christine M., 115
New London Group, xvi, xviii
New technologies, xiv, xvii, 26–27,
29, 32, 99, 110, 139

Okrent, Daniel, 161
Onians, Richard Broxton, 6
Open hand, 127, 129
Orlikowski, Wanda, 8–9, 190
Orson, Diane, 41, 124, 134, 137
Osborn, Michael, 151, 192

Palmeri, Jason, 191
Parr, Ben, 84
Pathos, xxv, 147, 149–150, 152
Pedagogy, xiii, xviii-xix, 25–26,
37, 48, 50, 74, 96, 108–112,
114–116, 118, 125, 146, 156,
169–174, 176, 179, 184, 187,
191–192
Performance, xiii-xiv, xxiii, 15, 19,
21, 31, 40, 58, 60–61, 92, 108,
112, 115, 140, 148, 157, 165,
168, 184, 186

Photograph, xvi, xxvi, 31–32,
34, 38–39, 62, 65–66, 87–91,
94–96, 123, 125–126, 129–135,
139, 141–143, 145–147, 152,
162, 164–166, 181
Photographic technologies, 154
Photography, 34–35, 130–131,
154, 184–185
Place, xii, xviii, 6–7, 13–14, 33,
61–63, 68, 72, 78, 87, 93,
99–100, 103, 141, 145–146,
149, 153, 155, 166–167, 171,
174, 180, 184
Plato, xviii, 12, 38–39, 42, 50, 149
Poesis: Multimodal poesis, 18–19,
21, 129, 143, 148–149, 152,
155, 157, 161, 175, 187, 192
Poetic world making, xvii, xxiv, xxviii, 18, 20, 128, 146–147, 149,
153, 157, 161, 164, 174–175
Poetics, 149–150
Poetry, 150, 157, 184
Porter, James E., xviii, 12, 61, 80,
126, 143
Poster, Mark, xi, 31–32
Post-Habermasian, 21, 146, 149,
153, 157
Pough, Gwendolyn D., 191
Presence, 10, 14, 59, 109, 150–
152
Press advisory, 81, 87–92, 178
Prior, Paul, 40
Pritzlaff, Mark, 145
Process, xv, xxi, 9, 15, 20, 30,
33–34, 52–53, 57, 60–61, 71,
73, 77, 79, 83, 97–98, 106,
110–112, 114, 117, 129–130,
135–136, 168, 174–175, 183,
187, 190
Production, xi-xii, xiv, xvii, xxii-
xxiii, xxv- xxviii, 9, 11, 30–33,
38, 45–46, 49, 53–55, 63–64,
66, 72, 74, 81–82, 93–94, 98,

110–114, 116–117, 124, 131,
143, 150, 157–158, 163–166,
168, 172, 175–178, 182,
185–188, 191
Public, xi-xix, xxi-xxv, xxvii-xxviii,
5, 12–15, 17–21, 25, 27–28,
31, 35, 38, 41, 44, 46, 50–51,
53, 55, 60, 63, 66, 69–71, 73,
77, 79, 86–87, 90, 100–101,
108–112, 114, 117–118,
125–29, 136–137, 139, 141,
143, 145–150, 152, 155–157,
161, 163, 165, 169–175,
178–180, 182, 184–185, 187,
189, 191–192; rhetoric, xv-xvii,
xxii-xxiii, xxvii-xxviii, 20, 21, 25,
50, 63, 70, 99, 108, 112, 114,
128–129, 136, 144, 148–149,
152, 155, 157, 161, 165, 169-
171, 173, 175, 182, 189
Public turn, xv

Radio, xi, xiv, 25, 31–32, 68, 156
Rational-critical, xxiv, xxviii, 13,
16–19, 21, 70, 128, 146, 147,
152, 164, 175; argument, xxviii,
147, 164, 175; debate, xxiv, 13,
17, 19, 21, 70, 128, 146, 152;
model, 152, 175
Recomposition, xxvi, 67–68,
74, 78–82, 84–87, 90–91, 93,
96–98, 115, 125, 139, 143,
166–167, 169, 175, 178
Reflexivity, 131, 137, 142
Remix, 78, 139–140, 142, 191
Reproduction, xxi, xxvi-xxviii, 11,
30, 32, 58, 60, 63, 66, 68, 70,
82, 97–98, 109–111, 113–116,
125, 165, 171–172, 175,
177–178, 183
Rhetor, xii-xiii, xvii, xix, xxi,
xxiii, xxv-xxvii, 7–13, 15, 21,
26, 38–39, 43–44, 50–52, 55,

58, 60, 61, 67, 71–73, 77–83,
96–97, 99–102, 106–111, 115,
117, 128, 139–141, 143, 146,
167–171, 175; Multiple public
rhetors, 5, 118; Public rhetor,
xvii, 25, 27, 32, 69, 77, 108–
110, 112, 117, 150, 172–173,
175
Rhetor-as-point-of-articulation,
108, 115
Rhetoric: alphabetic, xxvi, 42;
multimodal, xii, xiii, xv, xvi, xviii,
xxvi, xxvii, 38, 41, 52, 53, 55,
63, 84, 107, 113, 115, 116, 123,
125, 126, 129, 134, 135, 137,
141, 142, 147, 153, 155, 156,
158, 168, 175, 179, 189; public,
xv, xvi, xvii, xviii, xix, xxi, xxii,
xxiii, xxiv, xxv, xxvii, xxviii, 5,
12, 13, 19, 20, 21, 50, 51, 53,
55, 63, 70, 73, 78, 86, 108, 112,
114, 125, 126, 128, 129, 136,
139, 141, 146, 147, 148, 152,
155, 157, 161, 165, 169, 170,
171, 173, 174, 175, 182,184,
189, 190; visual, xvi, xviii, 40,
42, 49, 126, 135, 136, 154
Rhetorical: agency, xvii, xxiii, xxvii,
7–8, 98–100, 120, 191; composition, 67, 74, 78, 82–83, 92,
105, 111–112, 117, 126, 129,
139, 162, 165, 168, 171, 179,
183, 190; context, xxiv, xxv, 6,
70, 101, 112, 115, 178; ecologies, 71, 115, 174, 175, 178;
education, xiii, xix, xxvii, 10, 42,
48, 50, 96, 99, 100, 117, 119,
155, 168, 184, 187; intervention,
xxv-xxvi, xxviii, 53, 63, 71, 163,
176–177, 179–180; invention,
xxi, xxvi, xxvii, 15, 25, 27, 33,
48, 50, 53, 55, 66, 97, 98, 99,
100, 108, 109, 110, 115, 151,

172, 175, 183; options, xiv, 26, 36, 48, 63, 174; process, xxi, 60, 108, 110, 182; recomposition, xxvi, 67, 68, 74, 78, 79, 80, 81, 82, 84, 85, 86, 87, 90, 91, 93, 96, 97, 98, 115, 125, 139, 143, 166, 167, 169, 175, 178; strategy, 80; technologies, xxv, 27, 37, 38; velocity, xxvi, 67, 74, 77, 78, 79, 80, 81, 82, 83, 84, 85, 86, 87, 88, 89, 90, 93, 96, 97, 167

Rhetorical intervention: Distributed and ecological approach, xxv, xxvi, xxviii, 53, 63, 71, 163, 176, 179

Rice, Jeff, 71, 116, 153, 191

Rice, Jenny Edbauer, 14, 71, 115–116, 189

Richards, I. A., 151

Ridolfo, Jim, 52, 61, 77–78, 81, 86, 88–90, 93–94, 97

Roberts-Miller, Patricia, 189

Rose, Mike, 48

Ruby, Jay, 130–131, 137, 144

Rude, Carolyn D., 71

Sachs, Andrew, 151, 192

Scholes, Robert E., 47

SearchMTR, 180–183

Selber, Stuart A., 48, 116, 191

Selfe, Cynthia L., xv, 156

Selzer, Jack, 190

Semiosis: Multimodal semiosis, xvii, 38–39, 125, 131, 136, 139, 143, 156, 177

Semiotic, xiii, xxiii, xxv, xxvii, 11, 19, 31–32, 40–41, 44–45, 48, 74, 99–100, 103, 116, 119, 124–126, 132, 134, 136, 140, 143, 146, 148, 154, 165–166, 187–188; modes, 11, 165; potentials, xxv, 40, 44, 99, 187–188; resources, xiii, xxiii,

xxvii, 124–126, 132, 136, 140, 143, 146, 166

Semiotics: Critical semiotics, 129

Shapiro, Michael J., 39, 131, 137

Sheard, Cynthia Miecznikowski, 5, 6

Sheridan, David, 181, 190–191

Sherwin, Richard K., 39, 133, 135–136

Shipka, Jody, 61, 112–114, 174, 189–190

Shirky, Clay, 31–32

Sipiora, Phillip, 5–6

Skakel, Michael, xxvii, 12, 41, 123–126, 129, 131–137, 139–143, 153

Slater, Don, 34–38, 186

Sontag, Susan, 130

Sound, xiv, 30–31, 64, 79, 82, 132–133, 139

Sowards, Stacey, 191

Specialization: Practices of specialization, xxv, 38, 44–47, 49, 74, 99, 187–188, 190

Spectacle, xiii, 148

Spellmeyer, Kurt, xvii, xxviii, 46–47, 157, 176

Spivak, Gayatri: subaltern, 16, 189

Sproule, J. Michael, 137

Stolley, Karl, 80

Story, xxii, 39, 56, 80, 87, 89, 91, 105–106, 134, 145, 162, 164–166

Storytelling, xiv, 164

Streeter, Thomas, 155

Subaltern counterpublic, xiii, 16, 189

Subcultures, 176

Subjectivity: Public subjectivity, xxvii, 11, 102, 118, 152, 174

Sullivan, Patricia A., 156

Sutton, Jane, 5–7

Swistock, Janet, 46

Synchresis, 132–134, 136, 142
Syverson, Margaret A., 71, 100

Tagg, John, 34, 35, 38, 64
Taylor, Timothy D., 50, 140
Taylor, Todd, 50, 140
Technologies, xvi-xvii, xix, xxiii-
    xxiv, xxvii-xxviii, 25–26, 30–31,
    33–35, 37–40, 43–45, 47–48,
    63, 72, 92, 102–107, 111,
    114–117, 124–126, 136, 140,
    143, 169, 175, 183, 185–187
Television, xi, 25, 28–32, 54–55,
    58, 62, 82, 125, 130, 134, 146,
    154, 156, 163–166, 173, 177,
    179
The Moth: True Stories Told Live, xiv
Toulmin, Stephen, xviii
Townsend, Jim, 161–162, 166
Trimbur, John, 42, 45, 61, 78,
    109–110, 114, 116, 191
Twitter, 61, 84–86, 90, 191

Vatz, Richard E., 6
Video, 18, 30, 32, 36, 45–46,
    52–53, 55, 64, 68, 70, 72, 74,
    81, 83, 109, 113–114, 117–118,
    123–124, 134, 138, 146,
    162–163, 166, 179, 184, 190;
    digital, 33, 43–44, 45, 53, 63,
    139, 176, 187
Viewbooks, 113, 156, 173
View-Master, 62, 67
Visual rhetoric, xvi, xviii, 40, 42,
    49, 126, 135–136, 154
Voltmer, Katrin, xv

Wade, Lisa, 142
Walker, Jeffrey, xxv, 10–11, 50, 79,
    97, 150

Ward, Brad J., 84–86
Warner, Michael, xvii, xxiv, xxviii,
    15, 17–21, 28, 66, 70–71,
    100–101, 110, 114, 146–149,
    153, 157, 161, 165, 172, 175,
    189, 191
Warnick, Barbara, xvi
Wells, Susan, 171, 174, 189
Welsh, Scott, 146, 148–149, 163
Westside Neighborhood Associa-
    tion, 64–65, 66, 108
White, Ann Folino, xxi-xxiii
White, Eric Charles, xxv, 6, 9, 11,
    26, 37
Williams, Raymond, 37, 42, 54,
    107
Williams-Jones, Bryn, 107
Winston, Brian, 35, 37–38
Winter, Terence, 55–58, 60, 68,
    108
Wong, Shawn, 55–60, 67–68
Woodmansee, Martha, 191
World Wide Web, xv-xvi, 28, 30,
    32, 40, 58, 63, 66, 68, 90, 113,
    125, 146, 155–156, 161–162,
    165, 169, 180, 183
Writing assignment, 74, 177
Wysocki, Anne Frances, 40, 131,
    137, 189–191

Yates, JoAnne, 8–9, 190
Young, Iris Mario, 9, 16, 56,
    127–128, 144, 192
YouTube, 30, 63, 74, 81

Zimmermann, Patricia Rodden,
    35, 38, 64

About the Authors

David M. Sheridan is an assistant professor in Michigan State University's Residential College in the Arts and Humanities, where he teaches courses on writing, creativity, technology, and media. He also directs the RCAH Language and Media Center. His previous publications include articles in *JAC, Enculturation*, and *Computers and Composition*. He co-edited, with James Inman, *Multiliteracy Centers: Writing Center Work, New Media, and Multimodal Rhetoric* (Hampton, 2010). Under the sponsorship of MSU's Writing in Digital Environments (WIDE) Research Center, Sheridan is working with others to develop a game called INK—a multiplayer virtual world designed to function as a rich environment for public rhetorical practices. In 2012 Sheridan was the recipient of MSU's Teacher-Scholar Award.

Jim Ridolfo is Assistant Professor of Composition and Rhetoric at the University of Cincinnati. He received his PhD in 2009 from the Michigan State University Rhetoric and Writing program, where he worked for six years at the Writing in Digital Environments Research Center. His work has appeared in *Ariadne, Journal of Community Informatics, JAC, Enculturation, Journal of Community Literacy Studies, Pedagogy, Kairos*, and *Rhetoric Review*. He is currently a 2012 Fulbright Middle East and North Africa Regional Research Scholar and is working on his second book. He lives with his partner Janice Fernheimer and their two pet bearded dragons, Electra and Salsa.

Anthony J. Michel is currently Chair of the English Department at Avila University in Kansas City, where he teaches courses in American literature and composition and rhetoric. His research interests are in alternative rhetorics, social activism, new media, and writing theory. He has written on a variety of subjects, including Julie Dash's film *Daughters of the Dust*, hip hop culture in the writing classroom, and the role of new media in social movements. His articles and chapters have appeared in *JAC, Enculturation*, and in several edited collections.

CPSIA information can be obtained at www.ICGtesting.com
Printed in the USA
LVOW131809210413

330151LV00001B/19/P